90 0698139 X

7 Day

University of Plymouth Library

Subject to status this item may be renewed
via your Voyager account

http://voyager.plymouth.ac.uk

Exeter tel: (01392) 475049
Exmouth tel: (01395) 255331
Plymouth tel: (01752) 232323

The Future of Automated Freight Transport

TRANSPORT ECONOMICS, MANAGEMENT AND POLICY

Series Editor: Kenneth Button, *Professor of Public Policy, School of Public Policy, George Mason University, USA*

Transport is a critical input for economic development and for optimizing social and political interaction. Recent years have seen significant new developments in the way that transport is perceived by private industry and governments, and in the way academics look at it.

The aim of this series is to provide original material and up-to-date synthesis of the state of modern transport analysis. The coverage embraces all conventional modes of transport but also includes contributions from important related fields such as urban and regional planning and telecommunications where they interface with transport. The books draw from many disciplines and some cross disciplinary boundaries. They are concerned with economics, planning, sociology, geography, management science, psychology and public policy. They are intended to help improve the understanding of transport, the policy needs of the most economically advanced countries and the problems of resource-poor developing economies. The authors come from around the world and represent some of the outstanding young scholars as well as established names.

Titles in the series include:

The Future of Automated Freight Transport

Concepts, Design and Implementation

Edited by

Rob Konings

Senior Researcher Freight Transport Systems, OTB Research Institute for Housing, Urban and Mobility Studies, Delft University of Technology, The Netherlands

Hugo Priemus

Professor of System Innovation and Spatial Development, Faculty of Technology, Policy and Management, Delft University of Technology, The Netherlands

Peter Nijkamp

Professor of Regional, Urban and Environmental Economics, Faculty of Economics and Business Administration, Free University, Amsterdam, The Netherlands

TRANSPORT ECONOMICS, MANAGEMENT AND POLICY

Edward Elgar

Cheltenham, UK • Northampton, MA, USA

Published by
Edward Elgar Publishing Limited
Glensanda House
Montpellier Parade
Cheltenham
Glos GL50 1UA
UK

Edward Elgar Publishing, Inc.
136 West Street
Suite 202
Northampton
Massachusetts 01060
USA

A catalogue record for this book
is available from the British Library

Library of Congress Cataloguing in Publication Data

The future of automated freight transport : concepts, design and implementation /
    edited by Rob Konings, Hugo Priemus, Peter Nijkamp.
    p. cm.
    Includes bibliographical references and index.
        1. Freight and freightage–Technological innovations. 2.
    Transportation–Technological innovations. I. Konings, Rob. II. Priemus, Hugo.
    III. Nijkamp, Peter.

HE199.A2F88 2006
388'.044–dc22

2005049434

ISBN 1 84542 239 2

Printed and bound in Great Britain by MPG Books Ltd, Bodmin, Cornwall

Contents

Contributors

Arjan van Binsbergen, Transportation and Traffic Engineering Section, Faculty of Civil Engineering & Geosciences, Delft University of Technology, The Netherlands

André Bos, Parallel and Distributed Systems Group, Faculty of Electrical Engineering, Mathematics and Computer Science, Delft University of Technology, The Netherlands

Arnab Bose, Electrical Engineering Department, University of Southern California, Los Angeles, United States of America

Joy Dahlgren, University of California, Berkeley, United States of America

Joop Evers, Transport Policy and Logistics Organisation Section, Faculty of Technology, Policy and Management, Delft University of Technology, The Netherlands

Ernst-Dieter Gilles, Institute for System Dynamics and Control Engineering, University of Stuttgart, Germany

Ingo Hansen, Transportation and Traffic Engineering Section, Faculty of Civil Engineering & Geosciences, Delft University of Technology, The Netherlands

Sven Heidmeier, Institute of Track and Railway Operations, Technical University Berlin, Germany

Petros Ioannou, Electrical Engineering Department, University of Southern California, Los Angeles, United States of America

Rob Konings, OTB Research Institute for Housing, Urban and Mobility Studies, Delft University of Technology, The Netherlands

David Levinson, Department of Civil Engineering, University of Minnesota, Minneapolis, United States of America

Alexander Lutz, Institute for System Dynamics and Control Engineering, University of Stuttgart, Germany

Michiel Minderhoud, Transportation and Traffic Engineering Section, Faculty of Civil Engineering & Geosciences, Delft University of Technology, The Netherlands

Peter Nijkamp, Department of Economics, Free University, Amsterdam, The Netherlands

Ben-Jaap Pielage, Transport Engineering and Logistics Section, Faculty of Mechanical Engineering and Marine Technology, Delft University of Technology, The Netherlands

Hugo Priemus, Faculty of Technology, Policy and Management, Delft University of Technology, The Netherlands

Joan Rijsenbrij, Transport Engineering and Logistics Section, Faculty of Mechanical Engineering and Marine Technology, Delft University of Technology, The Netherlands

Claus Seibt, Department Technology Policy, ARC Systems Research GmbH, Seibersdorf, Austria

Steven Shladover, Institute of Transportation Studies, University of California, Berkeley, United States of America

Jürgen Siegmann, Institute of Track and Railway Operations, Technical University Berlin, Germany

John Stoop, Section Transport Policy and Logistics Organisation, Faculty of Technology, Policy and Management, Delft University of Technology, The Netherlands

Masoud Tabibi, Transportation and Traffic Engineering Section, Faculty of Civil Engineering & Geosciences, Delft University of Technology, The Netherlands

Alexander Verbraeck, Systems Engineering Section, Faculty of Technology, Policy and Management, Delft University of Technology, The Netherlands

Corné Versteegt, Systems Engineering Section, Faculty of Technology, Policy and Management, Delft University of Technology, The Netherlands

Matthias Weber, Department Technology Policy, ARC Systems Research GmbH, Seibersdorf, Austria

Mathijs de Weerdt, Parallel and Distributed Systems Group, Faculty of Electrical Engineering, Mathematics and Computer Science, Delft University of Technology, The Netherlands

Cees Witteveen, Parallel and Distributed Systems Group, Faculty of Electrical Engineering, Mathematics and Computer Science, Delft University of Technology, The Netherlands

Xi Zou, Department of Civil Engineering, University of Minnesota, Minneapolis, United States of America

Preface

The importance of freight transport for our society is beyond dispute, but transport volumes are ever growing and the problems of accommodating freight flows in an efficient and sustainable way become increasingly alarming. Traffic congestion is rapidly growing and the quality of freight transport is not able to keep pace with rising ambitions: shippers want higher reliability, lower prices, faster deliveries, more flexibility and higher service levels. In addition the side effects of freight transport, such as environmental deterioration, inefficient use of energy, space restrictions and traffic accidents become more and more acknowledged as serious problems. In light of these problems there is a great challenge to achieve a breakthrough in the improvement of the performance of freight transport systems.

Learning from experiences in the field of passenger transport, transport automation offers interesting opportunities to improve the performance of a transport system. There are many examples of automated people movers that are operated successfully. Automated passenger transport systems also receive a lot of attention in scientific research. Many publications exist in this field, but the subject of automation has not been covered extensively in literature on freight transport. This book aims to fill a gap in the literature on automated freight transport.

This volume gives an overview of the current concepts, design and evaluation tools and implementation issues related to automated freight transport. It starts with a presentation of the latest developments in automated freight transport and future perspectives in this field for the different transport modes (Part I of the book). Next, insights are provided into particular tools for designing and evaluating innovations in this transport area (Part II of the book). Finally, by drawing attention to the implementation issues we hope to contribute to bridging the gap between theory and practice in this particular transport field (Part III of the book).

The book is a collection of contributions by researchers from the research program, Freight Transport Automation and Multimodality (FTAM) Delft University of Technology, together with experts in this field from many different countries. Delft University of Technology has also financially supported the research program and this book project.

The Audience for the Book

The book is written from a multidisciplinary perspective, because of the complexity and diversity of relevant issues. Such an approach has the great advantage of presenting a more or less integrated view on the theme of automated freight transport, which in our opinion really helps us to understand the opportunities and threats for automated freight transport. A disadvantage could be that it leads to a set of contributions dealing with rather diverse topics, which could limit the value of the book to a reader having a very specific background or interest. However, since we have attempted to avoid contributions going into very much technical detail and using extensive mathematical formulations, we believe the book is accessible to a broad audience. The book is intended to be read by people in the academic world, but it could also appeal to policy makers as well as practitioners in the transport industry who are involved in the design, development or implementation of new technologies for freight transport.

Companion Volume

The idea for this book project arose from the completion of a five-year research program on Freight Transport Automation and Multimodality (FTAM) at Delft University of Technology. The goal of this research program was to provide knowledge and tools to design and develop technologies and organisational structures for an integrated, highly automated transport system for inland intermodal transport at different geographical levels. In addition to these scientific ambitions the program was also of course intended to contribute to improving the quality of freight transport, reducing its negative external effects and finally, increasing its scope.

The richness of both themes and our wish to present a coherent book structure and to avoid fragmentation persuaded us to produce two volumes: this volume dealing with freight transport automation, and a companion volume focussing on intermodal freight transport. Both intermodal transport and transport automation will become increasingly important solutions to cope with ever-increasing transport volumes in an efficient and sustainable way. Although both themes are treated separately it is obvious that they are also related strongly, e.g. with regard to developments regarding automated transport at intermodal terminals. The relationship between the books is expressed by the same general structure and comparable titles of both volumes.

For the composition of both volumes a selected number of researchers from the FTAM-research program together with experts in these fields from many different countries have been invited to contribute to the book. The chapters have been reviewed thoroughly by external experts.

Although it is impossible to cover all aspects of freight transport automation and intermodal transport in depth, we think that the collections in both volumes give a useful overview of the latest developments and tools regarding design and evaluation of innovations in these fields, as well as a fruitful discussion on the implementation issues. The different chapters of the books themselves can be viewed as an introduction to the specific topic. The literature reference lists of the chapters may be a useful guide for readers to go beyond the scope of these volumes. Finally, we hope that both books will contribute to the further scientific, societal and political debates on freight transport innovations.

Acknowledgements

This book project has been financially supported by Delft University of Technology within the framework of its research program Freight Transport Automation and Multimodality (FTAM). This support is gratefully acknowledged. Hugo Priemus was scientific director of this program; Rob Konings coordinated the program. TRAIL Research School also played a much-appreciated role in co-ordinating the FTAM program, which stimulated a multidisciplinary approach and enabled us to link scientific results to practical applications. We believe these aspects are also reflected very well in this book.

In addition, we wish to thank the participating authors for their contribution to this book, and the referees for their excellent reviews. We also owe much gratitude to Ineke Groeneveld, Herman Toneman, Dirk Dubbeling and Monique Hazewinkel, all working at the OTB Research Institute of Housing, Urban and Mobility Studies at Delft University of Technology, for their considerable efforts and endurance in copy-editing the manuscript. Finally, we also highly appreciated the help of Alexandra Minton and Kate Emmins of Edward Elgar Publishing in guiding us through the various stages of the production process of the book.

The editors
Rob Konings
Hugo Priemus
Peter Nijkamp

1. The future of automated freight transport: an overview

Rob Konings, Hugo Priemus and Peter Nijkamp

1.1 INTRODUCTION

In our rapidly changing society we observe a continuous drive to innovate in order to enlarge our prosperity and well being. The great impacts that mega innovations in information and telecommunication technology (ICT), like the introduction of the computer and Internet, have had on our daily life speak for themselves. Innovations take place in all sectors of our society, including the transport sector. Transport is of vital importance for enhancing the performance of the economic system as well as for fulfilling social needs. The transport system is sometimes called the blood circulation system of our society. Therefore, it is not surprising that improvement of the transport system has always received much attention. This also explains the long tradition of innovative development, where a great many technical innovations reshaped our transport system to what we have today.

History shows that major developments in transport systems resulted from radical changes in the propulsion system, i.e. the transition from horsepower to steam and combustion engines. This also had major implications for the competitiveness of different transport modes. Additionally, specific changes within a transport mode have also had substantial impacts on performance. For example, the transition from wooden rails to iron rails reduced maintenance costs and rolling resistance leading to a considerable cost reduction in rail transport. The introduction of the high-speed train enabled rail transport to compete with air transport and to develop a new transport market. For both these changes the development and extension of networks to accommodate these new types of rail transport services have been a prerequisite. Especially for the high-speed train, a new level of international standardisation of equipment and co-ordination between national governments in Europe has been shown to be of great importance. These examples show not only that radical technical innovations can improve transport system performance. They also demonstrate the importance of the political, organisational as well as logistic aspects of transport innovations. Incremental improvements in transport systems are a continuous process, and

1

have produced revolutionary changes in the last decades. The development of complete new transport systems usually takes at least fifty years. We argue that we are now on the eve of some major changes which can and will transform our transport system radically. The development of the fuel cell is still in its infancy but there is little doubt about its potential to replace the combustion engine, since the transition from a fossil fuel-based economy to a hydrogen-based economy is unavoidable. This transition will overcome environmental concerns about transport and could strengthen the competitiveness of individual transport modes. Parallel to this development towards a new propulsion system there is a great challenge and drive to develop, implement and improve automated transport systems.

Automated Transport is No Longer Science Fiction

For a long time automated transport, i.e. driverless transport, had a magical character and was often associated with science fiction. This notion is certainly no longer valid today, in either freight or passenger transport. As a matter of fact there are several fields of application where automated transport has developed so far. Most applications of automated passenger transport, so called automated people movers, are found in the USA, but Asia and Europe are fast growing markets. Within freight transport automated terminals are emerging, in particular in global mainports.

Probably the earliest application of what can be defined as automated transport is the elevator and later on the escalator. We have become so used to these systems that we are hardly aware of their usefulness. Also some variants have been developed for applications in horizontal transport, for instance, moving walkways at airports, but the distance covered by these systems has remained small, i.e. 100 to 200 metres.

One of the first projects that can be considered as pioneering work in the development of automated transport was realised at the airport of Tampa (Florida, USA) in 1972. Here an automated people mover was built to transport travellers from the land-side to the air-side area over a distance of 250 to 500 metres. This has been an important pilot project; since then many other automated people movers have been constructed at airports. Airports are the most important clients of automated people movers and provide the largest growth market for these systems. In view of fast growing passenger volumes at airports and the need for passenger friendly terminals (short walking distances and fast transits) and efficient handling of passengers, automated transport systems are becoming increasingly popular at airports. Airports as well as amusement parks form the oldest and most developed applications of automated passenger transport. Encouraged by the success of these systems, the fields of application have gradually broadened, however, in particular to urban public transport. The first application of a fully automated metro, the *Véhicule Automatique Léger* (VAL), dates from 1983 in

Lille (France). Since then the VAL has been copied in many other European and Asian cities. In addition, over the last decade there has been a growing interest in automated transport systems as local feeder transport to nodes of public transport, e.g. connecting business areas to public transport stations. One of the examples of this kind of application is the Park Shuttle in Capelle aan den Yssel in the Netherlands. Moreover, there are opportunities to operate these systems as a circulation transport system in large activity centres, such as clusters of medical centres (hospital buildings, medical/health care, research and academic institutes and their parking facilities) and campus universities, where employment, education, living and leisure functions are combined. Examples are found in the USA (e.g. Huntsville Hospital and West Virginia University) and in Europe (e.g. the Hospital of Milan and Dortmund University).

One of the latest developments in automated public transport systems is the extension of applications to bus-like systems, such as the 'Phileas' bus introduced in Eindhoven (the Netherlands) in 2004. A striking feature of this bus in addition to its ability to drive fully computer controlled, enabling a high efficiency and comfort performance comparable to tramcars and metros is that the design and propulsion system of this bus have innovative features to produce a high quality public transport system.

If we look back over developments in the passenger transport market, transport automation has indeed been successfully introduced in some specific market segments. Moreover, these applications have not been limited to private areas, but have been established in a public environment as well. Apparently the conditions for implementing those systems are favourable, although in terms of their share of passenger volumes their role is still modest. Nevertheless these automated systems have shown their viability and have been able to compete with traditional systems to gain market share.

This positive picture holds for the application of automated people movers, which have their roots in public transport. As regards the implementation of automated private cars, there is still a long way to go. Several driver-supporting systems have nearly become standard (i.e. cruise control, navigation systems) or will become widely available soon (i.e. adaptive cruise control, ultrasonic sensors to detect obstacles and lane departure warning systems). Others, such as driver fitness control systems, are still experimental, but are expected to enter the market in the near future. The ultimate phase of automated controlled cars, where the driving tasks themselves are delegated, is already technically feasible, but there are many institutional barriers to be overcome before this type of automated transport can be fully implemented, particularly in the sphere of safety requirements.

Automated Freight Transport is Still a Challenge

The present role of automated freight transport is quite different from that of automated passenger transport, although actually the driving forces and conditions for automation are at first sight rather similar.

Due to economic and societal developments, freight transport flows are growing and the difficulties of accommodating these flows in an efficient way are becoming increasingly alarming:

- traffic congestion is rapidly growing, leading to high economic and social costs;
- the quality of freight transport is not keeping pace with rising expectations: shippers want higher reliability, lower prices, faster deliveries, more flexibility and higher service levels, but the opportunities for the transport sector to cope with these increasing demands are lagging;
- negative side effects, such as environmental deterioration, inefficient use of energy, space restrictions, congestion and traffic accidents, are becoming more severe problems.

Therefore, within society there is an increasing need for freight transport systems which can cope with these problems now and in the future. Automation of transport processes could contribute substantially to solve these problems because there is:

- a potential reduction in operational costs due to savings in personnel costs;
- a better circulation of traffic flows by homogenising traffic, enabling potentially shorter transport times, higher reliability and energy cost savings;
- possible improvements in the utilisation of infrastructure, which enables accommodation of higher traffic volumes and thereby larger transport flows and/or increased transport frequencies;
- a possible improvement in the safety of transport, since the role of human actions is largely eliminated;
- a potential productivity gain in transport and the economy, because lower dependence on labour provides more opportunities for around-the-clock transport and production processes.

Although all these qualities seem appealing for infrastructure operators, transport service providers, shippers, governments as well as society as a whole, large-scale real world applications are very scarce and promising developments are exceptional. It is true that freight transport automation has become widely established in industry, where it has been applied to production and/or internal transport systems. In addition, transport systems at container terminals are one of the rare examples of automated freight transport systems that can be linked and integrated with existing external transport modes. The implementation of Automated Guided Vehicles at the ECT-Maasvlakte terminal at the port of Rotterdam in 1993 has been a pioneering development for automated terminal transport. However, automated operations in terminals take place in isolated private business areas, so these systems can actually also be considered as internal transport systems. Barriers seem to exist to the expansion of such automated transport operations onto a larger geographical scale, where such systems should be able to operate over longer distances, at higher speeds and in a public environment – with lower levels of supervision and protection – which is shared with different modes of manned transport. These barriers can be related to one or several of the following issues:

- low performing or incompatible vehicle and information technologies;
- uncertainties about positive cost–benefits ratios, both from a business perspective (shippers, operators) and from a societal perspective;
- lack of co-ordination with existing transport modes (physical and organisational): in particular problems in combining and linking automated and traditional freight transport systems;
- uncertainties about safety aspects and the vulnerability of the system;
- planning and legal restrictions, including institutional barriers;
- difficulties in arranging finance;
- uncertainties about the acceptance by shippers, operators, policy makers and citizens (behaviour).

Opportunities to introduce automated freight transport systems into the market will strongly depend on their performance in these aspects.

Despite the great potential benefits of automated freight transport for the transport sector and society, this theme has not been covered extensively in literature so far. Especially compared to literature on automated passenger transport it has got very little attention. This book aims to fill the gap in the literature on automated freight transport.

1.2   CONTENTS OF THE BOOK

In this book the issues surrounding the successful development and implementation of automated freight transport are discussed. This topic is elaborated through a three step-approach. Any possible development of automated freight transport starts from the generation of new ideas or extending the current knowledge on automation to new applications. Therefore the book starts with a presentation of the latest developments in automated freight transport and gives an outlook on desirable and likely future developments in this transport area. Next, the book provides insights into particular tools for designing and evaluating these transport innovations. Finally, by drawing attention to the implementation issues we hope to contribute to bridging the gap between theory and practice in this particular transport field. The book is structured according to these main strands and consists of three parts, each dealing with one of these themes. This structure can also be recognized in the subtitle of the book.

Part I: Concepts and Perspectives in Automated Freight Transport

The aim of this part of the book is to sketch the opportunities for automated freight transport within the different transport modalities. The chapters have a rather broad scope and introductory nature. They present an overview of the state-of-the-art in transport automation, i.e. results that have been achieved so far, current (research) developments and opportunities for and barriers to further development paths. In some sense these chapters can also be seen as setting the problems that have to be dealt with in order to make automated freight transport feasible from a technological, economical and societal point of view.

In this overview we focus on the inland freight transport system, i.e. road, rail and pipeline transport and inland shipping. In addition, a new hybrid transport mode, combining characteristics of road and rail transport, is presented. We are aware that this is not an exhaustive overview of modes. Of course aviation is a very advanced transport modality, in which the use of information and telecommunication technology (ICT) as well as automation (the autopilot) is deeply rooted. However, automation has not been of interest in improving the performance of freight transport in particular, except perhaps for ground-handling systems. Moreover, the market for aviation is pre-eminently the passenger market. In seaborne shipping ICT is now also widely applied, and there are strong similarities with the aviation sector. Sea and flight processes can be monitored continuously and can be adjusted autonomously. Information supply, communication, navigation and control are increasingly integrated, enabling more efficient and safe transport operations. In sea shipping, navigation tasks can also be taken over by sophisticated systems. Studies exist that have elaborated concepts for fully automated unmanned ships. According to these studies much of the technology already exists and other necessary systems are due to be implemented within a few years. However, perhaps the biggest barrier is that sea shipping operates in a global environment, which puts even higher demands on the required conditions. Of course the sea is also an unpredictable place, where the ability of a crew to cope with emergency situations is invaluable. Since there are several similarities between navigation processes in sea and inland shipping, some of the basic automation issues in waterway transport will be considered in chapter 4, where opportunities for automated inland navigation are discussed.

The first contribution in this part of the book, chapter 2, presented by Steven Shladover, gives an outlook for automation in road transport. It starts with a broad programmatic overview of projects around the world, where generally applicable technology development projects and location-specific projects are discussed. Ambitious projects are found in the USA as well as in Europe and Asia. A major observation in this chapter is that the purely technological issues tend to be universal, but that trade-offs, which must be considered in selecting the most appropriate technologies, are heavily dependent on local considerations such as the costs of alternatives, the institutional structure of the freight industry and its customers, and transportation system conditions. The most fundamental question remains whether to use a dedicated right of way or not.

In chapter 3 Jürgen Siegmann and Sven Heidmeier shed light on progress towards automated rail freight transport. In order to increase the role of the rail sector in freight transport in Europe the authors observe a need for a more flexible and customized rail freight product which is capable of transporting small-sized flows in a time- and cost-efficient way. Automated freight wagons are proposed as an opportunity to increase the flexibility of rail transport and to reduce costs. An overview of the most important developments and projects concerning automated freight transport shows that some ideas have indeed reached a test or pilot stage, but so far these systems have not achieved real and full implementation. Although the guidance device and the external control system of rail transport actually support possibilities for automated processes, there are still several technical issues to be solved. In addition, some institutional barriers exist. To implement automation a stepwise (three stage) development path for automated freight transport is presented, in which consecutive improvements in technologies are achieved. The authors conclude that shunting yard operations have the best opportunities to initiate automated processes, which could gradually be extended to long-distance trips.

In chapter 4 Alexander Lutz and Ernst-Dieter Gilles discuss the opportunities for automated transport in inland shipping. Traditionally, low cost operations and reliable and safe transport services have formed the competitive edge of inland shipping, but ever growing traffic volumes are due to endanger these comparative advantages. The authors argue that ICT and automation could be an apposite answer to these threats and would be helpful to further improve the capacity, punctuality and safety of waterway transport. Three levels of automation are distinguished and elaborated. The lowest level of automation covers the path-following ability of a single ship. It is capable of automatically guiding a ship under normal traffic conditions. The second level of automation deals with the co-ordination of several ships. The goal of this type of automation is to control conflicts on rivers with a lot of traffic or in especially narrow sections of rivers. The third level of automation does not deal with ship-to-ship interactions, but rather covers scheduling. The ship is considered as a unit that transports goods at a certain velocity, irrespective of path planning or path-following problems. The main relevant properties are the ship's position and its velocity. The goal is to optimize the overall shipping process by taking into account for instance lock operations and loading and unloading facilities. Lutz and Gilles conclude that in particular the first and third levels of automation have received a lot of attention, in both the research and business communities. At both levels systems are already available for commercial use and extensions of commercial applications are due soon. Nevertheless, legal issues have to be solved to further extend the degree of automation to fully autonomous vessels, but people will still supervise these vessels.

Ben-Jaap Pielage and Joan Rijsenbrij discuss the potential for automated underground freight transport in chapter 5. Underground freight transport has a long history and this probably explains the sophisticated transport techniques that have been developed for this transport mode. Due to one of its typical characteristics, i.e. operations in a dedicated environment without any outside disturbances, underground transport seems to have a high potential for automation. Pielage and Rijsenbrij give a brief historic overview of underground transport systems and discuss the two main directions in which innovative developments are explored and take place: capsule pipeline systems and automated vehicle systems. Capsule pipeline systems seem most promising for long distance transport through relatively small diameter tubes in point-to-point operations, while automatic vehicle systems would be more useful for short distance transport in more complex networks. Neither type of system has been widely implemented yet, but R&D efforts for these systems are likely to continue, partly because increasing problems with road transport will encourage the search for alternative transport modes, but also because innovative technological developments will increase the feasibility of underground freight transport systems.

In the next contribution in this part, chapter 6, Joop Evers elaborates a new type of transport mode in the form of an intelligent road–rail hybrid transport system. In addition to a description of the system characteristics, market potential is explored. The bottom line of Evers' idea for a hybrid transport system is to combine the favourable characteristics of road transport (speed, flexibility in time and space and door-to-door service) and rail transport (low rolling resistance) and to avoid their disadvantages (long braking distance of trains causing low frequencies and limited track capacity, high costs of road transport). Due to a smart mechanical engineering vehicle design and innovative logistic control, the proposed intelligent road–rail hybrid system would be able to offer economic, accessible, reliable and continuous transport services. Evers argues that the Betuwe Line, a dedicated rail line for freight transport connecting the port of Rotterdam to the hinterland in Germany, could be a perfect test bed for this system. Estimations of the potential market share, based on the model of McFadden, indicate that road–rail hybrid transport can be an interesting alternative to traditional road transport in hinterland transport.

In chapter 7 Petros Ioannou and Arnab Bose focus on a more general, but critical issue of transport automation, i.e. vehicle control. The control phase of vehicle driving is concerned with actuation of the steering wheel, accelerator and brakes in such a way that the vehicle follows its preceding vehicle or a desired path with a desired velocity and with acceptable precision. Their chapter outlines designs of controllers to perform these longitudinal and lateral functions. This topic also includes a discussion about the sensors that can be used together with such longitudinal and lateral controllers and which are indispensable for automated vehicle control. Another element in vehicle control is the communications capability of vehicles, which becomes increasingly important as the level of automation of vehicles increases. Ioannou and Bose highlight the issues and considerations in the design of such vehicle-to-vehicle communication systems. Finally, the authors have demonstrated by simulation models and real experiments that the introduction of automated traffic in today's traffic system can have considerable beneficial effects in terms of an improvement in traffic flow characteristics and a reduction in fuel consumption and air pollution.

The contribution of Michiel Minderhoud and Ingo Hansen (chapter 8), embroiders on the theme discussed by Ioannou and Bose. However, Minderhoud and Hansen do not focus on the control level of individual vehicles, but take a broader perspective by considering approaches for traffic control. The authors believe that traffic control for freight road transport has much in common with automated traffic control for passenger transport. The ideas developed for passenger transport could to a large extent be adopted for freight transport. The application of modern electronics provides a wide range of possibilities to control traffic. The chapter starts with an overview of traffic control systems, such as simple lane change prohibition of trucks and intelligent cruise control. One of the more sophisticated systems, the platoon-driving concept of trucks, is elaborated in detail because of its most promising benefits. The platoon-driving concept enables a group of vehicles to follow each other at small intervehicle distances. Simulation studies by Minderhoud and Hansen show that the application of automated trucks on a dedicated lane using the platoon concept is possible, although additional traffic control measures are required to ensure safe crossing of manually driven vehicles with the automated trucks. Due to the required safety measure of traffic lights, the performance of the studied roadway section decreases with respect to efficiency (fewer cars and trucks can pass the bottleneck), travel time (an increase for cars and trucks), and energy consumption (an increase for cars and trucks). The increased capacity of the dedicated truck lane, by means of automated platoons, could not be used optimally since platoons were forced to stop at traffic lights. From this preliminary assessment, it is concluded that application of fully automated trucks on a dedicated lane in metropolitan area with many on and off ramps is possible, but it will reduce performance compared to the case of manually driven trucks, although some safety benefits may be gained.

The requirements and implications for the use of infrastructure in accommodating automated transport are the central issues of chapter 9. Masoud Tabibi presents and assesses two key elements for the operation of automated controlled trucks (ACT) on existing motorways, as a new means of increasing the efficiency of road freight transport on motorways. The first element is the implementation of a dedicated freight lane for the operation of ACTs. His analysis indicates that in the case of a large share of trucks in the traffic flow (> 20%), a dedicated lane for trucks would be justified. As long as the share of ACTs is small, a dedicated freight lane could be assigned to the operation of ACTs at specific time periods of the day (or night). At other times the dedicated freight lane could be assigned to ordinary trucks. Simulation results also show that creating a dedicated freight lane on the shoulder lane of existing motorways is the best option. The second element is the application of buffer areas, which facilitate the flow control of ACTs while approaching on-/off-ramp areas. A buffer area could decrease interference with flows of ACTs by manually driven vehicles in on-/off-ramp areas, where crossing, merging or diverging of the flow of manually driven vehicles would be expected. Other functions like overruling the mode of driving (from automatically to manually and vice versa), dynamic traffic management of ACTs and incident management of ACTs could take place in buffer areas. Preliminary results of an optimization-based analysis confirm the effectiveness of buffer areas in improving the interactions of ACTs and manually driven vehicles at on-ramps.

Part II: Design and Evaluation Tools

The development of an automated transport system is a complex task. The design process is characterized by many complex and sometimes uncertain elements, as regards the technology, legal and economic aspects, and the fact that many actors with usually different interests are involved. The financial risks are, due to these uncertainties, usually high. What are the most promising choices as regards vehicle technology and infrastructural layout? Will the system performances meet expectations? Is the prospective automated transport system economically viable? Getting answers to such questions is of course always the ultimate goal before any new investment decision is made, but seems to be especially relevant to investment in automated transport systems, because of their innovative nature – generating high risks – high investment costs and large impacts on society. Therefore ex ante evaluation of the impacts of an automated transport system can be helpful in the design process. In this part of the book some tools are presented that are of particular interest in the design and evaluation of automated transport systems.

In chapter 10 Corné Versteegt and Alexander Verbraeck stress the importance of simulation in designing an automated transport system. Simulation models can play an important role because they can offer a common frame of reference for all designers involved, and provide both quantitative and qualitative answers for many different aspects of the system. In addition to the traditional approach to simulation the authors suggest including new tool kits in the models, which can extend the role of simulation from the evaluation of designs to supporting the design process itself. Recent developments from the field of simulation are discussed and the authors show how these new developments can support the design of automated transport systems. Innovative elements that are being discussed are object-oriented simulation, libraries of simulation building blocks, distributed simulation, real time control and emulation, and web-based simulation. The application of these tools and their merits are illustrated in a case study for an underground logistic system, planned at Schiphol Airport in the Netherlands.

Chapter 11, entitled 'Multi-agent systems for planning and operational management', presents a new view on modelling and development of software systems to support automation in the transport sector. Information and communication technology (ICT) has been contributing significantly to improvements in the performance of the transport system and their applications are divergent. However, André Bos, Mathijs de Weerdt and Cees Witteveen observe that the role of ICT in supporting the planning and co-ordination of interorganizational processes and management of incidents has still barely been explored. These issues are highly relevant in both a manned and unmanned transport environment. They could be dealt with by new techniques in two areas: multi-agent systems, and diagnosis and incident management systems. A multi-agent system is a system in which several interacting, intelligent agents pursue some set of goals or perform some set of tasks. For example, in international freight transport many different companies and organizations are involved. A computer program that communicates with other programs on behalf of its organisation can represent each of these parties. Such an artificial representative is called an agent. Techniques like multi-agent planning can then be used to better co-ordinate the activities of the organizations. Diagnosis and incident management systems support the derivation of the root cause of incidents and assist in finding remedial actions. For example, to control large numbers of automated guided vehicles (AGV), an incident management system monitors the course of action of each AGV. When an AGV gets stuck, the system determines the component that failed and creates an alternative sequence of actions. Bos, de

Weerdt and Witteveen show that the combination of multi-agent and incident management techniques allows organisations to cooperate more efficiently and react much more quickly to unexpected changes.

In chapter 12 Joy Dahlgren discusses the issue of how to evaluate an automated freight transport system. She examines the complexities of conducting a benefit–cost analysis and provides methods for addressing them. The process of benefit–cost analysis is broken down into its component tasks and each is discussed in detail. The way in which the benefits and costs of automated freight systems differ from those of conventional freight systems is noted, particularly the absence of human operators on the transport vehicle and the increased computer control of routing and scheduling of vehicles. Because the major benefits of an automated freight transport system are cost savings, benefit–cost analysis seems to be a convenient tool for the evaluation. For monetising the non-monetary benefits, such as safety or environmental benefits, tools already exist and they can be applied. Dahlgren concludes that a fair and careful evaluation of a proposed automated freight transport system is important, both to determine whether the project is worthwhile and if so, to gain support for system implementation. Evaluation of alternative system components is also useful in developing the optimal system. Once such a system has been implemented, an evaluation of its performance and cost can be used in planning future projects.

Part III: Implementation Issues

The technological development of an automated transport system or a system innovation in general is a time-consuming process in which several barriers must be overcome. The construction of a prototype is in itself already a major result, because most new concepts perish at a much earlier stage of development. However, although a prototype may be available and satisfying test results have been accomplished there is still a long way to go with many pitfalls before an automated transport system can be implemented in the market, and even then it may fail. The Dutch Combi Road project, an automated freight transport system that is described in chapter 2, is unfortunately a good example of the kind of critical problems that can be encountered on implementation.

In general many types of barriers to implementation may arise and the degree of success in overcoming them seems to depend on internal as well as external factors. To a large extent problems can be avoided if the potential barriers have been taken into account in the design process of the automated system. On the other hand specific circumstances at the time of market implementation that are not under the control of the designer of the system, such as government policy, will influence potential success.

Of course the quality of an automated transport system and the innovation process itself, which has different features, are the major determinants for success. *Business economic perspectives*, *technical complexity* and the degree of dependence on other technical developments, *compatibility* with other transport modes, opportunities to carry out experiments (*trialability*) and the extent of access to knowledge about experiences (*observability*) are all features that matter. In addition, there are other factors such as the selection of target markets and the appreciation of the system by potential customers, but also less obvious elements such as the role of suppliers of equipment as well as the suppliers of transport services. Nevertheless one should be aware that investment decisions are based on *perceptions* of the quality features of the system; therefore the communication channels used to inform and convince decision makers and other involved actors cannot be neglected either. In this part of the book we will take a closer look at these intriguing implementation challenges to bring automated freight transport into reality.

In chapter 13 David Levinson and Xi Zou address the issues of finance and deployment of automated freight transport systems. Since finance and deployment are very dependent on the characteristics of a mode, their discussion is structured around the most advanced modes for automated transport, i.e. pipeline, rail and road transport. However, even within each mode there are a large number of alternatives for the technology of automated transport systems and each results in different scenarios for finance and deployment. Ownership of the vehicles and the transport infrastructure as well as the conditions for operations appear to be crucial elements in financial and deployment structures. Levinson and Zou argue that government subsidies play a vital role in realising automated transport systems. According to the authors, finance and deployment are also highly correlated issues. Every deployment scheme can only be configured if financial resources are organized for capital and operating expenditures, while every financing scheme depends on the relationship of the actors responsible for deployment.

If we look at potential obstacles to the implementation of automated transport systems, uncertainties over whether a system can offer complete and sustainable safe operations are possibly one of the most underrated barriers. In chapter 14 John Stoop explains that these barriers have their origin in the fact that so far safety requirements have not been sufficiently incorporated during the different stages of the design process of transport systems. Stoop elaborates a series of fundamental changes that have occurred in transport system design and their relation to a safe operating performance. In order to integrate safety in fundamental changes a 'conceptual leap' in safety thinking is needed. New actors and safety aspects in the operating environment of transport systems have placed new demands on engineering design concepts and have triggered the development of various schools of safety thinking. A historical overview of railway system design principles gives an indication of their limitations with respect to the feasibility of a sustainable safe operation of such transport systems and the need for new notions in system design. Changes in the design environment and concurrent changes in the engineering design process put additional demands on assessing the design with respect to a system safety integrator role, failure mode identification, the role of the human factor and allocation of responsibilities. The author ends with a list of safety-critical decisions at various strategic levels in the design process concerning choices in the transport market, the transport process, the transport means and the infrastructure. Ultimately these choices determine the primary safety levels that can be achieved.

The scope of an automated freight transport system will to a large extent depend upon the way in which the automated transport infrastructure is connected with and embedded in the existing manned transport networks of roads, rail and waterways. Only if a seamless integration of both automated and manned transport networks is achieved, can the potential benefits of an automated system exceed its own system borders. The integration of manned and automated systems – both physically and from the perspective of operations – is a crucial element in the implementation process of automated systems. In chapter 15 Arjan van Binsbergen elaborates this compatibility issue by discussing the various infrastructural, technological and logistical aspects that must be taken into consideration when implementing automated systems for freight transport. To analyse the possibilities of integrating automated and manned freight transport the chapter starts by defining different types of freight transport automation, ranging from drivers' assistance systems to fully automated systems and different variants on these systems. Van Binsbergen argues that for operational and physical reasons automated transport systems are more likely to be used in dedicated infrastructure instead of mixed (automated/manned) traffic conditions and therefore specific transfer facilities – interfaces – are needed to integrate manned and automated systems. The transition between manned transport and the various types of automated transport require different types of interfaces, ranging from transition on the move or during a stop, change of driver or tractor to transshipment of cargo. The physical and operational forms of these interfaces are described. Regarding the consequences for the logistics organisation of these interfaces, an analogy is drawn with intermodal transport. This enables van Binsbergen to draw conclusions about the feasibility of the various automation concepts for specific niche markets in freight transport.

In chapter 16 Matthias Weber and Claus Seibt take a closer look at the possible role of government in introducing automated freight transport systems. The authors postulate that appropriate long-term policy strategies are needed to accompany the introduction of automated transport systems, because of the complexity and wide impacts of introducing such systems. As a starting point for analysis, theory on innovation diffusion and empirical evidence is presented to capture the notion of 'barriers to innovation' diffusion in large socio-technical systems. In addition, the possible roles of the government in promoting technological innovations is described and differentiated for the phases of innovation diffusion (invention, test, first application, market introduction, maturity, decline and replacement). The compatibility of these roles and innovations phases is assessed. Next the authors look more specifically at innovation barriers to automated freight transport. These general insights are used to analyse which roles of government would be appropriate to enable and support the development, introduction and to increase the scope of automated freight transport systems. Weber and Seibt conclude that a breakthrough in automated freight transport systems can only be accomplished with a supportive and active stance of government. Government actions should include the provision of financial support through R&D programmes to give incentives and direction in the early stages of the innovation process. Also predictable conditions, for instance in terms of safety regulations and liability rules, should be provided. In addition, the government should act as a moderator and facilitator to streamline major interorganizational co-ordination issues. Last but not least government should monitor and evaluate developments in order to change its role if necessary.

1.3   CONCLUDING REMARKS

The contributions to this book make clear that automation of freight transport systems is certainly no longer an unexplored field. As a matter of fact ideas for automated transport exist for all transport modes, but there are large differences in development stage between the different modalities, ranging from the conceptual design to the experimental phase. A major explanation for these differences in development seems to be the specific technical characteristics of transport modes. These conditions affect not only the ability of transport systems to overcome technical barriers to automation, but also institutional barriers including safety issues. From this point of view underground freight transport systems would have a great comparative advantage over the other transport modes. However, high investment costs appear to be the biggest bottleneck for the development of automated underground freight transport systems. In addition to technical issues, it is likely also that the driving forces for automation are an important explanation in the development phase of the transport modes. The problems road transport is faced with probably encourage efforts to develop automated systems. The fact that interest in road transport automation and also development projects in this field are worldwide will also be a stimulus. The contributions to this book also provide evidence of the potential benefits of automated freight transport, in particular with respect to an improvement of the utilization of infrastructure and a reduction of operational costs (fuel consumption) and environmental damage (air pollution).

In general promising developments for automated freight transport can be envisaged, but the route to a large-scale implementation of completely automated systems remains a long and difficult one, because there are still many barriers to overcome. In the end it will come down to the real quality of the automated transport system and a firm conviction that the system will bring the expected benefits. In this respect the development of new design and evaluation tools will be very useful to pave the way for automated freight transport.

PART I

Automated freight transport: concepts and perspectives

2. Road transport automation: current projects

Steven Shladover

2.1 INTRODUCTION

The movement of freight is a function vital for all human activities, but especially critical to the viability of modern industrialized society. Throughout the industrialized world, we need to move goods from one place to another, whether these be raw materials and manufactured parts within factories, finished goods within warehouses and transportation terminals, or all kinds of goods (from raw materials to finished products) from suppliers to consumers. The cost of moving these goods is an unavoidable part of the cost of production, but it can be reduced by use of the most efficient goods movement technologies.

The cost of unskilled manual labour is high in all modern industrialized countries, whether they be in Europe, North America or Asia. This produces strong economic incentives to replace that labour with automation technologies wherever it is feasible. Within recent decades, we have therefore seen the adoption of automated machine tools and assembly lines in factories, accompanied in some cases by automated guided vehicles (AGVs) to move everything from raw materials to the finished goods from place to place within those factories. These typically operate at very low speeds (walking pace) within a carefully structured environment (climate controlled, distinctively marked, protected from unexpected intrusions, carefully inspected and supervised). These restrictions make it feasible for first-generation automation technologies to operate safely and effectively.

The next step in the advancement of automated goods movement is the extension beyond the factory walls to the freight terminal, where shipments are transferred from one vehicle or transportation mode to another. These terminals are typically outdoors, and therefore not climate controlled, their large size requires higher operating speeds than the applications within factories, and they cannot be as well supervised or protected from intrusions. For example, the movements of shipping containers within the Europe Combined Terminals (ECT) near Rotterdam are currently effected by 120 automated container carriers operating at 14.5 km/h speed under all weather conditions. Although use of these automated vehicles increased the capital cost of the terminal, it produced savings in maintenance and operating costs, as well as increasing the terminal capacity and improving its logistical management.

The next logical advance in the automated movement of freight is to extend beyond the terminal to the broader road transportation system, including movements between terminals and even between different regions. These applications require the ability to operate at higher speeds, over longer distances, and with even lower levels of supervision and protection than the current applications. The road network is the dominant medium for freight movement because of its ubiquity and connectedness, so applications of automation to road transport are likely to have the largest economic impacts. The technological capabilities required to achieve these automated operations are consistent with those needed for automated movement of passenger vehicles on roads as well, providing opportunities for synergy with other transportation interests. This can be part of a broader advance toward automated highway systems in general.

2.2   CURRENT ROAD TRANSPORT AUTOMATION PROJECTS

Research, development and testing activities in support of road transport automation for freight movement are under way in Europe, North America and Asia. Although the transportation system needs and institutional environments are somewhat different on each continent, there are still significant similarities in the approaches that have been adopted. Some of the current projects are focused on development of generally applicable technological capabilities for freight transport automation, while others are focused on addressing location-specific needs. The focus of this review is on projects that have some significant public-agency involvement, because the available public information is very limited regarding those projects that are conducted entirely by private companies.

This review specifically addresses the automation of freight movement on roadways, using rubber-tyred vehicles operating at typical highway speeds, suitable for use within urban regions or between regions. We begin with generally applicable technology development projects and then proceed to location-specific projects.

CHAUFFEUR Project

The most ambitious recent activity is on the CHAUFFEUR Project (Schulze 1997), which is a collaboration involving the European Commission and a group of major industrial partners (DaimlerChrysler, IVECO, Renault Véhicules Industrielles, Bosch, WABCO, ZF, etc.). This project has been developing a variety of levels of automated capabilities for trucks:

- adaptive cruise control to enhance ease of vehicle following;
- lane departure warning and lane-keeping assistance to enhance lane-tracking capabilities;
- 'electronic towbar' to enable a lead truck driven by a skilled driver to 'tow' a following truck without a driver;
- automated platoon of three trucks, for application on truck-only lanes.

The first phase of CHAUFFEUR concentrated most prominently on the development and evaluation of the 'electronic towbar' capability, culminating in a public demonstration on an autobahn near Konstanz, Germany in June 1999. This showed the effectiveness of the automatic steering, speed and spacing control systems of the large tractor–trailer truck combinations, even while operating on a highway with significant grades and curves. The separation between the leading and following trucks varied from 6 m at low speeds to 12 m at the maximum speed of 90 km/h, and the towbar was demonstrated to work effectively for manoeuvres including lane changing and driving on curved exit ramps (Figure 2.1). The primary sensor for determining the relative lateral and longitudinal position between the trailer of the first truck and the tractor of the second truck was a two-camera infrared video image processing system, which observed a pattern of eight infrared lights mounted on the rear of the trailer. Coordination between the trucks was facilitated using data exchanged over a 2.4 GHz wireless radio link.

The CHAUFFEUR research has extended beyond the development and testing of technology to the evaluation of the impacts of system implementation, using computer simulation and economic evaluation models. This research has predicted significant fuel and emissions savings associated with the aerodynamic drag reductions from short-distance vehicle following (Bonnet and Fritz 2000), as well as increases in highway capacity and some safety improvements (Baum and Geissler 2000).

As the research has progressed, it has become evident that the 'towbar' capability can be applied to pairs of trucks (a leader and one follower), but not to longer platoons of trucks. It has also become evident that the platoons of three or more trucks could only be operated in truck lanes that are segregated from normal vehicle traffic and the disturbances that it can introduce (such as vehicles trying to cut between the electronically coupled

*Figure 2.1   CHAUFFEUR trucks using 'electronic towbar' capability for
                lane changing manoeuvre*

trucks). The second phase of CHAUFFEUR developed the platoon capability
and refined the nearer-term driver assist capabilities.

University of California PATH Program Automated Trucks

The University of California PATH Program, under the sponsorship of the
California Department of Transportation (Caltrans) has been developing
truck automation systems since 1997. This research is an outgrowth of
PATH's research on automated highway system technology for passenger
cars, recognizing that heavy trucks and transit buses are both likely to be
nearer-term applications of automation technology than passenger cars. The
PATH focus is on fully automated driving of trucks in segregated, protected
truck lanes, where they would not be mixed with passenger cars and would
have only limited interactions with conventional non-automated trucks. In
this way, the trucks can gain the maximum lane capacity, safety and fuel
consumption and emission reduction benefits. In addition, separation of the
trucks from lighter-duty vehicles makes it possible for the design and
construction of the roadway pavement and structures to be optimized for the
vehicles that will use them, potentially saving considerable infrastructure
capital and maintenance costs (Shladover 2001).

Figure 2.2   Three Freightliner Century-class trucks equipped for automated driving by California PATH Program

The PATH automation technology has been applied to one 1991 model Freightliner truck-tractor (Hingwe et al. 2000 and Tan et al. 1999) and three 2001 model Freightliner Century-class truck-tractor test vehicles (Figure 2.2). The lateral control of these trucks is based on use of permanent magnet reference markers in the lane centre and flux-gate magnetometer sensors mounted beneath the vehicles, providing for position measurement accuracy of about 1 mm. The longitudinal control of the trucks is based on using a combination of laser and millimetre-wave radar sensors, combined with a wireless LAN radio communication system to enable the vehicles to exchange their current state information with each other. These vehicles are designed to operate at full highway speeds (100 km/h) carrying a full range of loading (from empty to fully loaded) on highways including typical curves and grades. The newer vehicles are equipped for driver-initiated transitions between automated and manual driving modes, as well as merging into a traffic stream to form a three-truck automated platoon.

In addition to tests to prove smooth and accurate vehicle dynamics and control, the PATH research has also included evaluations of the aerodynamic drag reductions and fuel savings expected from operating the trucks in close-formation automated platoons. The drag reduction experiments have been based on scale-model tests in a wind tunnel (Hammache et al. 2002), followed by full-scale on-the-road tests for both fuel consumption and emissions, with two-truck platoons driving at separations of between 3 m and 10 m at about 100 km/h. The full-scale tests of the engine-forward trucks seen in Figure 2.2, pulling box trailers, have shown direct fuel consumption savings of 5-10% for the leading truck and 9-12% for the trailing truck (Browand et al. 2004). The wind-tunnel tests of scale models of cab-over-engine trucks showed larger potential fuel savings, especially at the shorter separations, because the cab-over-engine configuration left a smaller effective gap between the trailers behind the two trucks.

Minnesota 'Safetruck'

The University of Minnesota, under the sponsorship of the Minnesota Department of Transportation, has equipped one Navistar Class 8 truck-tractor with Global Positioning System (GPS) location sensing, combined with an accurate map database, to determine whether it is deviating from its lane and then to provide steering guidance (Alexander and Donath 1999). The intended application of this form of automation technology is to detect a driver's loss of alertness and then steer the vehicle automatically to a safe stop on the road shoulder, rather than for continuous automated driving.

US Army Truck Automation Research

The US Army is one of the largest, if not the largest, truck fleet operators in the world, with responsibility for a total of more than 200,000 trucks. The large majority of the driving of these trucks, and of the injuries and fatalities associated with their use, are related to normal daily supply operations rather than to military combat operations. The Army's Vehicle Intelligence Program is starting to explore how the Army could adopt some of the truck automation technologies developed elsewhere (electronic towbar, automated driving) and enhance them to address Army-specific needs (Gorsich and DiVito 2000), but this work is still in the formative stages and has not yet produced any experimental vehicles or test results.

Dual-mode Truck

Japan faces serious challenges of safety, productivity and congestion associated with heavy truck traffic on its expressways, and has therefore been considering concepts for automated freight movement for many years. The development of special lanes for automated trucks was considered as part of the planning for the New Tomei Expressway in the Tokyo–Osaka corridor, but this has not progressed beyond the planning stages. The use of light-duty, driverless, automated trucks has also been studied for urban freight movement in tunnels located beneath major urban centres, but this concept is still largely at the concept definition stage (Yamada et al. 1996) because of its costs and technical challenges.

Experiments were conducted on a test course of Japan's National Institute for Land and Infrastructure Management (formerly Public Works Research

Institute), showing the possibilities for automatic steering control of a single-unit truck at speeds of up to 80 km/h, using lateral guide wheels following a special curb (Tsunashima and Kaneko 1997). Longitudinal separations among vehicles were proposed to be measured by laser radar, and vehicle–vehicle coordination would be enhanced using wireless communications, while merging would be governed by a moving-block control system (Yamada et al. 1996).

Combi-Road

The Combi-Road project was established in the Netherlands to facilitate the movement of intermodal shipping containers from the port of Rotterdam to inland freight terminals where they could be transferred to long-distance trucks or trains for connections throughout Europe. It was developed as a public–private partnership between the government and the freight transport industry, both of whom had an interest in improving freight movement and in developing alternatives to conventional road and rail transport means. One of the key features of the concept was the use of special-purpose automated freight moving vehicles that would operate on their own guideway, completely segregated from other traffic in order to avoid congestion and safety problems.

Combi-Road was defined at several levels, ranging from a broad logistics concept for freight handling, to the development of its special-purpose freight guideway along a specific alignment, to the design of an automated, driverless, electrically propelled freight-moving vehicle (van der Heijden and Heere 1997, Scrase 1998). The Combi-Road vehicle was initially designed for lateral guidance using mechanical guide wheels rolling along a steel curb rail at the side of the track. However, the government requested that this be replaced with an electronic guidance system so that the vehicles would be more compatible with conventional roadway infrastructure. So, the PATH magnetic guidance system was then implemented on the prototype Combi-Road vehicle, which was tested and demonstrated on a short track in Ridderkerk, Netherlands in the summer of 1998 (Figure 2.3). The longitudinal control of the Combi-Road vehicles was based on use of track-mounted infrared beacons to detect vehicles passing.

Combi-Road did not advance beyond the concept definition and prototype vehicle testing stage, largely because of political challenges associated with the development of a competing rail freight line paralleling its intended route. The technology and logistics-operating concept could still be applicable to other locations, however.

*Figure 2.3   Combi-Road prototype vehicle on test track at Ridderkerk,
              Netherlands*

WesTrack Pavement Testing Trucks

A special-purpose application of automation technology to freight vehicles
was implemented for the testing of pavement endurance at the Nevada
Automotive Test Centre during 1996–8 (Ashmore and Mitchell 1997). This
test track was developed to provide maximum stress on the pavement within
a minimum period of time so that the endurance of different asphalt
pavement designs over a ten to twenty year period of normal use could be
compared within two years. In order to maximize the pavement loading, the
2.9 km track was driven virtually continuously at 65 km/h by three 69-ton
tractor-triple-trailer combination trucks. The driving of the trucks was
automated in order to save the labour cost of truck drivers and to avoid safety
concerns associated with driver boredom and fatigue if drivers were to be
expected to remain alert under these extremely boring driving conditions.

The WesTrack trucks were driven completely automatically, with nobody
on board, but with intensive monitoring from a roadside control centre
equipped with redundant computers and wireless communication links to the
trucks. The lane-keeping references were two continuous guide-wires
activated by 100 milliamp currents at two different frequencies, detected by
inductive loop antennas on the trucks. The trucks were designed to be
operated at constant speed on the test track and to be approximately equally
spaced along the track. The longitudinal locations were determined using
DGPS, combined with high-resolution odometers, and with an absolute

position update from a radio beacon once per lap of the track. Since the average spacing between trucks was close to 1 km, the longitudinal accuracy requirements were much less demanding than they would be in a more typical road transportation application.

Although the WesTrack operational requirements were very different from the requirements for typical freight movement systems, the results of the WesTrack testing still produced some relevant experience. These trucks were designed to operate for one million vehicle kilometres each, producing good experience regarding reliability and durability considerations. Their operations demonstrated the importance of designing the truck automation systems to address multiple simultaneous faults rather than only single faults. They also showed that if the trucks operate continuously with very accurate steering control they will significantly accelerate pavement wear, leading to the recommendation that 'wander' be deliberately introduced into the lateral control (standard deviation of at least 10 cm) in order to distribute pavement wear more evenly.

Freight Highway Case Studies in the United States

Interest has been growing in the United States in the concept of separating heavy-truck traffic from conventional light-vehicle traffic on major highway routes with high volumes of freight movement. This has been motivated in part by the economic considerations of the delays imposed on truck traffic by general traffic congestion, especially with the growth of 'just-in-time' delivery policies for both industrial and retail customers. However, it has also been motivated by public concerns about safety problems associated with mixing high-speed heavy trucks with light passenger cars on the same highway infrastructure, since the occupants of the light vehicles are much more likely to be injured or killed in the event of a collision.

The first consideration of truck-only lanes for long-distance freight movement was focused on Interstate Highway 10, which handles large volumes of truck traffic as it runs from the Atlantic to Pacific coasts (Jacksonville, FL to Los Angeles, CA). The states along this route recognized that the growing traffic volume along this highway was going to require the addition of lanes within the coming decades (much of the inter-urban length of this highway currently has only two lanes in each direction). Recognizing the importance of freight movement across this transcontinental corridor, they decided to consider the possibility of reserving the additional lanes exclusively for trucks, and to further consider how this could facilitate the application of automation technology to those trucks. However, the leading proponents of this concept retired before the study could be done, so it has not yet been studied in any depth.

In the Los Angeles region, the Southern California Association of Governments studied the possibility of adding truck-only lanes to a 60 km long section of an existing freeway that handles high volumes of truck traffic, State Route 60 (SR-60). That study determined that in order to handle the projected truck traffic volume it would be necessary to construct two truck lanes plus an emergency shoulder in each direction. Since the available right of way was not wide enough to accommodate this, it would have been necessary to build most of the facility on an elevated structure, causing the cost to exceed $4 billion (Kaku 2001). A follow-up study has shown that the ability to operate the trucks at shorter spacings using automation would make it possible to save one lane in each direction and thereby reduce the cost of the facility to $1.37 billion, representing a saving of two-thirds of the cost, even after including additional costs for separate access and egress ramps with check-in and check-out facilities (Sarakki 2003).

Researchers from the California PATH Program have explored the possibility of applying automation technology to facilitate the movement of shipping containers among multiple intermodal rail terminals in the Chicago region, as well as movements to and from major local industrial concentrations and the highway points of entry to the region. A study in the early 1980s considered the possibility of developing truck-only roads on unused rail rights of way to provide the inter-terminal connections in Chicago, but at that time automation technology was not even considered. The PATH study considered truck automation as a central element in the definition of an operating concept, with a focus on use of former railroad rights of way that could be available for use in the near future (especially those that are parallel to highly congested local streets and highways). This study showed that staging the introduction of the automation technologies after the initial construction of the truck lanes produced the highest benefit-cost ratio by providing time for the unit costs of the in-vehicle technologies to decline (Yin et al. 2004).

Finally, the Reason Foundation, a public-policy study organization, published a study promoting the economics of developing truck-only roads that would be financed using tolls collected from users (Samuel et al. 2002). This study focused on financial and economic efficiency arguments rather than technical issues, but concluded that use of vehicle automation and other related intelligent transportation system (ITS) technologies would improve the case for developing truck-only roads.

2.3   CROSS-CUTTING ISSUES

The diverse transportation system needs and perspectives from around the industrialized world have produced diversity in the approaches that have been taken to automating freight transportation. Although purely technological issues tend to be universal, the trade-offs that must be considered in selecting the most appropriate technologies are heavily dependent on local considerations such as the costs of alternatives, the institutional structure of the freight industry and its customers and transportation system conditions. The most fundamental issue that arises when reviewing all the current truck automation work is the question of whether to use a dedicated right of way. After that is addressed, other distinctions tend to become less significant.

Dedicated Right of Way

The cost of constructing new civil infrastructure (roadways, bridges, interchanges) is very high in the industrialized world because this kind of technology remains labour intensive and has not benefited significantly from the efficiency improvements of the information technology revolution. Therefore, any consideration of the costs of providing new means of improving freight movement is likely to be dominated by civil infrastructure concerns. It is generally assumed in the United States that once a lane of highway has been opened to the public for general use it is politically impossible to apply significant restrictions on access to that lane (only for high-occupancy vehicles or trucks, for example). Therefore, if a dedicated truck-only lane is to be provided, it will need to be by means of new construction rather than conversion of a pre-existing lane.

Nearly all of the current freight transport automation projects are founded on the assumption that the automation will be applied only in a facility that is dedicated to use of automated trucks, for a variety of good reasons:

- enabling all vehicles to operate at the highest levels of performance and predictability (accurate lane tracking for narrowest right of way, close vehicle following to maximize capacity per lane, coordination of manoeuvres with other vehicles and programmed consistency of vehicle behaviours to maximize safety and efficiency);
- enabling system-level operations to be optimized for highest performance, since individual vehicle movements can be managed definitively;
- avoiding hazards introduced by unpredictable and unsafe manoeuvring by individual drivers and thereby avoiding the need to implement extremely sophisticated, high-performance collision avoidance systems (which would exceed the state of the art);
- facilitating smooth speed trajectories and close vehicle following to reduce fuel consumption and pollutant emissions.

The projects that have assumed mixing of the automated trucks with conventional traffic have generally been based on providing partial, rather than complete, automation of the driving of the trucks. This applies to the Minnesota 'Safetruck' project, in which the automated driving function would only be invoked for a brief period of time when the driver was incapable, and the CHAUFFEUR project's 'assistants', which would leave much of the driving responsibility with the driver. The 'electronic towbar' concept of CHAUFFEUR is somewhat different because a driver would be fully responsible for the driving of the lead truck, while the automated system would control only the follower that is being 'towed'. However, the more advanced automation function of the CHAUFFEUR platoon operation (more than two trucks coupled together) would need to be restricted to use in a dedicated, protected lane.

It is worth exploring the possibility of operating automated trucks mixed with non-automated trucks in a facility that remains restricted only to trucks, if this can help address the economic and deployment staging challenges of implementing truck automation. In order for this type of operation to be safe without imposing unachievable technical requirements on the automation systems, it would probably be necessary to impose physical restrictions that preclude trucks from passing each other or otherwise creating complex operating conditions that exceed the capabilities of state-of-the-art vehicle control and collision avoidance systems.

Technical Challenges

The technical challenges that must be addressed in order to automate freight transport on roads are generally the same in all countries, once one accounts for the issue of whether or not a dedicated lane is assumed for the automated trucks. The technologies that are needed in all cases (and their current state of development) are:

- electronic control of steering (limited availability of prototype systems);
- electronic control of engine (generally commercially available);
- electronic control of braking (available in Europe but not generally in North America);
- wireless data communications among vehicles (becoming available via IEEE 802.11 wireless local area networks, and soon to be addressed as Dedicated Short-Range Communications (DSRC) at 5.9 GHz within North America);
- measuring vehicle longitudinal position on roadway and relative to forward vehicles (GPS, radar and lidar systems becoming available, but with somewhat limited capabilities);
- measuring vehicle lateral position relative to roadway and side and rear approaching vehicles (various methods becoming available, but selection depends on dedication of lane);

- human–machine interfaces to enable drivers to move between manual and automated driving (under development);
- fault-tolerant control software and computer(s) to maintain safety even when failures occur (major development work still needed).

The sensor requirements are most heavily dependent on whether the automated freight vehicles can be protected within their own lanes or whether they need to be able to operate on any public roadway, mixed with non-automated vehicles. When they are protected within their own lanes, special-purpose lane marking technologies can be applied to significantly increase the accuracy and robustness of the lane position measurements. If they must be able to operate on any public roadway, they are restricted to using machine vision technology, which has limited accuracy and is vulnerable to disruption by snow, ice and other adverse weather conditions. Alternatively, they might be able to use Differential Global Positioning Systems (DGPS), but Global Positioning Systems (GPS) remain vulnerable to signal interference of several types (Volpe 2001) and it would still need to be combined with a special, extremely high-accuracy (not commercially available) map database, which would need to be developed for any roads on which the trucks would operate.

In the dedicated, protected lane environment it would not be necessary to provide lateral and rearward sensing of other vehicles, but in the more general traffic environment these difficult functions would be needed to support crash avoidance capabilities. Similarly, the longitudinal sensing requirements would be much more demanding, particularly in terms of azimuthal accuracy and resolution, in order to support operations in mixed, multi-lane traffic as compared to dedicated, protected lanes.

Economic Challenges

Any new technology tends to be expensive when it is first introduced and to then decline in cost as suppliers gain experience in producing it and as production volumes increase. The freight transport industry can only be expected to adopt vehicle automation technologies when the benefits they provide exceed the costs, particularly when compared to the other available alternatives. Conventional trucking and intermodal rail remain viable means for transporting freight today, and are natural competitors to automated trucks. It would only make sense to introduce the automated trucks in situations where these competing means of transport have significant cost or quality of service disadvantages that can be overcome by means of the automation technologies. The challenge for the developers of automated trucks and truck-ways is to find the most promising initial applications, where the benefits exceed the initial costs of the new technology.

Deployment Staging

All deployments of new technologies that depend on cooperation between vehicle and infrastructure elements are confronted with a significant deployment staging challenge, which is often called the 'chicken and egg problem' (i.e. which comes first?). It is difficult to justify the construction of the new roadway infrastructure before vehicles are available to use it, but it is also difficult for vehicle purchasers to justify investments in new vehicle equipment if there are no roads on which they can use it. This is why most of the projects that have attempted to develop automation of road freight movement have had significant public agency involvement. It will be necessary for those public agencies to identify the targets of opportunity, in specific locations, where the roadway infrastructure can be installed to start the deployment sequence. This is where the emerging concept of truck-only lanes offers an opportunity to develop the infrastructure first, if technical solutions can be found to make it possible for the automated trucks to co-exist with non-automated trucks in those lanes.

REFERENCES

Alexander, L. and M. Donath (1999), Differential GPS Based Control of a Heavy Vehicle, *Proceedings of IEEE/IEEJ/JSAI International Conference on Intelligent Transportation Systems*, Tokyo, pp. 662–7.

Ashmore, C. and T. Mitchell (1997), WesTrack: Putting ITS to Work, *Public Roads*, Vol. 61, no. 1, pp. 8–15.

Baum, H. and T. Geissler (2000), Assessing Social Costs and Social Benefits of AHS: Methodological and Empirical Approach for the Introduction of CHAUFFEUR in Germany and Japan, *Seventh World Congress on Intelligent Transport Systems,* Torino, Italy, Paper no. 2224.

Bonnet, C. and H. Fritz (2000), Fuel Consumption Reduction Experienced by Two PROMOTE-CHAUFEUR Trucks in Electronic Towbar Operation, *Seventh World Congress on Intelligent Transport Systems,* Torino, Italy, Paper no. 2407.

Browand, F., J. McArthur and C. Radovich (2004), *Fuel Saving Achieved in the Field Test of Two Tandem Trucks*, California PATH Program Report UCB-ITS-PRR-2004-20.

Gorsich, D.J. and E. DiVito (2000), The Army's Vehicle Intelligence Program (AVIP): Bringing Telematics to the 21st Century Truck, SAE Paper no. 2000-01-3425.

Hammache, M., M. Michaelian and F. Browand (2002), Aerodynamic Forces on Truck Models, Including Two Trucks in Tandem, SAE Paper 2002-01-0530, SAE World Congress, Detroit.

Hingwe, P., A. Packard and M. Tomizuka (2000), Linear Parameter Varying Controller for Automated Lane Guidance Experimental Study on Tractor Semi-Trailers, *Proceedings of American Control Conference*, Chicago, pp. 2038–42.

Kaku Associates (2001), SR-60 Truck Lane Feasibility Study Final Report, Southern California Association of Governments.

Samuel, P., R.W. Poole, Jr. and J. Holguin-Veras (2002), Toll Truckways: A New Path toward Safer and More Efficient Freight Transportation, Reason Foundation Report.

Sarakki Associates (2003), *SR-60 Automated Truck Feasibility Study*, Report to California Department of Transportation.

Schulze, M. (1997), CHAUFFEUR – The European Way towards an Automated Highway System, *Proceedings of Fourth World Congress on Intelligent Transport Systems*, Berlin, Paper no. 2311.

Scrase, R. (1998), Driving Freight Forward, *ITS International*, Vol. 16, pp. 47–50.

Shladover, S.E. (2001), Opportunities in Truck Automation, *Proceedings of Eighth World Congress on Intelligent Transport Systems*, Sydney, Paper no. ITS00155.

Tan, Y., A. Robotis and I. Kanellakopoulos (1999), Speed Control Experiments with an Automated Heavy Vehicle, *Proceedings of the Eighth IEEE International Conference on Control Applications*, Kona, Hawaii, pp. 1353–8.

Tsunashima, H. and T. Kaneko (1997), Performance Analysis of Lateral Guidance System for Dual Mode Truck, *Proceedings of IEEE Conference on Intelligent Transportation Systems*, Boston, pp. 966–71.

van der Heijden, B. and E. Heere (1997), Combi-Road is on the Move, *Proceedings of Fourth World Congress on Intelligent Transport Systems*, Berlin, Paper no. 2284.

Volpe National Transportation Systems Center (2001), Vulnerability Assessment of the Transportation Infrastructure Relying on the Global Positioning System, USDOT Report.

Yamada, Harutoshi, S. Uedo, T. Kono and Y. Tanaka (1996), Development of the Dual Mode Truck Control Technology for the New Freight Transport System, *Proceedings of Third World Congress on Intelligent Transport Systems*, Orlando, Florida, Paper no. 3156.

Yin, Y., M.A. Miller and S.E. Shladover (2004), *Assessment of the Applicability of Cooperative Vehicle-Highway Automation Systems to Freight Movement in Chicago*, Transportation Research Board Annual Meeting, Washington DC, Paper No. 04-4755.

3. Improved quality of rail freight service by using self-propelled freight wagons

Jürgen Siegmann and Sven Heidmeier

3.1 INTRODUCTION

Rail transport is – like barge transport – very successful and nearly unbeatable in hauling huge masses over long distances. Small or medium sized flows require collection and transportation processes that are costly, time-consuming and susceptible to failures. Automation helps to accelerate collection and distribution processes and saves labour costs. In principle the railway system supports automation due to its guiding device and external control system. In the last few years promising developments and testing of automated rail freight systems have taken place but none of them has so far been developed into a commercial operating system.

This chapter will give an overview of the most important developments towards automated rail freight transport. Due to the fact that significant R&D effort is required to realise automated rail freight transport, a migration concept is introduced that supports the step-by-step development of the necessary basic technologies.

3.2 PRESENT SHORTCOMINGS OF RAIL TRANSPORT

Products of railway cargo companies in Europe consist mainly of block trains, single wagon load traffic and combined transport. Single customer block trains in specific, mostly cost-oriented markets have almost no problems in maintaining their market position. In single wagon load traffic and combined transport, however, the load has to be collected from several customers and transported to the marshalling yards or terminals. This feeder service is very inflexible and expensive resources (traction vehicles, personnel, slots) have to be used, which raises the price of the transport substantially. Shippers often complain that the use of wagons in private sidings is very inflexible especially as even small movements necessitate external power. In combined transport, good quality direct train connections between main industry centres are offered. The catchment area around terminals however is small; it forms an ellipse, which often covers not even the large population centres. The cost of handling the load twice in the terminals and of the road transport can swallow up the advantages of the cost-effective, bundled rail transport in the case of short transportation distances.

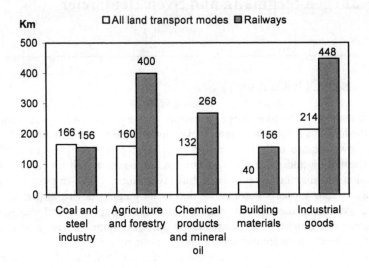

Source: MWMTV (1999).

Figure 3.1   Average transportation distance for freight in Germany (all land transport modes) compared with rail transport

The average transportation distance in rail freight transport is 245 km for all German railway companies. The average transportation distance for single wagon load traffic is 257 km, for combined transport 490 km and for block train services about 140 km (MWMTV 1999).

Figure 3.1 shows average transportation distances for different kinds of goods. The transportation distance by rail is much greater than for all other means of transportation, as a result mainly of the fact that railway transport today is not competitive over short distances. For example the share of goods transported by rail in Germany is well below 10% for chemical products/mineral oil and well below 5% for industrial goods. With respect to the growth prognoses for these markets rail transport urgently needs new production concepts.

Based on the drawbacks described, two principal directions for future rail freight traffic can be formulated.

More Individual Offers for the Customer

Supply and collection times of wagons in private sidings have to depend on customers' requirements and not on the service plan of shunting locomotives. That means that wagons needed by customers at short notice must be made available quickly and flexibly. Wagons must be able to move simply and flexibly in private sidings, without expensive shunting locomotives and high personnel expenditure. Substantial time and cost savings can be realized, particularly in the collection and distribution procedure, if wagons are able to move to the next marshalling yard autonomously, directly and without delay. In this way the entire transportation process can be tightened and made more attractive. Where it is desired and appreciated by customers, shorter transportation times must be offered, particularly by direct movement of wagons from origin to destination without any shunting. According to the requirements of shippers, telematics and sensor technology functions should be implemented, e.g. tracking and tracing, temperature monitoring or theft prevention. Wagons have to match customers' requirements, but the basic technology must be designed universally for as many classes of wagons as possible, thus allowing line production and low prices for the technology. A platform concept is also conceivable, comparable to a container wagon, on which customer-specific loading units can be placed.

Optimization of the Operational Mode

In order to use vehicle capacity in a highly-productive way, circulation times must be minimized. This requires the decrease of downtimes at the customer's siding and in marshalling yards, as well as the avoidance of detours during the collection and distribution process. Marshalling processes must be shortened by avoiding manual handlings as far as possible.

Time and cost for maintenance of vehicles should be minimised by telematic supervision of wear components. In this way the productivity of vehicles can be increased by reduced downtimes.

3.3 DEVELOPMENTS IN AUTOMATED RAIL SYSTEMS AND SELF-PROPELLED FREIGHT WAGONS

In principle railway traffic supports automatic operation due to its guiding device and external control system. There are already successful automated rail systems in operation such as automated metro lines. Other projects like Frederich's SST or the CargoMover developed by SIEMENS have shown the technical feasibility of rail automation. However these systems haven't achieved approval for general use yet. The important difference between automated metro systems and automated rail freight traffic is that the metro normally operates in a 'closed' area. For freight traffic such dedicated 'closed' lines are only reasonable for highly frequented links. If automated rail vehicles operate in a publicly accessible area, approval of safety is much more complex.

Another important step in achieving more flexibility can be realized by the adapted motorization of small train units or even single wagons. These vehicles can operate more cost-efficiently for forwarding small quantities of goods than conventional locomotives and allow more flexible wagon movements in private sidings or marshalling yards.

Historic Developments

The idea of self-propelled freight wagons is not new; however they have not yet achieved a widespread extension in rail transport. Self-propelled freight vehicles have been used for regular transportation on lines with limited traffic. Since the 1930s attempts were made to set self-propelled freight wagons against the growing rivalry of road transport (Rauschenberg 1999) (Figure 3.2).

Source: Rauschenberg (1999).

Figure 3.2   Self-propelled freight wagon ET 194.2 built in 1896 (left), self-propelled freight wagon VT 10 in operation 1938 (right)

CargoSprinter

The idea behind the CargoSprinter was to develop a small train unit that could serve private sidings and terminals autonomously. On long distance runs these train units can be coupled to save energy and track charges. The CargoSprinter has a driving trailer at each end powered by two 265 kW diesel engines. In between are four container wagons (Figure 3.3).

Except for the first application in Germany from 1997 to 1999 between Hamburg, Osnabrück and Frankfurt/Main the CargoSprinter has not yet been developed as a commercial operating system.

Source: www.windhoff.de

Figure 3.3   CargoSprinter

SST and SOG

Frederich presented the basic approach to adapting freight railways to the new transportation requirements of automation in 1992 (Frederich 1992). The ideal solution, named 'Selbstorganisierender Güterverkehr (SOG)' (self-organizing freight traffic), is based on self-propelled transportation units which are sent on their way immediately after loading. In order to meet customers' requirements for demand-oriented, flexible operation, the transportation units operate without a timetable and without coupling stop or shunting treatment between origin and destination. The vehicles communicate with signalling systems and other vehicles, compute their travel route autonomously, trigger necessary switching operations and recognize and solve conflicts with other vehicles (Figure 3.4). There is no longer any contact with conventional, signal- and timetable-oriented rail traffic.

This ideal concept of an automatic freight railway, however, first needs its own track network. This network must contain the main routes between densely populated areas and economic centres as well as a large number of feeder lines, in order to be able to satisfy as much transportation demand as possible. Since building of new lines is mostly not feasible both for financial reasons and for reasons of surface availability and acceptance by the population, existing lines must be used. These lines must be equipped with appropriate radio systems for communication between vehicles and infrastructure. The realization of such a network requires substantial financial expenditure and time, and is therefore probably not possible in the short term.

The use of separate tracks for automatic vehicles will remain limited to individual islands in the beginning, e.g. in-plant transport.

In all other cases the introduction of an automatic freight railway system requires it to operate alongside conventional, signal-led trains on conventionally equipped lines (Figure 3.4). Signal aspects and track clearance information is transferred to the vehicles by magnets or loops, which are fixed to the track. The control of infrastructure elements and signals is realized conventionally by signal towers.

The first tests of this 'Selbsttätig Signalgeführtes Triebfahrzeug' (SST) (self-operating signal-controlled transportation) took place on the route from Aachen main station to Aachen-West, Germany. A promising field test in the area of Braunschweig followed from 1996 to 1999. However, general permission for driverless operations could not be achieved (Molle 1998).

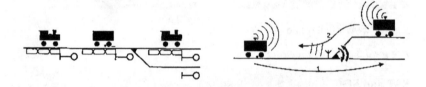

Source: Frederich (1992).

Figure 3.4   Selbsttätig Signalgeführtes Triebfahrzeug (SST) (self-operating signal-controlled transportation) (left) and Selbst-organisierender Güterverkehr (SOG) (self-organizing freight traffic) (right)

CargoMover

The CargoMover is a self-propelled automated freight wagon developed and lead-managed by Siemens Transportation Systems, Germany (Frederich et al. 2002).

As the system is not designed to operate in a closed area, the CargoMover is equipped with an obstacle-spot system to identify any obstructions on the track by means of on-board radar, laser and video sensors. If any obstacle is detected on the track, the CargoMover automatically stops.

The CargoMover operates on the basis of the European Train Control System (ETCS), level 2. The vehicle is controlled by GSM-R (Global System for Mobile Communication for Railways) radio data transmission. The track is fitted with balises to review the current position of the vehicle.

The first version of the CargoMover is based on a self-propelled CargoSprinter unit which is powered by two 265 kW diesel engines. This relatively high motor capacity results from the concept of the CargoSprinter, which is designed to haul additional freight wagons.

The CargoMover has proved the feasibility of an automated rail freight transport in promising tests at the Siemens test ring in Wegberg-Wildenrath, Germany. However, further research and engineering are required. The obstacle-spot system must be fitted to allow safe functioning at higher speeds and for cost-effective use the engine has to be adapted. The biggest hindrance to the use of the CargoMover in regular rail-freight traffic is that the schedule for an area-wide implementation of ETCS and GSM-R is not yet clear. Recent plans for a migration of ETCS following Directive 96/48/EC and 2001/16/EC of the European Union cover only the main lines in international corridors. However, it is uncertain if secondary lines and private sidings will be equipped with ETCS and GSM-R, where most of the potential for automated freight traffic is assumed to be.

Source: www.siemens.de

Figure 3.5   CargoMover

Automated Metro Systems

Worldwide several automated metro systems are in operation, e.g. the VAL in Lille, Toulouse, Chicago and Taipei, the SkyTrain in Vancouver or the METEOR in Paris. Characteristic for these metro systems is that they are fully segregated from public areas running in tunnels, on elevated tracks or guided by fences. At the passenger-train interface some of the systems operate with doors to protect the passengers at the stations like the VAL. Others use track-sided detection systems to stop the train in case of an intrusion into the guideway like the SkyTrain in Vancouver.

In most cases metro lines operate with a continuous train control system based on a track aerial cable to continuously transfer instructions (such as maximum authorized velocity or the distance to the next stop) into the vehicle. This continuous train control is a very good basis for automated train operation. For heavy rail a similar continuous train control is used only on major lines. Secondary lines are equipped with a conventional intermittent signalling system which is based on light signals.

For these two reasons, the separated track and the continuous train control, the experience with automated metro systems is very helpful but cannot be transferred in a direct way to rail-freight traffic operation.

3.4   NEW APPROACH IN THREE STEPS

Current research based on the latest technical developments has shown that the implementation of the ideal concept given by automatically, driverless operating rail vehicles still requires substantial derailed research (IVSGV 2002). According to previous estimates this ideal concept contains a large potential for rail freight traffic. However, this can be realized only in the medium term due to the necessary development steps. Taking these results, a basic implementation concept for automated rail freight traffic is introduced in the following sections considering the necessary step-by-step development and testing of fundamental technologies. The steps of development are selected in such a way that the implementation of the first step gains clear advantages regarding flexibility and individuality. Against this background the concept focuses not only on automation of rail-freight traffic, but analyses the entire range of possible technologies to realize its individualization. Therefore in the following sections the term 'Individualisierter Schienengüterverkehr (IVSGV)' (individualized rail freight traffic) is used for the entire implementation scenario. The three steps of development of IVSGV are:

Level 1: Wagon with Shunting Drive
The service of individual private sidings in rail freight traffic, in particular with small transport volumes, often requires operational expenditure which is out of all proportion to the yields attainable. Shunting locomotives and personnel must be able to meet peak demand, which however occurs rarely. The lack of flexibility of wagons in the work area has frequently been criticised by most shippers. These high costs led to the fact that the operation of many small private sidings has been shut down in the past. This again leads to a decrease of demand, which can endanger the economy of the whole system of single-wagon load traffic with its high share of fixed costs.

Self-propelled wagons offer flexibility at a reasonable price in private sidings and help to cut the number of shunting locos in sidings and feeder lines. Delivery traffic can perform with less expenditure of time, since collection and delivery of wagons in private sidings are simplified. Personnel and locomotives can be used more efficiently.

In combined transport self-propelled cars support operations (e.g. stopping under the crane in non-electrified areas of the terminal). Also alternative handling technologies such as 'Abroll-Container-System (ACTS)' (Roll-On-Roll-Off Container System), 'Wechselbehälter auf Schienen (WAS)' (swap-body handling) or horizontal container handling are supported by motorized wagons.

Figure 3.6   IVSGV Level 1: Car with shunting drive

Level 2: Driver-based IVSGV

While in the first step the drives of the wagons are used for shunting only, the second generation of IVSGV will be able to run on long-distance trips. Higher speeds are possible by coupling of the individual drives. The system combines the advantages of flexibility in the short range and saving of locomotives even in long-distance traffic.

This level supports new production concepts like Train Coupling and Sharing (TCS). It is possible to use small groups of wagons with adapted motorization for collection and distribution. These groups couple at rendezvous points and run together for long distances.

Figure 3.7   IVSGV Level 2: Driver-based operation

Level 3: Driverless Train Operation

Due to its specific characteristics such as vehicle guidance and external control the railway system has good prerequisites for automatic operation. At level 3 of IVSGV, distance trips can be realized without the time and cost-intensive requirements of locomotives or driving vans. This crucially affects the cost structure of the system and results in completely new perspectives for new flexible rail freight traffic with small IVSGV units.

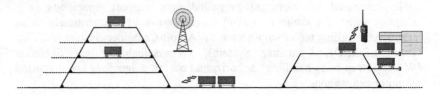

Figure 3.8   IVSGV Level 3: driverless train operation

3.5   TECHNICAL DETAILS

Basic Concept

The operation field of rail freight vehicles requires a drive which is able to cover even long distances on non-electrified feeder tracks. In the short term only diesel engines are available for this purpose. The use of electric drives with accumulator batteries, solar technology or a fuel cell is not recommended for economic and ecological reasons at the present stage of development.

The estimation of the necessary motor capacity for individually driving high-speed self-propelled freight wagons has shown that the drive units would exceed the budget. Also, in order to limit energy consumption, individual vehicles should not be used at higher speeds. The drive components should be designed in such a way that single vehicles can achieve speeds of approximately 60 to 80 km/h on regional routes, and about 120 km/h on long-distance routes within conjoint wagon groups by means of distributed power. For this purpose a suitable traction control has to be developed and optionally an appropriate coupling technique should be introduced.

It seems that virtual couplings, i.e. conjoint wagon groups without mechanical coupling but using an electronic distance control system, cannot be recommended. It is not possible to share traction; also failures or breakdowns of individual drives cannot be compensated by other vehicles.

At present the largest challenge is the development of control and safety devices for driverless train operation. Components that spot obstacles and take over track monitoring have not yet been developed for general use. Also, it has to be proved that driverless operation is as secure as the current state.

Vehicle control at low speed is possible by radio control. Such systems are available but have to be adapted to higher performance requirements. A considerable benefit can be realized through use of telematic components in the vehicle. Devices for vehicle location and tracking and tracing are the basis for an optimal fleet management, sensors reduce long and personnel-intensive checks (e.g. automatic brake checks) and allow maintenance depending on wear of components and a reduction of Life-Cycle Costs (LCC).

The use of self-propelled wagons requires less infrastructure in feeder lines and private sidings than operation by shunting locomotives. This also implies that operation frequency may be increased.

During the introduction phase individualized freight traffic will be integrated into the existing system of single wagon-load traffic. Wagons will be collected from private sidings e.g. by a ring or liner train system and sorted by route in marshalling yards. This procedure reduces expenditure on the use of shunting locomotives for delivery and collection and small quantities of wagons can even economically be forwarded by rail.

Bottlenecks for individual running wagons occur at the entrance and exit of marshalling yards. These problems can be solved by early forming of conjoint wagon groups. In the case of sufficient transport demand a train-coupling-and-sharing (TCS) system should be implemented.

The gradual development of technology for the implementation scenario is described as follows:

Level 1: Car with Shunting Drive
In order to design the drive components as economically as possible, mass production components from the motor vehicle industry should be used. A shunting drive for speeds of approximately 25 km/h needs a maximum power of 100 kW. The power transmission can be done mechanically, hydro-dynamically or electrically.

During the first implementation stage of the IVSGV such a drive unit has to be designed including power transmission, compressed air supply and support on the vehicle frame.

Important information about the state of the engine and diesel tank level will be measured. A telematics system for tracking and tracing and maintenance by state of components supports an optimal vehicle disposition and helps reducing the Life-Cycle Cost (LCC).

For simple and fast shunting, components of an automatic brake test have to be developed. The necessary technology is capable of being developed in the short term.

Vehicle brakes have to be compatible with conventional freight wagons. A cheap brake control system for wagons with shunting drive has to be developed. Driving of the wagon is realized by remote control. Applicable systems are available on the market. The still limited efficiency of these systems has to be increased with advancing implementation of the system

IVSGV. R&D is needed to upgrade the remote control to operate conjoint wagon groups.

An interesting extension of the basic version of IVSGV is the remote-controlled, video monitored piloting to reduce shunting personnel.

The basic variant of IVSGV, a wagon with shunting drive, is compatible with valid operational procedures concerning its operational handling and only slight changes in relation to today's regulations for the shunting service are necessary. To get permission for such operations should not be a problem. To drive a train in private sidings no train driver's licence is necessary but just the agreement of the local chief operation manager. Only internal personnel training is needed in this case. Work may be distributed between the shipper's and railway personnel. The wagons will be provided by the shipper at the connection point between private siding and network.

Of course the IVSGV vehicle with shunting drive will be higher priced than a conventional freight wagon. As the cost of external shunting increases for smaller traffic volumes, this higher price can be compensated by the decrease in the cost of external shunting. Nevertheless an adequate utilization ratio is needed for a return of investment, which means high kilometric performance and small downtimes for the vehicles.

A wagon with shunting drive can be realized in the short term. The development risk is limited due to the relatively low technical and operational requirements.

Level 2: Driver-based IVSGV

While in the first level of IVSGV the benefit is limited to shunting operations, the second level is aimed at improving the flexibility of the entire train operation. The goal is to develop a modular system that is based on self-propelled wagons. Due to the fact that single wagons travelling at high speed are not economically feasible because of the required motor power, energy consumption and track charges, the concept of coupling vehicles and using distributed power is essential for a flexible and cost-effective operation. The drives of the second modification phase of IVSGV will be designed in such a way that single vehicles will achieve about 60 km/h and conjoint wagon groups approximately 120 km/h. For these requirements power of 200–300 kW is needed. Appropriate drives are cheaply produced for commercial vehicles in line production.

For control of the distributed power a bus system is necessary which can be implemented as a cable- or radio-based solution. For this purpose the developments of the FEBIS project (Witte et al. 2001) should be used. Traction control systems between master and slave locos are already available but have to be adapted to IVSGV conjoint wagon groups. A particular problem of the control system is the consideration of different loading levels of the individual IVSGV vehicles. The fail-safe function of the system in case of an interruption of the radio communication still has to be established.

To realize a simple and quick coupling and splitting of conjoint wagon groups, the vehicles should be equipped with automatic couplers.

Due to the fact that automated operation will not be available in the short term the convoys have to be manned by a train driver in the first implementation phase. For higher speeds vehicles need train driver cabins and train safety devices. Because this causes high costs and a restriction of loading capacity for the wagons, a driving trailer should be developed. Keeping in mind that operation with driving trailers is associated with logistical disadvantages and may cause higher shunting activities, an interface between individual driving IVSGV wagons and IVSGV convoys has to be defined. For that reason single wagons will be used only in private sidings and at low speed on feeder lines. In these areas wagons will be driven by remote control or video monitoring. A driving trailer for movement on main lines collects single wagons or wagon groups by a ring or liner train system. These conjoint wagon groups will be connected with other groups over long distances by the TCS technique.

Level 2 is realizable in the short or medium term. The experience of level 1 will be very helpful for upgrading the motor power and concepts for local operation. Some of the required modules are already in existence or can be realized for a joined use in a widespread area of applications (e.g. distributed power control) so that the development risk can be minimized.

Level 3: Driverless Train Operation
The drive units of IVSGV vehicles from level 2 don't need major changes in the transition to automatic operation. Also, train-internal control and communication systems as well as the automatic coupler already exist in level 2.

There is still considerable need for research concerning the development of a simple signalling system for automatic driving on branch and feeder lines. Vehicle and infrastructure installations have to support low-cost operation procedures. Presently no technically or economically viable solutions are known. The noticeable trend of concentrating the intelligence on the vehicle and the simplification of infrastructure installations, e.g. the passive balises in ETCS, must also include rail-freight traffic. Automatic operation without a train driver requires the area-wide availability of operation control and communication technology for the transmission of control commands to the vehicle and from the vehicle's telematics equipment to a control centre, which is not available area-wide today. Branch lines in particular are equipped with personnel-intensive, simple operation control techniques only. Solving the problem of affordable operation control techniques is important for the future, not only for automatic operation but also for the entire rail service in low populated areas. Systems on which automatic operation can be based (e.g. ETCS 2) are available, but today the necessary vehicle equipment is too expensive for single wagons. Also investment in the infrastructure of branch and feeder lines seems too expensive. Unless the required vehicle and infrastructure equipment is available area-wide and at an affordable price, automated rail freight service will be limited to dedicated networks.

Units for obstacle detection are presently under development and still have to be made fit for series production. By now, safe obstacle detection is limited to a maximum speed of approximately 30 km/h (Frederich et al. 2002). A safety analysis has still to prove that unmanned operations meet today's safety standards. Additionally, driverless operation requires the development of emergency concepts, which are more complex for area-wide railways than for limited light rail systems.

With driverless, fully automated vehicles the production system will no longer be dominated by the need for economical management of employees, locomotives and driving trailers. Instead collection, distribution and long-distance transport of freight wagons can be made more flexible and locally managed.

The limits of an automatic IVSGV will probably depend on slot capacity limits and on the treatment of small IVSGV groups within the track access charging system. IVSGV vehicles are able to use the network individually over the shortest distance including secondary lines. If IVSGV-wagons are treated as whole trains in the track access charge calculation, slot costs must be distributed over many cars in a group for economical reasons. For small groups this will probably mean compromises in the choice of route.

Due to the direct travel and absence of dead time a maximum speed of 60 to 80 km/h will mostly be enough to bring IVSGV vehicles to their destination just as fast as a truck.

Although automated rail freight service is a very promising solution for the future of freight transport it should be noted that it will be realizable area-wide only in the medium or long term due to the required R&D work.

3.6   TOWARDS AUTOMATED FREIGHT WAGONS

The technical possibilities described above lead to the following 'timetable' for the realization of automated rail-freight traffic.

In the first implementation level of IVSGV the advantages of the autonomic drive can be achieved only in local areas. Over long distances wagons are forwarded within normal locomotive-driven trains. Even if only a shunting drive is implemented, the system has advantages over the current state. Private sidings with low quantities of wagons can be served more rationally and flexibly, because shunting locomotives are not needed any more. As this makes it possible for the customer to move wagons in private sidings without the use of external resources and allows the departure of wagons directly after loading, a large part of the aspired individualization of freight traffic can already be achieved in this first phase.

The first phase of IVSGV is not to be understood as a completely new production concept for the whole of rail freight traffic, but it enables users and operators to transport small numbers of wagons economically by rail, resulting in a better utilization of the single wagon system and increased efficiency of this production form.

In a systematic upgrading process, the operation limits of the autonomic drive should be tested, starting with self-propelled shunting operations in private sidings followed by local train operations and train convoys based on the distributed power of IVSGV wagons. This second implementation level of IVSGV requires the development of basic technologies which seem to be realizable in the short or medium term. On the vehicle side a remote controlled bus system and distributed power control have to be developed to an approved level. From the operational point of view, planning and disposition tools for effective vehicle routing and TCS administration have to be developed.

These technologies yield benefits not only for IVSGV, but also as basic components of the whole rail system. Therefore these technologies should be developed in cooperation with other rail departments including passenger transport.

The implementation of the third level will take place only in the medium or long term because of the necessary R&D work. The CargoMover has shown that automated freight wagons are technically feasible, but economic boundary conditions for operation systems, vehicle equipment and equipment for locating vehicles and obstacle detection still have to be specified. Automated freight wagons will maximize operational flexibility, but the vehicle equipment has to be economically feasible for single wagons. In development of infrastructure-based signalling systems and track monitoring it should be considered that these have to meet the economic requirements even of low usage lines. Nevertheless preliminary field tests on dedicated lines should take place in order to gain experience.

A conclusive evaluation of the technical and economical feasibility of automatic IVSGV without a train driver is only possible after clearance of the legal situation and the definition of the resulting safety requirements for vehicle and track. As yet, there is no technical solution that meets the financial limits of rail freight traffic. Anyhow it is to be expected that technological progress will result in affordable prices for the needed components. In the same way a concerted development of basic technology modules like distributed power control will help to reduce prices, and smoothes the way for automated freight traffic.

REFERENCES

Frederich, Fritz (1992), Eisenbahn, Quo Vadis? Betrachtungen Nicht nur zur Technik; *Glasers Annalen*, Vol. 116, no. 8/9, pp. 260–9.

Frederich, F., F. Mairhofer and H.M. Schabert (2002), Der CargoMover – eine Innovation für automatisierten Güterverkehr, *Glasers Annalen*, Vol. 126, no. 10, pp. 442–8.

IVSGV (2002), *Machbarkeitstudie Individualisierter Schienengüterverkehr*, Bundesministerium für Bildung und Forschung.

Molle, Peter (1998), Die Erprobung Selbsttätig Signalgeführter Triebfahrzeuge (SST) im Güterverkehr der Deutschen Bahn AG, *Eisenbahntechnische Rundschau*, Vol. 47, no. 7, pp. 443–6.

MWMTV (1999), *Marktstudie Schienengüterverkehr*, Ministerium für Wirtschaft, Energie, Mittelstand und Verkehr des Landes Nordrhein-Westfalen.

Rauschenberg, Rainer H. (1999), *Potentiale für die Verringerung der externen Effekte des Verkehrssektors durch einen dezentralisierten und automatisierten Gütertransport der Bahn*, Dissertation zur Erlangung des Doktorgrades des Fachbereichs Wirtschaftswissenschaften der Johann Wolfgang Goethe-Universität in Frankfurt am Main.

Witte, S., A. Launay, R. Tione and C. Coulange (2001), FEBIS System Aspects, World Congress on *Railway Research, Session 1.6*, Cologne.

4. Opportunities for automated inland navigation

Alexander Lutz and Ernst-Dieter Gilles

4.1 INTRODUCTION

The need to transport people and freight is ever increasing. For example, in Germany the national agency for traffic (Bundesministerium für Verkehr, Bau- und Wohnungswesen, BMVBW) predicts an increase of 20% in passenger transportation and an increase of 64% in freight transportation between 1997 and 2015 (BMVBW 2003). At the same time increasing the highway capacity to meet these needs is impossible due to spatial and financial restrictions. Therefore alternative methods of transportation, such as railway and inland waterway transportation, play a major role in coping with this capacity constraint.

Maintenance and extension costs of inland waterways in Germany make up only 5% of the total traffic budget predicted until 2015 while 12.7% of all goods are shipped on rivers according to the BMVBW.

Inland waterway transportation uses the least amount of energy when compared to road and railway transportation (see Figure 4.1).

Primary Energy Need in Freight Transport
Litres of diesel per 100 ton kilometres

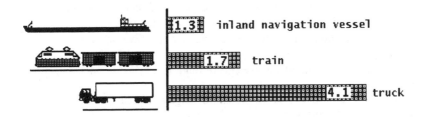

Figure 4.1   Energy costs for different transportation modalities

Inland vessels are mostly used to transport coal, oil, chemical goods, metal and food products over long distances from seaports to large industrial centres and vice versa. Nevertheless, container shipping is becoming more important. The average annual growth rate of container transport on inland waterways from 1999 to 2003 in Germany was more than 11%. It grew by 15.7% in the first three quarters of 2004 compared to one year earlier according to Statistisches Bundesamt (2004). Container transportation makes high demands on shipping times and their prediction. Containers are mostly transferred from seagoing to inland vessels at the seaports, shipped to container terminals using the waterways and then transferred to trucks. Low waiting times at the seaports and the container terminals are essential for the effectiveness of the transport chain. Automation in inland navigation strongly contributes to the satisfaction of these demands. Thereby substantially enhanced productivity of waterway transportation improves its competitiveness.

Inland navigation is considered to be the safest of the freight transport modalities. That is because the spacious waterways allow for large safety distances between the vessels for the current traffic volume. Automated navigation can also keep these qualities of inland shipping at a high level for growing traffic volumes and the larger average vessel sizes that go along with the growing volumes of container transport.

4.2   LEVELS OF AUTOMATION IN INLAND NAVIGATION

Inland navigation can be regarded as a complex system with many aspects, from the operators' navigational tasks to vessel fleet management. In order to properly deal with this complex system several design techniques are exploited:

- hierarchical structure: introduction of different levels of operation;
- modularity: definition of components based on common tasks;
- optimality techniques: application of optimization at all levels;
- partial autonomy: autonomous completion of well-defined tasks;
- redundancy and diversity: duplication of critical components and backup of critical components through functionally independent units.

Automation can be applied to the entire range of operations of inland vessel fleets from path following by a single vessel to the scheduling problems that shipping companies have to deal with.

A hierarchical structure with three levels of automation is proposed to divide the full system into several manageable subsystems. Two of these are depicted in Figure 4.2. Considering all aspects of inland navigation as an integrated automation design would be far too complex. Treating it as a system consisting of several subsystems is inherent to inland navigation since all the ships need to be considered as independent units. Furthermore, this partitioning comes naturally as the time constants of the different levels lie in different regions. The time constants of the path following module, for example, lie in an interval of several seconds up to one minute whereas the time constants of the highest level are in the domain of several hours or even days. Each of the sub-problems can be treated separately with some restrictions. Higher-level modules can influence lower levels' actions. Lower levels provide the higher levels with information about their state.

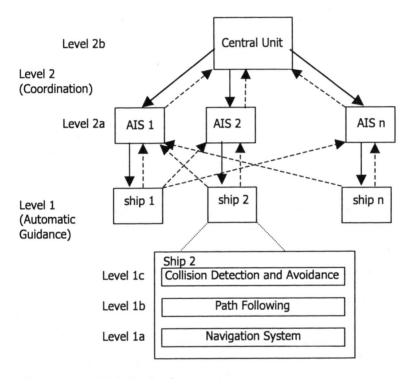

Figure 4.2   Different levels of automation

This chapter will cover in detail the lowest level of automation, namely path following by a single ship, but will also sketch the opportunities and technical and practical challenges that arise at higher levels of automation.

Level 1: Automatic Guidance
The lowest level of automation in inland waterway transportation deals with a single ship equipped with various sensors. The ship is passive in the sense that it does not communicate with its environment, namely other ships or supervision centres. Level 1 comprises three layers: the navigation system,

the path following module as well as a module for collision detection and avoidance.

A level 1 automation system is capable of automatically guiding a ship under normal traffic conditions without requiring any installations external to the ship.

Opportunities

The advantage of level 1 automation is a substantial improvement of safety on the waterways, by relieving the navigator of tiring routine work and providing support in complex situations, particularly at night and in foggy weather. This is of vital importance for protecting the environment by helping to avoid accidents since many dangerous goods such as chemical substances and fossil fuels are transported on inland waterways. A navigation system consists not only of various sensors that are installed on the ship but also of a detailed electronic nautical chart that is stored on an on-board computer and visible to the navigator. This chart contains much more information than the plain radar image that is normally the only visible aid with river information that is available to the navigator. Ideally, the radar image is plotted onto the electronic chart to allow both information sources to be available at the same time. The task of reading the radar image is then much easier, especially at times when visibility is limited because stationary objects such as radar reflecting buoys, bridges or small islands can be identified easily with the information given in the electronic chart.

A navigation system can combine the chart information with water depth data to calculate the fairway that is safe to navigate on for a certain draft. The depth information can be obtained from official agencies that keep track of these data, for example the ELWIS system (Elektronisches Wasserstraßen-Informationssystem) on the Rhine River. This feature can improve the capacity and safety of waterway transportation. In addition, it supports the competitiveness of waterway transportation, because accurate information about water depth enables maximum amount of freight for this depth (under safe conditions) to be transported.

In addition to the navigation system module, the path following module opens up many new opportunities in inland navigation. The path following module enables a ship to follow a guiding line autonomously without taking into account other traffic. In this case, the rudder angle is controlled by the navigation system according to the position and direction relative to the guiding line that is chosen by the navigator.

Automatic control of the rudder can lead to a reduction in fuel consumption. The computer determines the optimal guiding line with respect to the river's current, i.e. choosing the outer part of a turn going downstream and vice versa. The mechanical wear of the steering gear can also be reduced as shown in Sandler et al. (1996).

A high-precision path following module can be used to assist the navigator in the most complex navigational tasks. Automated docking manoeuvres and automatic navigation in locks require very accurate measurements and advanced algorithms.

Another interesting application of automatic guidance in inland navigation is the development of electronic trains of barges. The leading ship's trajectory serves as the target guiding line for the other vessels, which follow at a specified distance. Trains of barges can increase the safety of waterway transportation by the formation of virtual lanes. Furthermore, they permit shorter distances between vessels and thus increase the waterway transport capacity.

Developments

At the Institute for System Dynamics and Control at the University of Stuttgart, a self-contained, integrated navigation system for inland and coastal shipping is being developed.

The project started in the 1970s. Then the most reliable and accurate method to determine the position of a ship on a river was using a current-carrying pilot cable laid on the river bed (Stark 1976). To determine the position of a ship completely, several measuring methods were developed using the pilot cable. One of them determined the distance transverse to the cable, the height above the cable and the route angle. Another method determined the position along the course and indicated peculiarities such as sharp curves by generating markers that radiated coded frequency patterns in the form of alternating magnetic fields that were received and decoded on the ship using several coils. The system was tested successfully on several kilometres along the Neckar River in southern Germany.

Building an automatic guidance system in this way has some major drawbacks. The rivers need to be equipped with expensive pilot cables and relay stations that need constant maintenance. Moreover, rivers such as the Rhine River in Europe belong to several countries. International standardization of the automation infrastructure is necessary in order for such a system to be successful. The ships also need to install complicated coil systems that enable the detection of the pilot cables. The enormous costs and the huge installation requirements prevented the system from becoming relevant to commercial use.

The configuration of today's automation system is shown in Figure 4.3. A gyroscope on the ship provides a way to measure the vessel's turning rate above ground. The main output of a Global Positioning System (GPS) receiver consists of positional coordinates, based on an absolute coordinate system. It can also determine speed over ground. To enhance the accuracy of GPS, correction information to on-ship GPS measurements are available through differential GPS receivers (Driescher and Gilles 2000). They are transmitted from a reference station to the ship via radio link. Similar GPS receivers use differential methods based on the WAAS/EGNOS (Wide Area Augmentation System/European Geostationary Navigation Overlay Service) standard. For these systems special satellites transmit the correction information to the receivers. EGNOS provides an accuracy of 1–2 metres compared to 15–20 metres with raw GPS signals. Since the system is based on geostationary satellites it is difficult to receive the correction data if the ship is manoeuvring in deep river valleys. The vertical angle to these satellites is only approximately 30° for central Europe. The on board radar antenna is connected to the computer using a newly developed PCI (Peripheral Component Interconnect) bus computer card to deliver the radar image. The radar image provides information about stationary objects such as bridges, buoys and riverbanks as well as information about dynamic objects, for example other vessels.

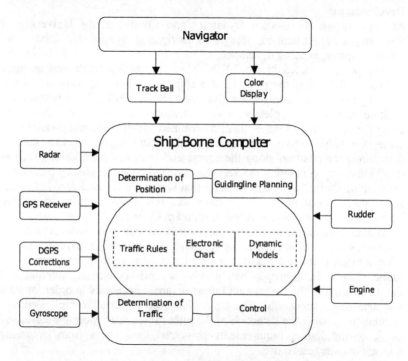

Figure 4.3   Configuration of integrated navigation system

A major resource for all the tasks of the integrated navigation system is the a priori knowledge deposited in knowledge databases within the computer. These data are displayed as dashed boxes in Figure 4.3. They consist of a database for the electronic chart based on the Inland ECDIS (Electronic Chart Display and Information System) standard, traffic rules and dynamic models of the vessels. Inland ECDIS is an extension of ECDIS that is standardized by the International Maritime Organization (IMO) to meet the needs of inland navigation by adding waterway-specific traffic signs to the charts. The ARGO (Advanced River Navigation) project that was carried out at the Institute for Systems Dynamics and Control at the University of Stuttgart integrated water depth information under certain water level conditions into the charts (Zimmerman et al. 1999).

The first task, represented by a box, is the determination of the position of the vessel. For this purpose, all the signals of the various sensors are combined in an extended Kalman filter in order to obtain the position, speed, heading and turning rate of the vessel. The matching of the radar image to the electronic chart is a peculiar feature of the system and further improves the positional information. Points on the radar contour are selected. Then the distance vectors from these points are evaluated to the nearest contour of the electronic chart. A vectorially weighted least squares algorithm is used to compute corrections to the initial position and direction of the vessel. For a typical radar image, some 200 points are processed in this way.

The radar image is also utilized for the determination of the traffic situation. The trajectories of other vessels are tracked over sequences of radar images using a multiple-target tracking algorithm (Plocher and Gilles 1992). Each track's position, direction, velocity and turning rate are estimated using Kalman filtering.

The results of the determination of the position and the traffic situation are fed into the third task of the navigation system, the planning of the trajectory of the ship. The goal is to calculate a safe guiding line with respect to other vessels on the river.

This collision detection and avoidance module is still part of ongoing research. In order to automatically find safe trajectories, a prediction of future trajectories of other ships needs to be available. Several issues arise that make such a task difficult. The relatively low accuracy of the other vessels' position and velocity measurements resulting from radar image analysis prevent a prediction that is only based on the extrapolation of a dynamic model from being successful in all cases. Furthermore, information that is needed for prediction is not always present in these measurements. A turning rate close to zero before a curve might be used to predict the future trajectory, resulting in a straight trajectory even for the curve. A prediction that is only based on measurements and a dynamic model would also provide unreliable results for vessels in curves, i.e. for a turning rate not equal to zero. In this case, a curved trajectory would be predicted even beyond the actual curve. Therefore, other information such as knowledge about the river course, typical manoeuvres and traffic rules need to be used in making a prediction. Unlike in road traffic, rules in inland navigation play a minor role. Only some parts of the river have rules for right or left hand traffic, for example. Nevertheless, the electronic chart in combination with object tracking is an important source of information. An increasing turning rate just before a port entrance may well indicate entry into this port. The integration of this static information is done using a Bayesian approach with plan hypotheses as described in Barthel (1999). For all relevant vessels conflict probabilities are assigned to the different plan hypotheses according to how likely a plan hypothesis is and when a conflict might occur. The conflict probabilities decrease with time since the predictions become more accurate with time.

Another approach to combining measurement information with a priori knowledge uses fuzzy logic to model the behaviour of a navigator. The plans 'following guiding line', 'using model-based prediction' and 'ferry crossing river' are proposed. In the fuzzification, step membership functions are evaluated that assign a numerical value between 0 and 1 to fuzzy values like 'quite parallel to guiding line' according to measurements. If–then rules that combine the different fuzzy values in the inference step model the navigator's knowledge. The defuzzification step provides a transformation back to numerical values that are a measure of the likelihood of the different plans.

The main drawback of these methods is the number of tuning parameters. The more plans that are used, the more parameters have to be identified. Different navigators may behave in different ways due to the lack of traffic rules. This makes the identification step difficult.

The other vessels' trajectories are fed into a risk analysis module. The river is spatially divided using a grid. A risk value is assigned to every grid point according to the predicted trajectories. A grid-based search algorithm calculates the future guiding line by finding the path with the lowest risk.

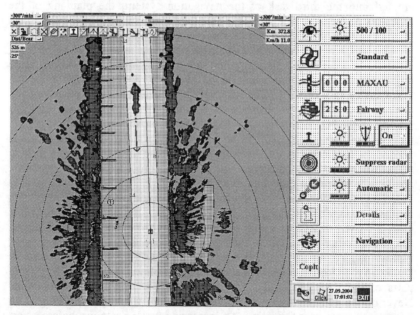

Figure 4.4   ECDIS chart with overlayed radar image (colour display)

The planned trajectory is input into the control task. Control signals are generated for the rudder and also for the engine throttle of the ship if electrically available. The controller is based on a standard Riccati approach that has turned out to fulfil the robustness demands. For performance improvement a feed-forward controller is used that is derived in Bittner et al. (2002) from inversion of the ship dynamics that are modelled in Bittner et al. (2003). Neglecting disturbances and model uncertainties, the rudder angle that is calculated by this feed-forward controller would keep the ship on its given trajectory. Therefore, the feedback Riccati controller only compensates for disturbances and model uncertainties.

The human navigator of the vessel supervises the integrated navigation system. The results of the different tasks are presented on a colour display as shown in Figure 4.4. The navigator can interact with the system by means of a track ball and a keyboard, supplementing or overriding the results of the guidance task.

The navigation system without path following and without the collision detection and avoidance module is commercially available through a university spin-off company. The path following module has been tested intensively on two research vessels that belong to the University of Stuttgart and the Max-Planck-Institute in Magdeburg as well as on several commercial vessels. One of these is a push tow with up to four full barges with a total weight of 10,000 t, a length of 180 m and a width of 22.5 m.

In order for the path following and collision detection and avoidance modules to become commercially available, legal issues have first to be resolved. An inland vessel navigating on public waterways will most likely always need the supervisory function of a navigator who is held responsible for safety.

Level 2: Coordination
The second level of automation deals with the coordination of several ships on narrow stretches of river. The ships are active in the sense that they can communicate with other ships or central stations. The goal of level 2 is the automation of conflict resolution on rivers with a lot of traffic or especially narrow stretches. Two sub-layers are proposed, namely a centralized and a decentralized conflict resolution layer. The coordination layer results in optimized guiding lines with assigned velocities for the coordinated vessels with respect to time.

The level 1 systems provide the coordination layer with information about the position, direction, velocity and turning rate of the vessels. On the other hand, the guiding lines that are calculated at level 2 are fed back into level 1 as set points.

Centralized conflict resolution
Centralized conflict resolution is a topic of ongoing research. Therefore, only the main concepts are presented here. Many prerequisites make implementation in the near future difficult.

All vessels need to be equipped with standardized communication units. AIS (Automatic Information System) transponders, mandatory for new seagoing vessels since 2002 (according to IMO – International Maritime

Organization), could offer the necessary capabilities. In order to provide sufficiently accurate information about position and velocity, navigation systems need to be available on all vessels. Path following modules are required so that the vessels accurately follow the optimized guiding lines that are transmitted from the central supervision centre.

Coordination on narrow river stretches can increase waterway capacity by more effectively controlling the traffic flow. The goods can be transported faster since the waiting time before narrow stretches like the so-called Gebirgsstrecke on the Rhine River can be reduced. A traffic light system that is supervized by human operators ensures safe passage there at the moment. Traffic signals tell upstream traffic what size vessels are currently navigating downstream in the supervised area. The passage can be closed off for upstream or downstream traffic. The goal is to replace the traffic signal system with an automated guiding line calculation in the supervision centre. These optimized guiding lines would be transmitted back to the vessels. As in air traffic, controllers would still be necessary for responsibility reasons and for exception handling.

The river is spatially discretized using an undirected graph as shown in Figure 4.5. The use of these virtual lanes reduces the complexity enormously. The spatial graph is shared by all the vessels in the supervized zone. However, for each vessel an individual time-expanded network is created based on the spatial graph. Each node in the individual network has an associated time stamp according to the time of entry into the zone and the velocity of the vessel. Costs are assigned to the edges in the network according to length and other properties. The cost of a straight edge is set lower than that of a lane-switching edge since staying in lane is preferred. In order to distinguish between the importance of different vessels, costs also depend on priorities. High priorities are assigned to larger vessels to account for the fact that small vessels need to give way to larger ones. From the set of individual time-expanded networks for the supervised vessels, a multicommodity network flow problem is constructed. A network optimization algorithm calculates optimal guiding lines for vessels by minimizing flow costs. Optimization constraints make sure that calculated guiding lines do not cross in the time–space domain. The guiding lines are transmitted back to the vessels.

Large vessels navigating through tight curves in a downstream direction produce large drift angles, i.e. the direction of movement differs substantially from the ship's length axis. Therefore, the size of the virtual lanes needs to be chosen accordingly to ensure safe passage.

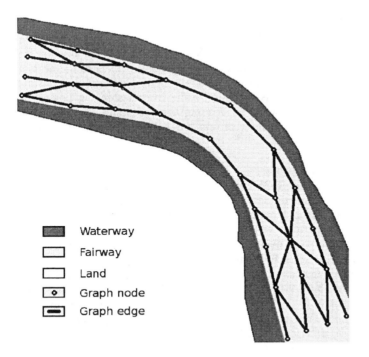

Figure 4.5   Coordination graph in ECDIS chart

Decentralized conflict resolution
The decentralized conflict-resolving layer is an extension of the collision detection and avoidance module of the previous layer. The information about other vessels that have AIS transponders (Automatic Information System) becomes much more accurate when actual guiding lines are transmitted. AIS transponders are mandatory equipment for seagoing vessels but are not yet required for inland vessels. Local optimizations can be carried out to generate new guiding lines. Since each vessel's objective is to minimize a certain cost function, the calculated guiding lines are in general not the solution to the global optimization problem that would be carried out by a central supervision centre. In fact, conflicts generally develop among vessels. Therefore, explicit rules are necessary to deal with such situations. One solution to competition problems like this is the introduction of priorities according to the size of vessels. Large vessels get a large priority and calculate their guiding lines without regard to vessels with lower priority. Vessels with lower priority compute their guiding lines using the higher priority vessels' guiding lines as constraints to their optimization algorithm. Such an inner-level hierarchy can solve this competition dilemma but does not necessarily correspond to the global optimization solution of a central station.

Level 3: Scheduling
The third level of automation in inland navigation does not deal with ship-to-ship interactions as at the previous level. Rather, the ship is seen as a unit that transports goods at a certain velocity not regarding path planning or even path following problems. The main relevant properties are the ship's position and its velocity. The goal is to optimize the overall shipping process by taking into account lock operation, loading and unloading facilities. Many international level 3 automation efforts are combined in the COMPRIS project.

European COMPRIS project
The ambitious European COMPRIS (Consortium Operational Management Platform River Information Services) project started in September 2002 with the goal of improving and implementing River Information Services (RIS) on the main inland waterways in Europe by 2005. Forty-four research institutes and companies from all over Europe are participating in the project. The project does not aim for full automation of level 3 processes but tries to establish a common platform for level 3 services. Therefore, RISs do not directly influence level 2 in the sense of setting level 2 parameters but rather provide information on the basis of which navigators or vessel fleet managers can optimize inland navigation efficiency. The specific project objectives are the following (as described in COMPRIS):

- spatial information: further development of the Inland ECDIS standard described earlier;
- vessel traffic management and tracking and tracing: development of standard procedures for traffic monitoring and lock and terminal planning. Evaluation of AIS transponders for tracking and tracing purposes;
- value added services from RIS: development of a logistic data platform (LDP) combining existing RIS applications and providing logistic companies with additional information such as estimated times of arrival (ETA) and route planning;
- cross-border traffic and transport information: development of cross-border operation enhancements. Evaluation of information needs for customs and emigration authorities to facilitate satisfaction of these.

The operation of the RIS will be tested using several vessels and three vessel traffic service (VTS) centres.

Automation at this level is on the verge of becoming commercially successful. Besides the COMPRIS project there already exist first proprietary systems that support logistic providers with different kind of information, including the vessels' location and expected time of arrival (ETA).

4.3   CONCLUSIONS

Automation in inland navigation at levels 1 and 3 have received a lot of attention, both in the research community and the business world. The first systems are available for commercial use.

Commercial level 1 systems provide the navigator with additional information, such as electronic charts, precise positional information, information about the traffic situation, river depth data and so on, to ease the navigator's work. In addition to an increase in safety, the productivity of inland navigation is enhanced because vessels can operate in difficult weather situations and loads are optimized with respect to the current water depth.

Vessel fleet management becomes substantially easier with commercial level 3 systems. Information about the fleet's vessels, such as their position, their load information, their estimated times of arrival, can be monitored by the manager. This information is used to optimize the scheduling of the vessels resulting in fewer empty trips and higher efficiency.

All of these commercial systems restrict their functionality to the support of the navigator's or vessel fleet manager's work. They are not aimed at replacing the human operator. However, several research projects have proved the technical feasibility of automatic guidance of ships on waterways. Automated path following has been achieved on many types of inland vessels. Like the developments in the automotive industry where driver assistant systems slowly push towards automation, several small steps will be necessary to promote fully autonomous vessels with human supervisors. Legal issues also have to be resolved in order to implement full automatic guidance at level 1 on commercial vessels. Only after this step is completed can level 2 coordination of several vessels on narrow rivers be achieved.

REFERENCES

Barthel, R. (1999), Szeneninterpretation zur Erkennung von Konflikten an Engstellen, Diplomarbeit Universität Stuttgart.

Bittner, R., A. Driescher and E.D. Gilles (2002), Entwurf einer Vorsteuerung zur hochgenauen Bahnführung von Binnenschiffen. In *3. Wismarer Automatisierungssymposium*, September, pp. 4–9.

Bittner, R., A. Driescher, and E.D. Gilles (2003), Drift Dynamics Modeling for Automatic Track-keeping of Inland Vessels. Tenth Saint Petersburg International Conference on Integrated Navigation Systems, State Research Center of the Russian Federation 'Elektropribor', May, pp. 218–27.

Bundesministerium für Verkehr, Bau- und Wohnungswesen (BMVBW) (2003), Verkehrsprognose 2015, Bundesverkehrswegeplan 2003, http://www.bmvbw.de/Bundesverkehrswegeplan-.806.5923/.htm

Consortium Operational Management Platform River Information Services: http://www.euro-compris.org

Driescher, A., and E.D. Gilles (2000), GPS-basierte Navigationssysteme in der Binnenschifffahrt, Tagungsband DGON-Symposium *Ortung und Navigation*, Vol. 1, pp. 197–206.

Plocher, T., and E.D. Gilles (1992), Rekursive Objektverfolgung in Bildsequenzen. *At – Automatisierungstechnik*, Vol. 40, pp. 59–63.

Sandler, M., A. Wahl, R. Zimmermann, M. Faul, U. Kabatek and E.D. Gilles (1996), Autonomous Guidance of Ships on Waterways, *Robotics and Autonomous Systems*, Vol. 18, pp. 327–35.

Stark, K. (1976), *A Measuring System for the Automation of Inland Shipping*, IMEKO VII Congress, London, Preprint Vol. 1, Paper no. ATT 127.

Statistisches Bundesamt (2004), *Gütertransport per Binnenschiff erreicht wieder Niveau von 2002*, Press release, December.

Zimmermann, R., T. Gern, and E.D. Gilles (1999), Advanced River Navigation with Inland ECDIS, *First European Inland Waterway Navigation Conference*, Balatonfüred, Hungary.

5. Developments in underground freight transportation

Ben-Jaap Pielage and Joan Rijsenbrij

5.1 INTRODUCTION

Underground transportation is not new; there have been operational underground freight transportation systems for at least 150 years. Underground Freight Transportation (UFT) focuses on transporting freight, using subterranean tunnels or tubes. Although we all know about underground pipeline systems for transporting gases, liquids or slurry, few people know about underground transportation systems for (solid) freight. This chapter first gives a brief overview of some historical systems and then discusses some of the more recent developments in underground freight transportation.

Why is UFT interesting? In the last 10 to 20 years, many studies focusing on UFT have been carried out in different countries. With increasing transport demands, problems arise in the transportation and distribution of freight, especially in high density urban areas. Expansion and improvement of existing systems is not always possible and does not always lead to efficiency improvements or a better living environment. Society demands efficient sustainable transport systems for the future. This creates opportunities for UFT. At the same time, there have been many technological developments in freight transport automation, further increasing the potential of UFT.

Two different types of systems are distinguished: capsule pipeline systems and automated vehicle systems. Capsule pipeline systems use capsules to transport freight through a pipe. Automated vehicle systems use automated vehicles to transport freight through a tunnel. Developments in both types of systems are discussed.

5.2 HISTORIC DEVELOPMENTS

Underground freight transportation has a history of at least 150 years. In 1853 an underground pipeline was installed in London, using pneumatic techniques, to transport messages between two offices of the Electric and

International Telegraph Company. Although this first system used felt bags to carry the messages, capsules were soon introduced. Throughout the second half of the 19th century and the first half of the 20th century, various cities all over the world installed and used these pneumatic capsule systems to carry post. Apart from London, systems were installed in for example New York, Paris, Berlin and Prague. Figure 5.1 (left) shows some pictures of the pneumatic capsule system in New York. These systems typically used small diameter capsules (2 to 8 inches) often capable of reaching speeds of up to 30 mph.

Larger diameter pneumatic capsule systems were also developed. The London Pneumatic Despatch Company developed and installed an underground tube system with tubes 30 inches in diameter. A first full-scale trial was performed in 1861 (see Figure 5.1, right). A single tube, 452 yards long with curves of up to 300 ft radius and gradients of up to 1 in 22, was installed on the surface. The capsules were fitted with vulcanised rubber flaps to seal the air and steel wheels, which ran on 24 inch gauge tracks inside the tube. Powered by a 30 horsepower engine, a single capsule weighing 3 tons achieved speeds up to 40 mph. A permanent line was constructed and put into operation in 1863. The system was used to carry mail and parcels and was expanded in the following years. However, unlike the small diameter capsule systems, it was not a success. The Post Office found only limited time savings by using the system, and furthermore doubted the system's reliability. In 1874, with only a little income and no guarantees from the Post Office, the company was closed down.

New York post office pneumatic tube terminal   *Rail guided pneumatic driven capsule*

Source: R. Cohen, US Postal Services.   *Source:* Beach (1868).

Figure 5.1   Pneumatic capsule systems

Large diameter pneumatic systems were also developed for conveying passengers. During the Crystal Palace Exhibition of 1864 a capsule carriage was demonstrated as a prototype. In North America, Alfred Beach proposed several systems during the 1860s for the transportation of passengers and mail. Although several prototypes were developed, these large diameter systems never achieved full commercial operation. For more information on capsule pipeline systems and their history please visit www.capsu.org, an extensive website on capsule pipeline systems with many references.

A different historic development is that of underground rail systems. The Chicago Tunnel Company in the USA developed an underground freight transportation system using tunnels, originally intended for telephone and telegraph wires. The construction of the tunnels began around 1900 and developed into an extensive gridlike network of approximately 60 miles under nearly every street in downtown Chicago. The system used electric locomotives and had many different types of freight-cars to transport different types of cargo. Although many types of cargo were transported, the system was mainly used to transport coal. The system was shut down in 1959, due to financial problems. Figure 5.2 (left) shows a photograph of the Chicago tunnels.

Another historic underground rail system can still be found in London. Royal Mail has been operating an underground transportation system for mail since 1928. This MailRail system uses unmanned electrically driven rail vehicles to transport mail between several posting offices in the centre of London. The system is still in use today and is probably one of the oldest operational automated underground freight transportation systems in the world. Figure 5.2 (right) shows a photo of the London MailRail system.

Chicago Tunnel Company   *London MailRail System*

Source: www.ameritech.net   *Source:* Royal Mail.

Figure 5.2   Chicago's freight tunnels (left) and MailRail London (right)

In Tokyo, an underground railway system was constructed in 1915 between Tokyo Central Station and the central post office. This system was several hundreds of metres long and dedicated to carry freight. More recent developments in both capsule pipeline systems and automated vehicle systems are discussed in the following sections.

5.3   DEVELOPMENTS IN CAPSULE PIPELINE SYSTEMS

Although most of the older pneumatic pipeline systems discussed in the previous section have been shut down, new and improved systems are still being developed and implemented today. This section first shows some examples of modern pneumatic capsule systems in operation today and then discusses two interesting fields of research: Hydraulic Capsule Pipeline systems and Electro Magnetic Propulsion for pipeline systems.

Pneumatic Capsule Systems

The principle of pumping air into (or out of) a tube to drive a capsule has been used for many years. Although modern systems use the same basic principle, many improvements have been made in mechanical components, materials used and the control system. Figure 5.3 shows two modern pneumatic capsule systems. Today, these systems are mainly found within buildings to transport smaller/lighter items between fixed locations within buildings (Figure 5.3 left). Examples are medical samples within hospitals, industrial samples within a factory, documents within an office and cash within a bank or shop.

For larger/heavier cargo, capsules with wheels are used for support and guidance. Figure 5.3 (right) presents the Capsule Liner from Sumitomo Metals, currently being used to transport limestone between a mine and a processing plant in Japan. This system with a tube diameter of 1 metre, was opened in 1983 and is still operational today. Each capsule has wheels and can carry up to 1.6 tons. Earlier developments on these larger/heavier systems were performed in the USA by 'Tubexpress' and in Russia by 'Transprogress'.

Modern pneumatic capsule system for offices   *Sumitomo Capsule liner*

Source: Hörtig Rohrpost.   *Source:* Sumitomo Metals Japan.

Figure 5.3   Modern pneumatic capsule systems

Source: www.tubexpress.com   *Source:* Sumitomo Metals Japan.

Figure 5.4   Possible future developments for capsule pipeline systems

Future developments on pneumatic capsule systems do not focus only on smaller lighter items or bulk material, but also on general cargo as one of the main areas of interest. A vision for the future by Tubexpress (left) and Sumitomo (right) is shown in Figure 5.4. Both consider palletised goods as a possible future development.

Hydraulic Capsule Pipeline Systems

Apart from air, liquids can also be used as a transport medium. Although the idea of using water, oil or other liquids as a medium for pumping capsules through a tube is not new, commercial operations have not yet evolved. Hydraulic pipeline systems can transport (watertight) capsules which hold the cargo, or so-called Coal Logs. These Coal Logs are solidly compressed coal cylinders, which are both water-resistant and wear-resistant. Recent developments in this field are concentrated at the Capsule Pipeline Research Center (CPRC) at the University of Missouri-Columbia in the USA. Figure 5.5 shows the construction of the Coal Log pilot plant.

Source: Henry Lui CPRC.

Figure 5.5   Construction of Coal Log pilot plant at University of Missouri-Columbia in the USA

Electro-magnetic Propulsion

One of the main disadvantages of traditional pneumatic pipelines is the throughput capacity limitation imposed by the valves and airlocks needed to enable the capsules to bypass the airpumps. By using electro-magnetic propulsion, the capsules can be driven and controlled directly, thus increasing the potential capacity of the system. Research and development in this field is taking place at different locations. Figure 5.6 shows pictures of two different R&D projects. On the left, a Linear Induction Motor (LIM) is being tested at the Capsule Pipeline Research Center (CPRC) at the University of Missouri-Columbia, using steel capsules with a thin outer layer of aluminium. On the right, tests are being done with a Linear Synchronous Motor (LSM) developed by Magplane Technology. This demonstration project was constructed at IMC-Global, a phosphate mining company in Florida, and uses capsules with permanent magnets on the bottom.

Where the LIM technology requires a tight fit (small air gap) for the motor to be efficient, the LSM technology allows a larger air gap, which is an advantage for the cost of infrastructure. On the other hand, LSM requires permanent magnets to be fitted to the capsules. Both options have advantages and disadvantages.

Research on Linear Induction Motor at CPRS

Demo of Linear Synchronous Motor for Florida Phosphate Industry (capsule on left rotated 180 degrees for inspection of magnets)

Source: Henry Lui CPRS.

Source: Bruce Montgomery, Magplane Technology.

Figure 5.6   R&D on electro magnetic propulsion

The linear motors do not have to be installed throughout the full length of the tube. By positioning them at certain intervals, the capsule (when in the linear motor) acts as a piston, driving the other capsules in the tube (outside the motor). This principle was already patented by William Vandersteel in 1984 (William Vandersteel US patent No. 4.458.602 1984).

5.4 DEVELOPMENTS IN AUTOMATED VEHICLE SYSTEMS

The last decades have shown some interesting developments in automated vehicle systems. Two interesting operational examples are automated metro systems and automated guided vehicles at container terminals (ECT Rotterdam and HHLA, Hamburg). Figure 5.7 shows a picture of the automated metro system in Toulouse, France (left) and an Automated Guided Vehicle (AGV) at the ECT container terminal in Rotterdam, the Netherlands. Although these vehicles were not developed specifically for underground freight transport, future UFT systems can benefit from the experience gained from these existing systems. Both types of automated transportation systems share the same important characteristic: an 'undisturbed' infrastructure fitted with control equipment (transponders, sensors etc.).

VAL / automated metro Toulouse   *Automated Guided Vehicle (AGV)*

Source: www.railway-technology.com   *Source:* ECT.

Figure 5.7   Operational automated vehicle systems

Automated vehicle systems are interesting, especially for underground freight transportation. Automated vehicles can operate underground without any outside disturbances, which contributes to a more reliable and efficient transportation. Furthermore, expensive and maintenance requiring provisions normally found in tunnels can be avoided, making automated vehicle systems interesting also from a cost perspective. In this respect it is relevant to focus on the developments in automated trucking, large automated guided vehicle (AGV) systems and automated rail transportation.

Automated Trucks

Today most freight is transported by road, making trucks one of the most important vehicles for transporting freight. Worldwide, several developments have taken place involving the automation of trucks. One of the first developments involving the automation of small trucks and their use underground can be found in Japan. During the 1980s, the Public Works Research Institute (PWRI) of the Ministry of Construction in Japan started research on underground freight transportation and developed the Dual Mode Truck (DMT). This automated electric truck could travel through underground tunnels without a driver. Unmanned, the electric vehicle used side wheels for guidance and had an external power supply while travelling on an exclusive track. The DTM could also be used for normal operation on the streets, driven by a driver and powered by batteries. Figure 5.8 shows a picture taken at the DMT Test Track. Although the tests were promising and social and economical studies showed encouraging results, the DMT system has not been developed into a commercial operational system.

Source: Ministry of Construction Japan.

Figure 5.8   Dual Mode Truck in Japan

Two other interesting projects involving truck automation are CombiRoad and PATH. Figure 5.9 shows a prototype of the CombiRoad vehicle on the left and a truck demo by PATH on the right.

CombiRoad Truck   *Trucks developed within the PATH project*

Source: CombiRoad project.   *Source:* PATH.

Figure 5.9   Automated truck projects

CombiRoad was developed during the mid 1990s in the Netherlands for transporting containers. The containers are placed on normal semi-trailers, which can be pulled by automatically controlled, unmanned vehicles. Similar to the DMT, the vehicle runs in a separate lane using electric propulsion, powered by a rail system. For off-track operation, an onboard diesel generator is available for supplying electricity. Latest developments include the implementation of the guidance systems developed by PATH. The Partners for Advanced Transit and Highways (PATH) program started in 1986 in California, focussing on the automation of passenger cars on highways (see also Shladover, chapter 2 in this volume). Today, one of the main focus areas is the automation of trucks, using the same basic technology developed and tested for passenger cars. The positioning system is based on magnetic markers placed in the road. The fully automated trucks can travel at free-flow highway speeds, and are capable of performing various manoeuvres.

AGV Systems

The first Automatic Guided Vehicles (AGVs) were wire guided, using magnetic field sensors measuring the magnetic field induced by a floor-mounted electric wire. Today, many more track-keeping technologies are available, such as transponder reading, magnet reading, laser triangulation, radar triangulation and visual recognition sensors (digital cameras).

Some interesting developments have taken place in underground freight transportation in the Netherlands. Following several studies on underground freight transportation, several 'OLS' projects were defined. OLS is the Dutch abbreviation for Underground Logistic System (see also Versteegt and Verbraeck, chapter 10 in this volume). Two different fields of application were distinguished and artist's impressions of these two types of systems are presented in Figure 5.10.

The picture on the left presents an OLS for urban areas, servicing retailers, hotels and catering, offices and other urban consumers. Typical load units here are pallets and roll-containers, requiring a tube diameter of 2 to 2.5 metres. The picture on the right shows an OLS connecting industrial areas, logistic centres and multi-modal hubs like airports. Here, larger load units (air cargo Unit Load Devices (ULDs) or city boxes, carrying various weights of cargo) are envisaged which require a tube diameter of up to five metres.

Feasibility studies were performed for the cities of Utrecht, Twente, Arnhem Nijmegen, Tilburg and Leiden. The OLS–ASH (Ondergronds Logistiek Systeem–Aalsmeer Schiphol Hoofddorp) project was the largest project. The goal of the OLS–ASH was to transport flowers and other time critical cargo through an underground transportation system between the flower auction in Aalsmeer, Schiphol Airport and a rail cargo terminal near Hoofddorp. The OLS–ASH project started in 1995 with a feasibility scan,

Source: Marcel Schöningh – Element.

Figure 5.10   Artist's impression of UFT in urban areas (left) and at Schiphol Airport (right)

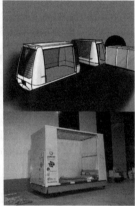  

Rubber-tyred AGV with full electronic guidance
Front-wheel steering
Front and side loading
DC electric drive
Battery powered

Rail mounted AGV in tunnel and rubber-tyred electronically guided at terminal
Four-wheel steering
Two side loading
AC electric drive
Battery powered at terminal and power rail in the tunnel

Rubber-tyred AGV, self-guidance in tube (wheels on tube surface) electronic guidance at terminal Front-wheel steering
One side loading
AC electric drive
Battery powered

Source: OLS–ASH project documentation.

Figure 5.11   Vehicle concepts and 1:1 prototypes tested for OLS–ASH

and after several other phases, some interesting concepts for the vehicles, material handling, layout and control of the system were developed. Figure 5.11 shows the three different vehicle concepts developed for the OLS–ASH project, with the 1:1 scale prototypes which were built and tested at a test site in Delft. Each prototype has its own characteristics (see Figure 5.11 labels), but all are fully automated vehicles. More information on OLS can be found on the web (www.het-ols.nl and www.connekt.nl).

Similar ideas, using AGVs for transporting freight underground, exist in London and Houston. In London, consideration is being given to the renovation and expansion of the existing Royal Mail tunnels and the development of a new automated freight distribution system called Metrofreight. This system would use rubber-tyred, battery-driven, driverless vehicles to supply goods to major retail outlets in the congested city of London. In Houston, Texas, research is being done into the feasibility of an underground logistic system for transporting containerised cargo within the city of Houston. In the Netherlands the OLS Tilburg and OLS–ASH projects look most promising and could become the first automated underground freight transportation systems in the Netherlands.

Rail Bound Vehicles

There have been some interesting developments in rail bound systems since the first rail system emerged. In Japan, several studies were performed in the 1990s on possible underground freight transportation systems with rail bound vehicles driven by linear motors. The Tokyo L-net project, for instance, proposed an underground network for trains with linear motors to connect post offices in the central area of Tokyo. Two more recent projects focussing on rail bound underground freight transportation systems are CargoCap in Germany and a study performed by the Texas Transportation Institute (TTI) in Texas, USA.

CargoCap is a project which was initiated in 1999 at the Ruhr University, Bochum. The aim is to develop an underground freight transportation system in the Ruhr area connecting inner urban areas, industrial estates, business centres, logistic parks, airports etc. The proposed tunnels with an inner diameter of 1.6 metres run mainly under heavily congested public roads and motorways. The proposed CargoCap vehicles (Figure 5.12, left) can carry two Euro pallets (W*L*H = 800*1200*1050 mm) run on rails, and are guided by side guide rollers. The on-board computer, controls the autonomously propelled vehicles travelling at 36 km/hour with a minimum spacing of two metres between the vehicles. It is planned to develop the system in several stages, starting with basic components and scaled prototypes, eventually arriving at an operational system for the Ruhr area. Possible extensions into the Rhineland are also foreseen.

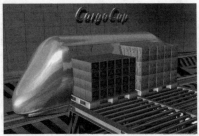
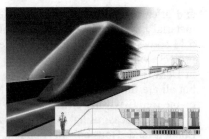

CargoCap Germany   UFT by TTI in Texas USA

Source: Ruhr University, Bochum.   *Source:* Texas Transportation Institute.

Figure 5.12   New concepts for rail-bound UFT systems

In Texas, the Multi Modal Freight Transportation Center of TTI is investigating whether non-traditional systems can alleviate the congestion and wear problems encountered on Texas highways. Texas, because of its location, serves as the principal landside gateway to Mexico and as a consequence hosts truck traffic from all over the USA, Mexico and Canada, and these are beginning to dominate certain Texas highways. Underground freight transportation is being considered as an alternative to truck transport along the most problematic routes. An underground freight transportation system is being designed to transport palletised goods along the state's most heavily travelled trade corridor, the highway Interstate 35 (I35). The system would connect Dallas in the northern part of Texas with Laredo at the Mexican border, a distance of more than 400 miles. The proposed vehicle (Figure 5.12 right) could carry up to 30 pallets, travel on steel wheels with steel tracks and be driven by linear induction motors, reaching speeds of up to 60 mph. So far this is a preliminary design. A lot of research is still to be done, not only on the technological side, but also taking into consideration economic, social and political aspects. Here again, investment in infrastructure may become a critical factor for successful development.

In general, developments in rail-bound vehicles focus on high speeds and/or electro-magnetic propulsion, sometimes even combined with magnetic levitation (maglev). An interesting development for smaller/lighter applications is the Bagtrax system developed by Vanderlande for transporting baggage at airports. This system uses carts, guided by a rail and driven by linear induction motors, reaching speeds of up to 10 m/s. A picture of the system at Schiphol Airport is shown in Figure 5.13 (left). Another well-known development is the high speed train, currently operating in Japan (SHINKANSEN), Germany (ICE) and France (TGV). Figure 5.13 (right) shows a TGV used to transport mail in France.

Baggage transportation system at   *TGV for transporting mail*
Schiphol Airport

Source: Vanderlande Industries.   *Source:* SNCF.

Figure 5.13   Existing rail-bound systems for freight

These high speed trains already carry small shipments of cargo; moreover the French SNCF is developing a cargo transportation network focussed on the fast movement of perishable, high value and time critical cargo (TGV Fret). In Europe the first pilot projects have been launched to operate fast rail connections between the major European airports and industrial conglomerates. It is expected that rail freight transportation will be further encouraged in the future.

In this respect another potential application may become of interest: the combined transportation of passengers and freight. Rail transportation systems for passengers have a considerable surplus in transportation capacity outside the daily rush-hour periods. The combination of freight and passengers is achievable with the help of standardised load units (city boxes), standardised handling techniques and standardised vehicles for the fast delivery of goods between stations and the final consumer. The required short stopping time at stations for a fast interchange of cargo will require (partly) automated handling systems, separated from the passenger access areas. Figure 5.14 shows two possible concepts for fast automated handling at rail terminals.

The latest developments in rail transportation cover magnetic levitation and linear motor propulsion. These developments are taking place in Japan and Germany. After a long development period, the first commercially operated 'maglev' train system is now being built in Shanghai. This German system, called Transrapid, will connect Shanghai Airport with the city centre. Other projects are expected to develop, and although these high speed systems focus on passenger transport, freight is also considered (Figure 5.15 (left) shows an artist's impression of a transrapid system for transporting air cargo). Apart from these high speed rail bound systems 'in open air', there are also research developments for high speed underground transportation. Swissmetro for instance, envisages a high speed underground transport system comprising of two tunnels of five-metre interior diameter with reduced pressure (partial vacuum) to reduce energy consumption. The vehicles

(Figure 5.15 right) will be driven by linear motors, allowing for speeds of up to 500 km/hr.

Combined passenger freight concept   *Fast handling of freight for high speed trains*

Source: Marcel Schöningh – Element.   *Source:* Marcel Schöningh – Element.

Figure 5.14   Concepts for rapid automated freight handling at rail terminals

Transrapid system transporting Aircargo   *Swissmetro vehicle*

Source: Transrapid   *Source:* Swissmetro
www.transrapid.de/en/index.html   www.swissmetro.com

Figure 5.15   High speed rail bound freight systems for the future

In general, existing and future rail transportation systems have real potential for underground freight transportation. Costs of infrastructure, increasing road traffic congestion and priorities in society, will eventually determine whether these high-capacity systems will finally mature for underground transportation.

5.5   SUMMARY AND CONCLUSIONS

There are many interesting developments concerning underground freight transportation (UFT) systems. On the one hand, increasing congestion problems with road transportation encourage the search for alternative modes of transport. On the other hand, there are interesting technological developments, increasing the feasibility of underground freight transportation.

Furthermore, automation and underground freight transport seem to fit one another. While the undisturbed underground infrastructure makes it possible to develop an automated freight transport system within a reasonably controlled environment (a favourable condition for developing an automated transport system), automation makes it possible to transport freight underground without any people in the tunnels, which improves working conditions and safety and reduces operational cost.

Development in UFT systems can be divided into two main areas: Capsule Pipeline Systems and Automated Vehicle Systems. The difference between them is that capsule systems actually need a pipeline as a closed infrastructure to travel through, whereas automated vehicle systems can travel through underground tunnels but do not need such a closed infrastructure. Both can however be used to transport freight underground without a driver.

Capsule pipeline systems today, are mostly used to transport documents or smaller items in buildings. Apart from this successful application, several other larger diameter systems can be found for transporting bulk materials. Research in the field of capsule pipeline systems focuses mainly on possibilities for electro-magnetic propulsion (linear motors), and to a somewhat lesser extent on hydraulic systems, using water as a medium to carry the capsules. Future applications focus not only on transporting smaller items or bulk material, but also on transporting palletised goods over long distances.

Automated vehicle systems were discussed, distinguishing between automated trucks, AGV systems and rail-bound systems. Although automated trucks and automated guided vehicles (AGVs) have different backgrounds, the technology developed for both is coming closer together. Rubber-tyred fully automated vehicles can operate autonomously and are capable of performing various manoeuvres. Different types of fully automated rubber-tyred vehicles are considered for future underground freight transportation (UFT) systems. Rail-bound systems are being also considered for UFT. Rail-bound systems make use of a rail for lateral guidance, and when using steel wheels on steel tracks have a lower rolling resistance. New developments in rail-bound systems focus on high speed applications and/or electro-magnetic propulsion and levitation.

High speed, a typical rail-bound development, could prove feasible for long distance freight transportation. It is important to remember with high speed transport that air resistance increases with the square of the speed. This is the case in open-air situations; in tunnels the pressure build-up in front of the train only exacerbates the problem. Although lowering the air pressure in the tube reduces this problem, this generates other air-related problems such as the air tightness of the tunnels and the need for airlocks. The 'need for speed' is therefore always an interesting dilemma, especially in tunnels.

Investment costs in infrastructure are always a key factor, specifically for underground tube or tunnel systems. As a rule of thumb, tunnel costs quadruple when the tunnel diameter doubles. This is why, for extensive underground freight transportation systems, the tunnel diameter should be optimised. Smaller tunnels are easier and cheaper to build. Larger tunnels can accommodate more (larger) types of load units, but are more expensive to build.

In spite of the developments over more than a century, UFT has not (yet) developed into a widespread standard mode of transport. Plausible reasons are the high investment, operating and maintenance costs, but probably also the fact that adequate alternative modes of transport such as road and rail still function. However, ongoing urbanisation and increasing demands from society for sustainable mobility and faster, reliable deliveries of consumer goods will require better transportation systems. Densely populated areas may eventually need the application of UFT-like systems. This is why these developments should continue.

So far, none of the discussed UFT systems has shown its dominance over the others, and there are still many technical and operational issues to be further developed. However, when comparing the different types of systems, some comments can be made on their best field of application.

The capsule pipeline systems could prove promising for long distance transport of freight, which can be transported through relatively small diameter tubes (lower investment costs), from point to point, e.g. from city to city in the USA or Trans-Europe. Capsule pipeline systems are less suitable for complex network–like structures with many terminals, intersections, load and unload stations etc.

The automated vehicle systems look more promising for transporting freight over shorter distances within a more complex network, with many intersections and many origins and destinations. These vehicles offer more routing flexibility and could also be used outside the tunnel above ground. In this respect, automatically guided rubber-tyred vehicles are most flexible as they require no physical rail for guidance, making it easier to change routes and interact with other transport systems. The rail-bound systems become interesting when higher speeds are required or rolling resistance is an important issue. Compared to the rubber-tyred vehicles, rail-bound vehicles are of course less flexible as they require rails and switching points. In general, one could state that rubber-tyred vehicles should perform better for dense network-like systems with many origins and destinations. Rail-bound systems could be better for 'wide' networks with longer distances between the nodes.

Continuing economical growth and increasing demands from society will stimulate further developments in UFT systems. Different technologies are available to serve the transportation industry in the most optimal way.

REFERENCES

Beach, A. (1868), *The Pneumatic Dispatch*, New York: American News Co.

Bliss, D. (2000), MailRail – 70 Years of Automated Underground Freight Transport, in *Proceedings 2nd International Symposium on Underground Freight Transportation (ISUFT)*, Delft, The Netherlands, September.

Clarke, M. and D. Wright (1993), *Metro Freight, A New Direction for Transport, an Introduction*, Bedfordshire: Cranfield School of Management.

Cohen, R.A. (1999), *The Pneumatic Mail Tubes: New York's Hidden Highway and its Development*, Columbia, Missouri: ISUFT.

Combi-Road (1996), *Eindrapport, CTT* (Centrum Transport Technologie), Krimpen aan den Yssel.

DMT described in: New Freight Transportation System brochure published by Ministry of Construction Japan.

Dunselman, J.R., B.A. Pielage and J.C. Rijsenbrij (eds) (2000), *OLS Project Document: Transport Technology and Control System, Underground Logistic System ASH*, Delft/Rotterdam: TRAIL Research School/Connekt.

Hörtig, M. (2002), *Pneumatic Tube Systems – Through Big Pipes into the Future*, Bochum, Germany: ISUFT.

Interdepartementale Projectorganisatie Ondergronds Transport (IPOT) (1998), *Transport onder ons*, Den Haag: Ministerie van Verkeer en Waterstaat.

Interdepartementale Projectorganisatie Ondergronds Transport (IPOT) (1999), *Transport onder ons: schakel in de keten*, Den Haag: Ministerie van Verkeer en Waterstaat.

James, A.P., F.M. Sanders and G. Arends (2002), *Houston Projects 2000 and 2001 – Research Leading to the Design of a Palletised Cargo Consolidation and Distribution ULS for Houston Texas,* Bochum, Germany: ISUFT.

Kosugi, S. (1999), *Pneumatic Capsule Pipelines in Japan and Future Developments*, Columbia, Missouri: ISUFT.

Liu, H. (2002), *Freight Transport by Underground Pipelines: State-of-the-art assessment*, Bochum, Germany: ISUFT.

Montgomery, B. et al. (2000), *Electromagnetic Pipeline Demonstration Project*, Delft, The Netherlands: ISUFT.

O'Connell, R.M. and W. Plodpradista (2002), *Design of a 1 meter Tubular Induction Motor for a Pneumatic Capsule Pipeline System*, Bochum, Germany: ISUFT.

Pielage, B.A. (2000), *Design Approach and Prototyping of Automated Underground Freight Transportation Systems in the Netherlands*, Delft, The Netherlands: ISUFT.

Pielage, B.A. (2001), *Underground Freight Transportation. A New Development for Automated Freight Transportation in the Netherlands,*

Oakland, CA: IEEE Intelligent Transportation Systems Conference Proceedings.

Rijsenbrij, J.C. (1994), *Automation: A Process Redesign*, Oakland, CA: Europe Combined Terminals, October.

Roop, S. (2002), *The Economic and Technical Feasibility of an Underground Freight Pipeline in Texas*, Bochum, Germany: ISUFT.

Stein, D. and B. Schösser (2002), CargoCap – A Vision becomes Reality, *Tunnel, International Journal for Underground Construction, Issues 3/2002*, ISSN 0722-6241.

Taniguchi, E., R. Ooishi and T. Kono (2000), *Development and Future Perspectives for Underground Freight Transport Systems in Japan*, Delft: ISUFT.

US Department of Transportation Research and Special Programs Administration and Volpe National Transportation Systems Center (1994), *Tube Transportation*, Cambridge, MA.

Visser, J.G.S.N (2003), Underground Freight Transport Systems, in E. Taniguchi and R.G. Thompson (eds), *Innovations in Freight Transport*, Southampton: WIT Press.

www.ameritech.net/users/chicagotunnel/tunnel1.html

www.capsu.org

www.tubexpress.com

www.path.berkeley.edu

www.railway-technology.com

6. Road–rail hybrid transport: a new modality for the Rhine–Schelde Delta area

Joop Evers

6.1 INTRODUCTION

In this chapter a new transport modality which can be described as a road–rail hybrid transport system is presented. This transport system combines the favourable characteristics of road transport (speed, flexibility in time and space and door-to-door service) and rail transport (low rolling resistance) and avoids their disadvantages (long braking distance of trains causing low frequencies and high costs of road transport). Due to a smart mechanical engineering vehicle design and innovative logistic control, the proposed intelligent road–rail hybrid system would be able to offer economic, accessible, reliable and continuous transport services. Hence it could be a good alternative for the conventional modalities.

The chapter starts with a description of the geographical context and planned infrastructural investments in this area. This is a starting-point for a case study that has been elaborated for the road–rail hybrid transport system. Next the characteristics of the road–rail hybrid transport system, and the related logistic control system, are discussed. To explore the market potential of this new transport system a model has been applied in which the future market share of the road–rail hybrid system has been estimated in relation to road transport and inland shipping. The chapter ends with conclusions on this market analysis.

6.2 TRANSPORT WITHIN THE RHINE–SCHELDE DELTA

The Rhine–Schelde Delta as Logistic Area

The area encompassed by Amsterdam, Rotterdam, Antwerp and Duisburg is densely populated and highly industrialised. The ports of Rotterdam, Antwerp and Amsterdam accommodate transport over sea. The port of

Rotterdam is one of the largest seaports in the world with respect to intercontinental container transport. Within this area, called the Rhine–Schelde Delta, container transport is intensive. The Rhine offers an excellent waterway for large-scale inland shipping between Rotterdam, Duisburg and Mannheim. However, most of the containers are transported via trucking.

Table 6.1. shows the modal split of transport over land related to the port of Rotterdam. The figures are deduced from data on container transport in 1995 between the port of Rotterdam and 122 hinterland regions published by the Rotterdam Port Authority (Gemeentelijk Havenbedrijf Rotterdam 1998). In Table 6.1. these data are aggregated in five regions. Exports and imports are distinguished: the term export-containers indicates containers that depart from Rotterdam via intercontinental shipping, while import-containers concern the arrivals.

In general, the choice of a transport modality is determined by costs and the quality of the logistics service; national boundaries are of lesser importance. In this respect the Rhine–Schelde Delta is exemplary.

For inland transport within the area of the Rhine–Schelde Delta, road transport has an advantage over rail transport owing its high speed, its flexibility and its door-to-door service. For transport over distances longer than 300 km, rail transport begins to gain the advantage owing to the lower costs.

Table 6.1   *Container transport volumes to and from Rotterdam, number of units (x 1000) and modal split (%), 1995*

	Volume (export) x 1000	Road transport %	Inland shipping %	Rail transport %
West Netherlands	221	95	2	3
East Netherlands	84	75	15	10
Duisburg + Mannheim	153	87	10	3
South Germany (+ Italy)	166	50	25	25
Antwerp Harbour	210	43	54	3

	Volume (import) x 1000	Road transport %	Inland shipping %	Rail transport %
West Netherlands	219	93	1	6
East Netherlands	51	78	12	10
Duisburg + Mannheim	73	75	15	10
South Germany (+ Italy)	106	45	21	34
Antwerp Harbour	142	37	60	3

Investments in Transport Infrastructures

Accessibility is an essential issue in the logistics of the Randstad, the major conurbation in the Netherlands including cities such as Rotterdam, The Hague, Amsterdam and Utrecht. The problems are well-known: congestion, noise, pollution, space use and high energy consumption by road transport. It is expected that the volume of freight transport will double within 20 years. The government's policy aims to anticipate this and to extend the infrastructure while considering environmental and spatial aspects.

It was decided to construct the Betuwe Line as a railroad to provide a direct link between the port of Rotterdam and the German railway system. The line runs from the Maasvlakte harbour area to the German border at Zevenaar. Transfer stations will be built at the Maasvlakte, Eemhaven and at Valburg. At present, the construction is almost completed.

It was decided to build the Maasvlakte-2 (MV2) as an extension of the current Maasvlakte, especially aimed to accommodate a new generation of intercontinental container vessels. There are also plans for a dedicated freight railway between Rotterdam and Antwerp with a connection to the Betuwe Line, to provide an alternative to road transport. Furthermore, there are also projects for the development of a multimodal node in Valburg and a logistics centre at Moerdijkse Hoek.

Towards a New Dedicated Transport Infrastructure

As a matter of fact, with the creation of the Betuwe Line and the special Rotterdam–Antwerp railway, a dedicated transport infrastructure has come into being which may offer exceptional logistic opportunities. So far, the governmental investment program is rather conventional. Thus the question is what an ideal dedicated transport system along the main axes of the Rhine–Schelde Delta would look like.

The favourable characteristics of road transport are speed, flexibility, door-to-door service and individual handling of freight units. In addition there is two-dimensional freedom of movement on transshipment platforms; as a result the space requirements of these platforms are relatively small. With respect to these aspects rail transport falls short, certainly with regard to the transport distances within the Rhine–Schelde Delta. Another disadvantage of the railway is the long braking distance it needs. This means that the rail track can be used only at low frequencies, which is logistically unfavourable and reduces capacity. Low rolling resistance when travelling on rails, however, is favourable from the points of view of energy consumption and economy. With increasing scarcity of energy, this aspect is becoming increasingly important. From this point of view road transport is at a disadvantage.

It is thus desirable to create an energy economical, generally accessible and reliable transport system, with a high capacity, that can combine the advantages of both means of transport, avoid their disadvantages and is suitable for continuous operations. With respect to the Rhine–Schelde Delta, this system must provide an alternative to road and to rail transport and be able to function in a way that is complementary to each. Part of the innovation lies in logistics coordination, while another part involves mechanical engineering. The intention of this study is to describe such a system on the basis of what we call an intelligent road–rail hybrid transport modality and to investigate its market potential.

6.3   ROAD–RAIL HYBRID VEHICLES

The Road–rail Hybrid Betuwe Line as Infrastructural Basis

A system working with automated vehicles driving on dedicated traffic lanes fits these ideas. Speed can be restricted to 50 km/hr; after all there are no (expensive) drivers with the associated limitations on driving times. The low constant speed reduces energy consumption and noise production. These considerations lead to an intelligent Rhine Delta Transport System (RTS).

Such an RTS is to be designed as a dedicated system for the transport of freight, providing a computer guided link between the Maasvlakte and Zevenaar, with branches to Rijswijk and Moerdijk. Transition centres for road transport are situated at so-called RTS stations at Rijswijk, Eemhaven, Moerdijk, Geldermalsen, Valburg and Zevenaar. The connections with the Maasvlakte and the Eemhaven give access to the marine terminals.

Although the system is suitable as a general alternative to road transport, this study covers only container transport that is related to the marine terminals of the Maasvlakte and the Eemhaven. Figure 6.1 shows the proposed layout of this RTS-network. The Maasvlakte–Zevenaar link can be a road–rail hybrid-equipped Betuwe Line. Figure 6.2 shows a design by construction company VolkerStevin for such a road–rail hybrid track.

Both trains and RTS vehicles can use this link during one-hour cycles. For example, every cycle could consist of 15 minutes for trains, 30 minutes for the RTS and 15 minutes for over-running, to be allocated by a system of dynamic trip booking. According to this design the extra investment in traffic lanes for the Betuwe Line is estimated to be 100 million euro.

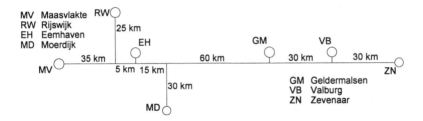

Figure 6.1   The network for the Rhine Delta Transport System

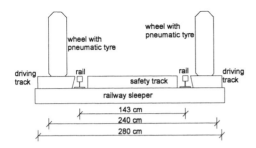

Figure 6.2   Cross-section of a road–rail hybrid driving track

The RTS is intended to be an open computer-guided system; in principle every vehicle that satisfies the stipulated requirements for the communication interfaces, mechanical behaviour and safety will be admitted. The speed is 50 to 60 km/hr. The technology is available and is being vigorously developed internationally under the Intelligent Transport Systems program.

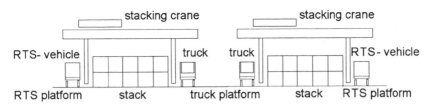

Figure 6.3   Profile of a duo RTS station

The RTS operates with robot vehicles that can participate fully in operations at the marine terminals. This affords new opportunities for the efficient layout of intersections. In the system the RTS stations take over the services of the truck service centres at the Maasvlakte that are currently operating. The road transport is then handled at the RTS stations and does not need to travel through to a terminal at the Eemhaven or the Maasvlakte. Thus no extra transshipment is needed. The proposed RTS station combines three functions: handling of road trucks, handling of RTS vehicles and short-term storage of containers. Figure 6.3 shows a setup for such an RTS station; (see van Rijswijk 2001).

The ICT Base of an Intelligent Transport System

Transport concerns the visible world of physical handling and the invisible world of co-ordination. Under the name AgileFrames, a generic logistics co-ordination system has been designed, partly in the context of the research program Freight Transport Automation and Multi-modality (FTAM) of Delft University of Technology. The system models the logistics world in a way analogous to the Internet and is suitable for any large logistics network. This involves a model with distributed intelligent actors, communicating with each other online in response to events or messages. Three segments are distinguished: one for logistics services and internal capacity allocation, one for concurrent use of common infrastructure (including traffic control) and one for internal control of machines (such as vehicles). Characteristic is the absence of centralised control authorities. All actors are autonomous and intelligent. They include clients, service providers, brokers (with co-ordinating functions), and executing actors.

Dynamic Trip Booking

When online logistics are applied to the control of public transport facilities, new possibilities arise. Road capacity can be interactively allocated via dynamic trip booking. This proceeds as follows. Anyone wishing to book a trip makes an advanced request for a place on a section of the road to be travelled within a specific time-window. The request is made via the Internet or by telephone and an agreement reached about the actual allocation. If necessary, the time-window may be adjusted in relation to the road capacity that is still available. This is automated via the allocation computer of a road capacity manager. It is also possible to cancel reservations. The charge depends on the time for which the reservation is made. If the journey is made on time, part of the charge is refunded. On cancellation, part of the charge is refunded, the proportion of this refund being smaller, the closer the time of cancellation approaches the reserved time. If the journey lasts longer than a specified guaranteed time, there is a partial refund. If no reservation is made, the full charge is paid and there is no entitlement to a refund.

In this model 'false reservations' and 'random behaviour' are costly, and will be avoided. This results in reliable information about the future and current capacity occupation. The advantage is clear: dynamic trip booking gives information and certainty about the duration of the trip and also the possibility to plan trips, thereby increasing effective road capacity. This is pre-eminently suitable for an open accessible infrastructure such as the road where any vehicle is admitted if it satisfies standards relating to roadworthiness, control and safety.

A system of dynamic trip booking is elaborated and studied with the help of simulation by de Feijter and Evers (2002).

A Booking System for Vehicles

The efficient deployment of vehicles is essential to the success of the RTS. In this context, there are two types of autonomous actors in organisational terms: vehicle providers, who provide transport services and vehicle rental services; and site operators who contract transport to these providers further to the processes on these sites. It is assumed that there are online procedures to support the request for and allocation of vehicles, to ensure that the autonomy of providers and operators is respected.

Terminal transport is the responsibility of the site operator. He can rent vehicles as required if agreed in time with the vehicle provider. He will be responsible for the deployment of vehicles which he has hired from the vehicle provider. The use of vehicles will be monitored online and this information is used for vehicle maintenance and invoicing.

Planning by the provider depends on requests made by the site operators. These requests concern required transport capacity in terms of the number of containers to be transported to specified terminals, and the number of vehicles to be rented for transport on the terminals, all in the form of specified time profiles. In essence, this amounts to categorical planning. The instruction to a vehicle to transport a specific container is given by the site operator at the time the transport process has to be implemented, in such a way that it fits in with current categorical planning. When the vehicle arrives, the receiver instructs it about further transport at the terminal.

The internal planning of a site operator will result in a request in the form of a profile of minimum transport capacity requirements, and a maximum capacity profile based on the margin to anticipate these minimal capacity requirements. The provider will then have to present a proposal which does not exceed the upper limit, but is above the lower limit. The site operator then issues a binding booking, which may be between the proposal and the lower limit specified earlier. This interaction is illustrated in Figure 6.4.

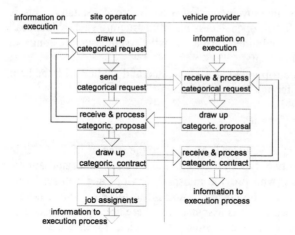

*Figure 6.4   Capacity deployment interaction between principals and a
              provider*

The demand profile will be known in outline a day ahead, but will have to
be updated frequently to reflect the actual situation. A multi-period approach
will be needed to follow the dynamics. In view of the transport times, a
period of 10 to 20 minutes would appear to be appropriate. The planning time
horizon should be long enough for efficient capacity deployment. A period of
18 hours would appear to be adequate in view of the daily cycle.

The interaction can be supported by a sophisticated charging system to
create a win–win situation. This procedure should include the following
rules:

- allocations above the minimum level are charged at a lower rate than
  those up to the minimum level. This means that the site operator is
  rewarded for the margin between the upper and lower levels which the
  provider uses to deploy capacity efficiently;
- the rate includes a fee for supplying the capacity, as well as a small
  fee for the booking. On cancellation, booking costs are only partly
  refunded, if at all;
- hiring more capacity at a later stage is also possible, but the likelihood
  of rejection due to a capacity constraint will normally increase the
  closer the request for additional capacity is made to implementation;
- if transport capacity demand shows peaks and troughs, a low-demand
  rate could be introduced to encourage peak demand shaving;
- there are fines for providers who fail to provide the agreed minimum
  capacity allocation.

Clearly, a procedure of this nature can only operate if both site operators and providers have computer-supported management systems, connected online. Information can be updated at the start of each planning cycle. In each planning cycle the provider will have to use all the information to make a feasible and efficient proposal for every principal. Feasible means that the relevant constraints must be fulfilled in every modelling cycle, for every destination, and for every principal. These constraints are:

- the conservation conditions on the sites, parking areas and RTS roadways;
- capacity restrictions affecting handling capacity and roadways;
- upper and lower limits of specified capacity demand.

Within these conditions, preference is given to a proposal which maximises revenues for the vehicle provider. Revenues are based on the rates for the capacity to be provided, while costs depend on the time and distance and use of the number of vehicles suggested in the proposal. This setup can be reduced to a linear programming model and optimised with the help of commercial software (Fourer et al. 1990).

For local transport, the procedure could issue transport assignments to vehicles at the micro level, within the volumes of the categorical planning. Jobs and vehicles can be matched by assignment techniques known from operations research. These techniques aim to minimise trip distances, including empty trips.

More details of the broking system can be found in Evers (2004), where the models are implemented and tested on models of hypothetical (small) configurations; the results are very promising. We conclude that it is technically feasible to optimise the allocations online, while respecting the autonomy of site operators and vehicle providers. In principle, this means that a major organisational problem associated with the autonomy of the actors might be solved.

Capacity of the Hybrid Road–rail Betuwe Line

Management of the road–rail hybrid Betuwe Line will require a trip booking system to accommodate hybrid use of the Betuwe Line, serving both conventional freight trains and the RTS. The system would be based on hourly cycles, moving along in the direction of travel, with a quarter hour slot for railway traffic and half an hour for road vehicles, (see also de Feiter and Evers 2002).

Table 6.2 describes how the time slots can be calculated, for a train (with length: trainLength) on a route section (with length: trackLength), assuming that the speed of the train (trainSpeed) is not lower than that of the RTS vehicles (vehicleSpeed) and also assuming that, given the long braking distance of a train, a minimal time lag (timeLag) has to be preserved between the RTS in front and the train behind.

Table 6.2 Blocking and unblocking RTS-vehicle access – train faster than RTS vehicle

---

blockTM = trackLength / vehicleSpeed + trackLength / trainSpeed – timeLag
deblockTm = trainLength / trainSpeed + timeLag2

If a train is admitted at time point '0', then the section must be closed some time in advance (denoted: blockTm, which has a negative value) to RTS vehicles to ensure that these will not obstruct the train on this track section. The section can be re-opened to RTS vehicles when the train has passed (passing time span: trainLength/trainSpeed) and a set period (denoted: timeLag2, being shorter than timeLag) has elapsed. The formula shows that the blocking time (blockTm) must start earlier as the difference in speed between train and RTS vehicle is greater, and the track section is longer. If the two speeds are identical only a minimum period (timeLag2) is required.

Table 6.3 gives a numerical example for a train leaving at 00.00 h from Eemhaven and travelling non-stop to Zevenaar. The train travels at 20 m/s and the RTS vehicles at 16 m/s, the length of the train is 600 m, and the lead time is 4 minutes.

The first three columns show the blocking times for vehicles travelling on the sections 'Eemhaven–Geldermalsen', 'Geldermalsen–Valburg' and 'Valburg–Zevenaar'. The last three columns show the blocking times for RTS vehicles making non-stop trips on the sections 'Eemhaven–Valburg' and 'Eemhaven–Zevenaar'. In future timetables, all freight trains will stop at Eemhaven and Valburg; thus the blocking periods will be at most half an hour.

Table 6.3 Numerical example on blocking sections on the Betuwe Line

	EH-GM	*GM-VB*	*VB-ZN*	*EH-VB*	*EH-ZN*
Distance, km	*75 km*	*30 km*	*30 km*	*105 km*	*135 km*
Blocked, hour min.	–00.20	01.17	01.17	–00.26	–00.32
Unblocked, hour min.	00.03	01.30	01.30	00.03	00.03
Duration train slot, min.	23 min.	13 min.	13 min.	29 min.	35 min.

Table 6.4   Basic data, estimates for 2010 and beyond, number of containers by road

Terminal		Area served	Eemhaven	Maasvlakte
Rijswijk	RW	North Holland, Rijnland,	160,000	196,000
Eemhaven	EH	Delfland, Westland;	349,000	427,000
Moerdijk	MD	Rotterdam and environs, Gouda, Drecht; Zeeland, Roosendaal, Bergen op Zoom, Belgian border	201,000	246,000
Geldermalsen	GM	Utrecht, North Brabant, South	140,000	171,000
Valburg	VB	Limburg	144,000	176,000
Zevenaar	ZN	North-east, Nijmegen, Limburg, borders Venlo, Twente, Arnhem, Zevenaar	90,000	109,000
Total number of containers			1,084,000	1,325,000

A distinction is made between journeys associated with Eemhaven and those associated with the Maasvlakte. The largest volumes are transported between the Maasvlakte and Eemhaven and between Eemhaven and Kijfhoek. Given six operating days per week this amounts to an average of 2,200 containers per day. The capacity of the Betuwe Line for RTS operations is estimated at 7,200 containers per day in each direction, assuming that 10 hours per operating day will be available for RTS-operations and that the gap between the vehicles will be 5 seconds on average.

We conclude that capacity is clearly adequate to cope with even a major increase in the demand for transport.

The Road–rail Hybrid Vehicle

Because of the mechanical lateral guiding by rails, rail wagons do not have two-dimensional freedom of movement. Compared with road trucks, this is unfavourable at logistics centres. In addition, railways operate with rigid schedules which do not accommodate the current logistics agility. In fact the only favourable characteristic is the low rolling resistance.

Now given the road–rail hybrid Betuwe Line, it is possible to profit from this favourable property, but to avoid the disadvantages. For this the system uses vehicles which, in addition to the usual road wheel sets, are equipped with rail wheel sets (see Figure 6.5). The road wheels are fitted with pneumatic tyres, are actively steered and are equipped with brakes and possibly also with drives. The lateral control is electronic. The rail wheel sets can move vertically, so that in the low position they roll on rails, which reduces the support forces on the road wheels. They are mounted on the chassis with some free margin for lateral movements and they are self-centring. The rail wheels are about 15 cm wide and have no flanges and they are not used for braking. Therefore noise production is low.

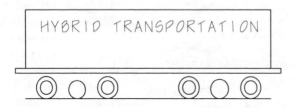

Figure 6.5   An example of a road–rail hybrid vehicle

Figure 6.5 shows the scheme of a hybrid vehicle with two rail wheel sets, each of which is mounted between two road wheel sets. With raised rail wheels the vehicle functions as a vehicle running on pneumatic tyres. With the rail wheels lowered the axle pressure is automatically controlled in such a way that a stable and skid-free movement is maintained. When braking, the vertical forces on the rail wheel sets are reduced as the braking force of the road wheel sets increases. The length of the braking distance thus is equivalent to that of a road vehicle, even when rails are being used. The hybrid track can thus facilitate intensive traffic with these hybrid vehicles.

When moving over a terminal platform the rail wheels are raised. The road wheel sets are controlled independently of the rails according to instructions about the route to be followed. Depending on the nature of the logistics environment, this control can be fully automated, manually operated, or a hybrid combination of automated and manual operation. Travelling in this way, the freight vehicle has the flexibility of a vehicle with tyres. As to implementation there are many possible variations, for example as intelligent robot trailer, or as semi-trailer. The concept is protected by Dutch patent P54316NL00.

A road–rail hybrid freight vehicle can be almost entirely constructed on the basis of proven technology. The rail wheel set is based on well-known engineering principles, but must be further developed. A preliminary engineering verification has been carried out with the aid of a simulation model for the dynamic–mechanical properties of a vehicle according to Figure 6.5. These demonstrate mechanical behaviour that is adequate in every respect. Table 6.5 gives an estimation of the energy consumption for the transport of marine containers.

Table 6.5   Estimation of power and energy use 'at the wheels'

	Speed	Average situation		Heavy load
		Power	Energy use	Power
Truck	100 km/hr	244 kW	100%	930 kW
Truck	50 km/hr	72 kW	60%	400 kW
Hybrid	50 km/hr	37 kW	30%	350 kW

The first row shows the power required for a freight vehicle without rail wheels at a speed of 100 km/hr; the next row shows power at a speed of 50 km/hr. The bottom row gives an estimate for a road–rail hybrid vehicle that is 60% supported on rails at a speed of 50 km/hr. The column 'average situation' shows the situation without a gradient, with normal loading and some wind effect. The situation 'heavy load' indicates heavy loading, a gradient of 3% and a strong head wind. Kinetic energy and the effects of variations in speed are not included.

The RTS versus Conventional Road Transport

When comparing the merits of the RTS versus road transport, the following points must be taken into consideration.

- with an automated system the wage costs are primarily related to supervision; this is estimated at 10% in comparison to wage costs for conventional road transport;
- for the RTS it is possible to introduce optimised co-ordination for the exploitation of RTS vehicles, which avoids empty driving and exploits opportunities for peak shaving;
- the investment costs for an RTS vehicle are higher than for a truck. However, because the RTS vehicles operate continuously at constant speeds, depreciation and maintenance costs are the same as those for a truck;
- the extra investment costs for traffic lanes are low in comparison with those for normal road transport. It is only necessary to separate traffic lanes. Little hardware is needed for traffic and vehicle control; the robot vehicles are themselves 'intelligent';
- in comparison with future road transport, the RTS stations do not require extra investment. After all the automated stations are located in the hinterland instead of on the Maas Area (Maasvlakte);
- when operating with road–rail hybrid vehicles, expected average energy consumption will be only 40% compared with conventional road transport.

6.4   ESTIMATION OF THE FUTURE MARKET FOR ARHINE DELTA TRANSPORT SYSTEM

The Methodological Basis for Estimating Future Market Shares

The primary objective of the Rhine Delta Transport System (RTS) is to provide an alternative to road transport. However, the RTS will also compete with inland shipping and with rail transport. Therefore the second part of this study concerns the future market shares of the RTS; it is based on earlier work by Evers et al. (2002) and the work of Evers and Konings (2001).

The methodological basis of the research is a model with which the market shares of various competing modes of transport can be calculated. To assess the results, an existing model for the estimation of market shares for various modes of transport that can use generally available data has been chosen. The mathematical model of McFadden (McFadden 1976; Ben-Akiva and Lerman 1985) in which the choice of modality is assumed to be dependent on tariffs and throughput times, is eminently suitable for this, providing an aggregated approach under some simplifying modelling assumptions. More precisely we assume that the transport market for containers is homogeneous and that frequency of a transport link can be neglected. Clearly, the results will give no more than a raw indication of market shares.

A characteristic of the model is that the calculated market shares are invariant with respect to the addition (or subtraction) of a similar amount to the tariff of each of the competing modalities and similarly invariant with reference to an increase (or decrease) in the throughput time by the same time span. For the section of the transport chain between the sea ship and the gateway to the hinterland, this means that in the calculation it is sufficient to include the parts in which variations may occur. The study can therefore be restricted to the section between the landside platforms of the marine container-stacks and the origin or destination locations in the hinterland.

For the application of the model, data is collected about the network, the transport chains between the marine quays and the origin/destination, the tariffs, the transport times and handling times on the transition platforms. In order to determine the parameters of the model for the choice of mode and to gain insight into the accuracy of the model, data about the present modal split is also collected. These data permit an estimate to be made for a basis year for three model parameters. With the model thus specified exploratory calculations are then made for the modal split in the coming year.

Data and Assumptions on Volumes and Distances

The research used data from the Ministry of Transport, Communications and Water Management (see Gemeentelijk Havenbedrijf Rotterdam 1998) about container transport in 1995 between the port of Rotterdam and 122 hinterland regions, broken down into conventional modalities. At the moment of writing (2002) these are the most recent data with such a degree of specification.

The reports also contain a specification of the transport distance between Rotterdam and these regions. Table 6.1 is derived from the volumes of the hinterland regions by combining these into regions with the shortest road distance from one of the RTS stations. Thus, West Netherlands is served by the stations Rijswijk, Eemhaven and Moerdijk (see Figure 6.1); the stations Geldermalsen, Valburg and Zevenaar serve East Netherlands; the areas Ruhr and Germany+ are served by the stations Valburg and Zevenaar; Antwerp goes via RTS station Moerdijk. Exports and imports are distinguished: the term export-containers indicates containers that depart from Rotterdam by sea, while import-containers arrive by sea.

Transport between Rotterdam and North Germany is partly carried out by coasters which thus provide an alternative to inland shipping. Because this will distort the market this transport relation is not included. Transport between Rotterdam and France is also not considered because the waterways and railways are considerably poorer in quality than the other means of transport. The volumes of the West and East Netherlands areas are relatively homogeneous and small. The South Germany+ area does not include the Ruhr area, but includes more distant areas extending to Italy.

Table 6.6 gives the transportation distances. The column headed >/< gives the distances by road to and from RTS stations. These distances are irrelevant for the mode of road transport, because this mode does not have movements to RTS stations. The column headed 'New Rail' relates to the operational Betuwe Line; in the column 'RTS' the distances relate to the RTS stations and the gravity centre of the terminal of the port of Rotterdam, which lies 14 km east of the Maasvlakte.

Table 6.6   Transport distances (km) to Maasvlakte per mode and road links to and from RTS stations (>/<)

	Road	Inland Shipping		Existing Rail		New Rail		RTS	
	road	I.S.	>/<	rail	>/<	rail	>/<	RTS	>/<
West Netherlands	85	110	30	110	30	110	30	60	40
East Netherlands	155	150	40	150	40	130	40	130	40
Ruhr area	300	310	75	310	75	290	75	165	120
South Germany+	865	965	150	885	150	865	150	135	700
Antwerp Harbour	195	175	20	195	20	195	20	140	60

Data and Assumptions on Tariffs

The tariffs for transport found in the literature are highly divergent. Use is made of research carried out by TNO Inro (Maas 2001; Weibel and Henriques 2001) and that of Runhaar et al. (2001). The cost distribution derived from these is shown in Table 6.7 for 2001. In this time-dependent and distance-dependent costs are distinguished, the latter excluding travelling time. The data shown in the Barge, Rail and Road columns are taken from the literature.

The columns entitled 2007+ relate to a future reference year. It is considered that by then inland shipping companies will use ships that are three times the size of those used now and these will be considerably cheaper to run per container. In addition, since Barge 2007+ is supposed to avoid interim stops, it will be faster than Barge 2001. In the calculations the average sailing speed of the conventional inland shipping vessels at Antwerp is taken as 10 km/hr. The average speed of the downstream Rhine traffic is 10 km/hr, while the upstream speed averages around 8 km/hr. In the Randstad area the average speed of ships is 8 km/hr. In 1995 the effective speed of rail traffic was around 22.5 km/hr. A speed of 45 km/hr is calculated for the New Rail.

The data in the column headed 'RTS-R' refers to an automated guided road vehicle moving at a constant speed of 50 km/hr. Fuel consumption is therefore lower than that of a truck, while wage costs are only 10%. With the RTS-H, using hybrid road–rail robot vehicles, fuel consumption is half that of the non-hybrid RTS vehicles.

Table 6.7   *Cost distribution per transported container over 'the hinterland' and the speeds*

| | | 2001 | | |
		Barge	Rail	Road
€/hour	salaries	0.45	6.40	31.3
	diverse	0.34	–	16.2
€/km	fuel	0.014	0.07	0.26
	diverse	0.042	0.29	0.22
Speed, km/hr		10–8	22.5	65

| | | 2007+ | | | | |
		Barge	Rail	Road	RTS-R	RTS-H
€/hour	salaries	0.15	6.40	31.3	3.1	3.1
	diverse	0.22	–	16.2	17.0	17.0
€/km	fuel	0.010	0.07	0.26	0.20	0.10
	diverse	0.028	0.29	0.22	0.24	0.24
Speed, km/hr		13–8	45	65	50	50

To relate 2001 tariffs to transport flows in 1995, the price level of 1995 must be used. In accordance with the literature, the price increases between 1995 and 2001 are thus assumed to be +10% for transshipment; +15% for rail transport; +20% for road transport and +5% for inland shipping. The general price increase is assumed to be +10%.

Data on Transition Throughput Times and Costs

Table 6.8 gives an overview of throughput times and costs at the Maasvlakte and in the hinterland sites and the possible road transport to and from the station. A distinction is made between the situation in 1995 and the future reference year 2007+. For example it is assumed that, because of better co-ordination and more intensive use of the system, future throughput times will be considerably shorter than those of 1995. The costs of transshipment at the Maasvlakte correspond with those that can be derived from the studies of the R&D Management Institute for Traffic and Transport, Connekt. The total costs of handling a visiting container there are estimated as €80 (see FAMAS-MV2 2002). However, in this chapter the transportation chain is restricted to the section between the landside transshipment platforms of the marine stacks and the hinterland carrier, which can be estimated as 30% of the integral throughput costs on the marine terminals.

The throughput times are derived from data on transshipment times plus the time margins that are needed to ensure that the links of the transport chain are reliably connected to each other. For the RTS one hour is calculated at the Maasvlakte, plus one hour for transport to and from the terminal. For road transport only three hours at the Maasvlakte is assumed. The difference of one hour in favour of the RTS derives from the fact that the RTS, as a dedicated transport system with a reliable 24-hour service, functions as part of the transshipment company on the Maasvlakte (and the Eemhaven).

The difference between the throughput Barge in 1995 and Barge 2007+ arises from the assumed greater carrying capacity of the new style inland shipping. This means that there is only a three-stop procedure on the Maasvlakte and loading and unloading take less time. Road 1995 refers to loading and unloading at the Maasvlakte using straddle carriers, while Road 2007+ is assumed to use an integrated service station, such as that shown in Figure 6.2 for example, with which short throughput can be achieved.

RTS vehicles can be handled directly at the maritime stacks, so in this context the cost of transshipment is zero. For inland shipping, railway and RTS, road transport to and from the stations in question is needed (of course this does not apply to road transport). In the market analysis the following aspects are also included.

Table 6.8   Logistic throughput times and costs of handling at the transshipment points

		1995		
		Barge	Rail	Road
Maas-	ProcTime carrier	12.0 h	8.0 h	1.0 h
Vlakte	ProcTime container	10.0 h	8.0 h	3.0 h
	ProcCosts container	€25.0	€25.0	€30.0
Inland	ProcTime carrier	9.0 h	4.0 h	–
Sites	ProcTime container	9.0 h	4.0 h	–
	ProcCosts container	€20.0	€20.0	–
Trans to	ProcTime truck	1.0 h	1.0 h	–
and	ProcTime container	1.0 h	1.0 h	–
from	ProcCosts container	€15.0	€15.0	–

		2007+			
		Barge	Rail	Road	RTS
Maas-	ProcTime carrier	4.0 h	4.0 h	0.5 h	–
Vlakte	ProcTime container	4.0 h	4.0 h	3.0 h	1.0 h
	ProcCosts container	€27.5	€27.5	€33.0	–
Inland	ProcTime carrier	4.0 h	2.0 h	–	0.25 h
Sites	ProcTime container	4.0 h	2.0 h	–	0.25 h
	ProcCosts container	€22.0	€22.0	–	€16.5
Trans to	ProcTime truck	0.5 h	0.5 h	–	0.5 h
and	ProcTime container	1.0 h	1.0 h	–	1.0 h
from	ProcCosts container	€16.5	€16.5	–	€16.5

In Antwerp a considerable part of the inland shipping is directly related to the port, so transport to and from the station is not needed. It is assumed that this applies to 50% of the transport via inland shipping.

With road transport the acquisition of loads for journeys to and from the station must be taken into consideration. The literature presents widely divergent data. Here it is assumed that, on average, road transport needs an hour for this purpose for every trip, while, as a co-ordinated system, the RTS is assumed to require only 30 minutes.

In due course in Europe all modalities will be subject to a kilometre levy. It is intended that all marginal social costs of freight transport should be passed on and the levy is also intended to cover the costs of the infrastructure. According to Dings et al. (1999) this will amount to €0.80 per kilometre for road transport. For rail and barge transport respectively tariffs of €0.35 and €0.30 are anticipated; for the RTS we propose a tariff of €0.60.

The Model for the Estimation of Market Shares

In McFadden's model, the modal split is calculated via a probability approach: a shipper chooses a specific modality (road, rail, barge or RTS) with a probability $P(i)$. This probability is assumed to depend on the logistic costs on that section, which are specified in the form of a function $F(.)$ of the monetary tariff and on the monetary assessment of the throughput time. A probability $P(i)$ with respect to the choice of modality is derived from a suitably chosen declining positive function $G(.)$, in the following form: $P(i) = G(\beta*F(i)) / \Sigma j \{G(\beta*F(j))\}$.

With the coefficient β the model can be adjusted to the sensitivity of the market: A high β value corresponds with a high sensitivity. As shown in Table 6.9, the so-called logit-function occurs with an exponential form of $G(.)$ and in this form it is used in a variety of traffic and transport studies (see Tavasszy (1999) for an application to freight transport). $S(i)$ can be interpreted as the market share of modality i at a specific origin/destination relation. The logistic costs $F(i)$ comprise the monetary tariff $p(i)$ and the monetary value $\alpha*d(i)$ of the throughput time $d(i)$. In this context α can thus be interpreted as the logistic tariff of the throughput time.

Table 6.9   The model for the choice of modality

$S(i) = \exp(-\beta*F(i)) / (\Sigma\{\exp(-\beta*F(j)), \text{j from } M\})$
$F(i) = (p[i] \uparrow \gamma + (\alpha * d[i]) \uparrow \gamma) \uparrow (1/\gamma))$

$S(i)$: market share 'i'	M: modalities
$F(i)$: logistic tariff 'i'	$p[i]$ tariff for 'i'
α: time value	$d[i]$ = throughput time 'i'
β: market sensitivity	γ: linearity

	Influence of coefficient γ					
	$\alpha * d = 0, \frac{1}{2}, 1, 2, 4, 8;$ with $p = 1$					
γ	0.0	0.5	1.0	2.0	4.0	8.0
0.90	1.00	1.61	2.16	3.22	5.30	9.38
0.95	1.00	1.55	2.07	3.10	5.14	9.17
1.00	1.00	1.50	2.00	3.00	5.00	9.00
1.10	1.00	1.42	1.88	2.83	4.78	8.74

The specification proposed here permits the estimation of an optimal functional form for the function $F(i)$ (see Table 6.9). Usually in such models for freight transport only a linear specification is used which corresponds with the value $\gamma = 1$. However, it is not clear whether this assumption is valid. After all, if the type of freight that is carried in containers is variable in relation to different origins and destinations, it might be possible that the time values will differ according to distance. The form of *F(.)* we propose gives the model an additional degree of freedom which can solve this problem. With $\gamma = 1$, *F(i)* depends only on the weighted sum of throughput time and tariff, which corresponds to the usual studies of this type. With $\gamma < 1$, *F(i)* is superlinear in the throughput time and with $\gamma > 1$ it is sublinear (see Table 6.9). For increasing throughput time, the relative deviation in relation to the linear form (thus with $\gamma = 1$) becomes zero. For pragmatic considerations the economically well-known CES-function is chosen for *F(.)*, but this is not related to any economic interpretation.

Calculation of Model Coefficients

The coefficients α, β and γ are estimated from data and assumptions about the modal split, tariffs and throughput times. The data on tariffs and throughput times are summarised in Table 6.10. The figures in the column 'barge upstream' refer to shipping moving upstream and those in the column headed 'barge downstream' refer to shipping moving downstream; this is only relevant for the Rhine traffic. In contrast, in the column 'average inland shipping' data for the average sailing are shown.

Table 6.10   Calculated logistic throughput times (hours) and tariffs (€) for a container in 1995

	Road transport		Barge upstream		Barge down-stream		Average inland shipping		Rail transport	
	h.	€	h.	€	h.	€	h.	€	h.	€
Randstad	4.3	199	–	–	–	–	34.2	203	18.4	294
East Neth.	5.4	274	39.4	220	36.6	217	37.3	218	20.3	327
Ruhr area	7.6	427	59.9	280	52.2	274	55.6	277	27.9	454
South Germany+	16.3	1026	142.9	457	118.8	438	129.5	446	54.6	855
Antwerp Harbour	6.0	316	–	–	–	–	36.2	148	22.0	331

In the calculation the chosen coefficients are such that the sum of the (volume weighted) quadratic deviations of the calculation, as opposed to the given modal split of Table 6.10, is minimal (see de Feiter and Evers 2002). The result of the calculation is shown in the form of the standard deviations summarised in Table 6.11. The deviations arising from the separate calculations for export and import container flows are shown in the columns headed 'exports' and 'imports'. The result of the calculation for the market in which exports and imports are taken together is given in the columns headed 'Total', in which the sailing speeds for upstream and downstream transport are averaged. The average deviation over the whole is 6% for exports and 3% for imports. The value of ±1 for γ implies that a linear combination of the monetary tariff and the costs for throughput time is possible. When $\gamma = 1$, the combined optimum values for α and β are equal to 5.4 and 0.019, in which the weighted deviation is 5%.

Table 6.11   The model coefficients corresponding with the tariffs for 1995 and 2001

| | 1995 | | | 2001 | | |
	Export	Import	Total	Export	Import	Total
A €/h	5.95	4.90	5.40	6.55	5.39	5.94
B 1/€	0.018	0.019	0.019	0.0164	0.0173	0.0173
Γ	1.00	1.01	1.00	1.00	1.01	1.01
Dev. %	6	3	4			

The model coefficients for 1995 are given on the left-hand side of Table 6.10. On the right-hand side of Table 6.11 these have been adjusted to the general inflation level of 10% over the period 1995–2001; this is possible because $F(i)$ is homogeneous from zero degrees.

In the further calculations no distinction is made between imports and exports or between upstream and downstream transport. To obtain an impression of the sensitivity of the tariff to time, calculations are based on both high and low tariffs, these being $\alpha = 6.60$ and $\alpha = 5.40$ €/hours, with $\beta = 0.019$ and $\gamma = 1$ in both cases.

Future Market Shares of the RTS versus the Other Modalities

There are considerable differences between the starting-points of the calculations for a future reference year 2007+ and those for 1995. These are:

- freight trains travel at an average speed of 45 km/hr instead of 22.5 km/hr and the transshipment is more efficient. The Betuwe route is operational;
- handling of the trucks at the Maasvlakte is semi-automated, and throughput time is reduced to 30 minutes;
- the inland ships are bigger and make few or no stops en route. Moreover the transport facilities are more efficient. Therefore on average the transport process is quicker and cheaper than in 1995;
- in Rotterdam the volumes are divided into 75% for the Maasvlakte and 25% for the Eemhaven area. The 'gravity point of the transport' then comes to lie about 10 km east of the Maasvlakte;
- possibly by then general kilometre levies will be in force; the calculations are therefore made with and without a kilometre levy.

It is also assumed that, in relation to 2001, fuel prices remain unchanged and that no inflation occurs. In the mathematical model the latter is equivalent to the assumption that the mutual relations of the tariffs for transport and for transshipment remain the same.

Compared with 1995, Table 6.12 shows that 2007+ inland shipping and rail are assumed to achieve shorter throughput times, and also lower costs. Road transport is not assumed to develop in this way and will therefore lose market share. The kilometre levy that is highest for road transport strengthens this effect. The calculated estimates are given in Table 6.13. It appears that the decline in road transport over longer distances is considerable, as is the small share of rail in all transport relations with the exception of South Germany+.

Table 6.12   *Calculated logistic throughput times (hours) and 2007+ tariffs (€) with and without and with kilometre levy*

Without kilometre levy	Road h.	€	Barge h.	€	Rail h.	€	RTS-Road h.	€	RTS-Hybrid h.	€
Randstad	4.3	207	25.2	187	9.9	267	3.8	218	3.8	212
East Neth.	5.4	292	22.1	199	10.5	289	5.2	277	5.2	264
Ruhr area	7.6	467	36.0	252	14.6	411	7.1	403	7.1	386
South Germ.+	16.3	1151	91.7	388	28.5	790	15.5	1080	15.5	1066
Antw. Harbour	6.0	340	28.7	114	11.6	297	5.7	310	5.7	296

With kilometre levy	Road h.	€	Barge h.	€	Rail h.	€	RTS-Road h.	€	RTS-Hybrid h.	€
Randstad	4.3	275	25.2	244	9.9	330	3.8	286	3.8	280
East Neth.	5.4	419	22.1	276	10.5	367	5.2	387	5.2	374
Ruhr area	7.6	707	36.0	405	14.6	573	7.1	598	7.1	581
South Germ.+	16.3	1843	91.7	798	28.5	1211	15.5	1721	15.5	1707
Antw. Harbour	6.0	496	28.7	175	11.6	381	5.7	422	5.7	408

A further step could be to include the RTS, road transport, inland shipping and railways in the model simultaneously and to determine the corresponding market shares. This has no practical meaning, because the model used has very specific limitations: it cannot cope with the fact that the RTS and road transport differ very little with respect to tariffs and throughput times. This can be compared with the situation in which road transport is twice included as a separate modality in the model: the combined share according to the model would then be greater than that of road transport as a single modality.

In contrast to this, road transport, inland shipping and the railway differ to such an extent that the choice of modality is largely determined by the shipper. The road shipper largely determines the choice between RTS and truck-trailer. His principal consideration will be whether the truck-trailer is handled at the Maasvlakte/Eemhaven or at one of the RTS stations. The choice is determined by the costs, the travelling time restrictions on the driver, the likelihood of a return load and similar factors. It is clear that the model of modality choices under consideration cannot process such information. Therefore a hypothetical exercise is used to calculate what the result would be if all road transport runs via the RTS stations. Table 6.14 gives the results when non-hybrid RTS vehicles are used, while Table 6.15 shows the results when the system makes use of road-railroad hybrid RTS vehicles. Note: using the RTS, costs and throughput times of road transport between RTS stations and the related inland sites.

In comparison to Table 6.13, Tables 6.11 and 6.12 show that the RTS is a relatively attractive alternative to road transport, in that the use of the RTS leads to a greater market share. In particular this applies to the Maasvlakte–Valburg–Zevenaar and Maasvlakte–Moerdijk sections connecting with Germany and Antwerp. With the associated road transport to and from it, the RTS takes considerably more of the market of the East Netherlands, the Ruhr and Antwerp Harbour areas than road transport does.

For the direct transport relation between the Maasvlakte and Eemhaven the situation is different. This typically involves the two-way transport between terminals that can be done completely by RTS, by train or barge, without additional road transport. The use of the RTS is now primarily triggered by terminal operators, who therefore take on the role of shipper. In this context the RTS clearly operates differently from road transport and thus can be introduced into the choice model with the other modalities. Table 6.16 shows calculated market shares using of the above parameters α, β and γ. This relates to a distance of 40 kilometres, without transport to and from the station.

Table 6.13   Estimate of future market shares (in %), 2007+, without RTS

With kilometre levy	Road High TmVal.	Road Low TmVal.	Barge High TmVal.	Barge Low TmVal.	Rail High TmVal.	Rail Low TmVal.
Randstad	79	74	8	13	13	13
East Netherlands	44	37	32	39	24	23
Ruhr area	26	18	43	57	31	25
South Germany+	0	0	43	76	57	24
Antwerp Harbour	16	11	67	76	17	13

With kilometre levy	Road High TmVal.	Road Low TmVal.	Barge High TmVal.	Barge Low TmVal.	Rail High TmVal.	Rail Low TmVal.
Randstad	77	71	10	15	13	14
East Netherlands	23	19	44	51	33	30
Ruhr area	7	4	58	70	35	26
South Germany+	0	0	48	80	52	20
Antwerp Harbour	3	2	83	88	14	10

Table 6.14   Future market shares (in %), 2007+, with RTS replacing road transport along the RTS network

Without kilometre levy	RTS-Road High TmVal.	RTS-Road Low TmVal.	Barge High TmVal.	Barge Low TmVal.	Rail High TmVal.	Rail Low TmVal.
Randstad	77	71	9	14	14	15
East Netherlands	52	45	27	35	21	20
Ruhr area	55	44	26	39	19	17
South Germany+	1	0	42	76	56	24
Antwerp Harbour	25	18	59	70	16	12

With kilometre levy	RTS-Road High TmVal.	RTS-Road Low TmVal.	Barge High TmVal.	Barge Low TmVal.	Rail transport High TmVal.	Rail transport Low TmVal.
Randstad	74	67	11	18	15	15
East Netherlands	37	30	36	44	27	26
Ruhr area	37	26	39	54	24	20
South Germany+	0	0	48	80	52	20
Antwerp Harbour	12	8	75	82	13	10

Table 6.15   Market share of RTS-Hybrid as alternative to road transport along the RTS network (in %)

Without kilometre levy	RTS-Hybrid		Barge 2007+		Rail 2007+	
	High TmVal.	Low TmVal.	High TmVal.	Low TmVal.	High TmVal.	Low TmVal.
Randstad	78	73	9	13	13	14
East Netherlands	58	51	24	31	18	18
Ruhr area	63	51	22	34	15	15
South Germany+	2	0	42	76	56	24
Antwerp Harbour	31	22	55	66	14	12
With kilometre levy	RTS-Hybrid		Barge 2007+		Rail 2007+	
	High TmVal.	Low TmVal.	High TmVal.	Low TmVal.	High TmVal.	Low TmVal.
Randstad	76	70	10	15	14	15
East Netherlands	42	36	33	40	25	24
Ruhr area	45	33	34	49	21	18
South Germany+	0	0	48	80	52	20
Antwerp Harbour	16	10	72	81	12	9

Table 6.16   The market shares at Maasvlakte–Eemhaven (MV–EH) (in %), with and without kilometre levy

	RTS-Hybrid		Road 2007+		Barge 2007+		Rail 2007+	
	High TmVal.	Low TmVal.	High TmVal.	Low TmVal.	High TmVal.	Low TmVal.	High TmVal.	Low TmVal.
Without levy	64	61	9	9	12	15	9	9
With levy	61	58	8	7	15	18	17	17

In this context the RTS appears superior to the other modalities. Possibly locating a RTS between the terminals at the Maasvlakte and those in Eemhaven area may lead to integration of the logistic operations and thereby to synergetic advantages. In fact, this would mean that the Maasvlakte would be extended to the Eemhaven.

6.5 CONCLUSIONS

Because of its functional characteristics, an intelligent road–rail hybrid transport in the context of the proposed Rhine Delta Transport System has to be considered as a new transport modality. It can be integrated directly with the terminal's operations, whereas special RTS stations take care of the transition interface between conventional road transport and the RTS. These RTS stations do not require extra investment; they are located in the hinterland instead of on the Maasvlakte. For the RTS it is possible to introduce optimised co-ordination for the exploitation of RTS vehicles, which avoids driving empty vehicles and exploits opportunities to carry out transport orders in a larger space of time (peak shaving). When operating with road–rail hybrid vehicles, expected average energy consumption will be only 30 to 40% compared with conventional road transport.

To study its market potential, the well-known model of McFadden is used. This model explains the modal split from the tariffs and throughput times, calculated over the entire transport chain. The model is calibrated against numerical data from 1995. The results indicate that the model adequately represents the modal split of 1995.

By applying the model to a future situation with shorter throughput times and lower costs both for inland shipping and for railway transport, but with unchanged characteristics for road transport, it appears that the market share of road transport becomes marginal at distances over 400 km and that large-scale inland shipping is dominant at the connections with Antwerp and the Ruhr area. Rail transport is more important on the link to South Germany.

Separate studies of the RTS and road transport in combination with the other modalities provide insight into possible market shares: the RTS (with road transport to and from RTS stations) will perform better than road transport. This is primarily the case with the Maasvlakte–Valburg and Maasvlakte–Moerdijk links, where the proposed RTS (with associated road transport to and from the RTS stations) will on average take about half of the market, whereas the other half will go to inland shipping.

For direct transport between the terminals at the Maasvlakte and the Eemhaven where the linking transport over the road is not included, the RTS functions in a different way than road transport. Our calculations indicate that by this means the RTS can acquire a large market share at the expense of road transport: 60% versus 10%. Possibly a RTS between the terminals at the Maasvlakte and Eemhaven could even lead to the integration of the logistics operations and thereby generate further synergetic advantages.

It is recommended that a model approach should be taken for the policy investigation in preparation for more advanced studies of layout for transport infrastructure, such as the Iron Rhine (a railway, connecting Antwerp and Germany), possibly in road–rail hybrid form.

REFERENCES

Ben-Akiva, M. and S.R. Lerman (1985), *Discrete Choice Analysis*, Massachusetts: MIT.

de Feiter, R. and J.J.M. Evers (2002), *An Interactive Program to Calculate Shares on Multi-modal Transport Markets*, to be published electronically, www.rstrail.nl. TU-Delft, January.

Dings, J.M.W., B.A. Leurs, M.J. Blom, E.H. Buckmann, L.M. Bus, H.W.J. van Haselen and S.A. Rienstra (1999), *Prijselasticiteiten in het goederentransport*, Rotterdam/Delft: NEI/CE.

Evers, J.J.M. (2004), Centralized versus Distributed Feeder Ship Service, *Transportation Planning and Technology*, Vol. 27, no. 5, October.

Evers, J.J.M. and R. Konings (2001), De slimme rail-weg hybride Betuwe Lijn in relatie tot het wegtransport, *Tijdschrift vervoerswetenschap*, Vol. 36e, no. 6, June.

Evers, J.J.M., L.A. Tavasszy and A.D. Heyning (2002), Een intelligent transportsysteem voor de Rijndelta kan een reëel alternatief bieden voor het Randstedelijk containertransport, *Tijdschrift Vervoerwetenschap*, Vol. 37, no. 1.

McFadden, D. (1976), The Mathematical Theory of Demand Models, in P. Stopher and A. Meyburg (eds.) *Behavioural Travel Demand Models*, Lexington, MA: Lexington Books.

FAMAS-MV2 (2002), *Cost Analysis Model for Container Terminal Operations*, Delft: Connekt.

Fourer, R., D.M. Gay and B.W. Kernighan (1990), A Modelling Language for Mathematical Programming, *Management Science, 36*, 5.

Gemeentelijk Havenbedrijf Rotterdam (1998), *Integrale verkenningen voor haven en industrie 2020*, Rotterdam.

Maas, N. (2001), Recordit, Identification of Taxes, Charges and Subsidies, TNO INRO, Draft.

Runhaar, H.A.C., B. Kuipers, R.E.C.M. van der Heijden and W.H. Melody (2001), *Het goederentransport in 2001*, TRAIL Research School, October.

Tavasszy, L.A. (1999), *Model Praktijkoefening College Goederentransportmodellen en Beleidsanalyse*, TNO Inro, TU Delft.

van Rijswijk, H. (2001), *Compacte containerterminals voor de Slimme Betuwe Lijn*, Ontwerp-opdracht TU-Delft, Begeleiding J.J.M. Evers, September.

Weibel G. and M. Henriques (2001), *Real Cost Reduction Door-to-door Intermodal Transport, Imbalances and Inefficiencies of Current Pricing System*, Tetraplan (DK), Draft.

7. Automated vehicle control

Petros Ioannou and Arnab Bose

7.1 INTRODUCTION

The introduction of vehicles with automatic vehicle following capability in the market has drawn considerable interest to automated vehicle control. This chapter discusses longitudinal and lateral controller designs for automated vehicle control. It also outlines automated vehicle sensor requirements and vehicle-to-vehicle communication considerations. Subsequently, two benefits of vehicle automation are discussed.

Longitudinal and lateral control of a vehicle are the major functions performed by human beings while driving an automobile. The human driver reacts to stimuli by pressing the gas pedals, the brakes or turning the steering wheel. This defines the driving behaviour of an individual. Automated vehicle control deals with automation of the different functions of driving behaviour.

In the last decade considerable research has been done into the automation of the vehicle-highway system in an effort to improve safety, capacity and traffic flow characteristics. It has been envisioned that removing the human from the vehicle–driver control loop will eliminate the randomness associated with today's manual traffic and satisfy the above requirements (Stevens 1997 and Ioannou 1997). The degree of automation in a vehicle determines the involvement of the human driver in the driving loop (Bose and Ioannou 1998). Full automation in the longitudinal direction is expected to benefit safety, capacity and traffic flow characteristics. Likewise, replacing the human driver in the driving loop with longitudinal and lateral automation, as in a fully automated vehicle, is expected to further improve safety. Different system configurations for automated vehicle deployment have been outlined in Hall (1997).

The use of actuators and sensors is deemed to improve safety, capacity and traffic flow characteristics for the following reasons: firstly, electronic sensors do not get fatigued, tired or distracted and are therefore more reliable (Ward 1997). Secondly, actuators react much faster than the average alert human driver, who has a time delay of about 1.0 s to 1.5 s (Milestone 2 Report, 1996b). This implies that vehicles can travel closer, which translates into higher capacity/throughput (Bose and Ioannou 1998). Thirdly, the deterministic response of the controllers in comparison to the random behaviour of human drivers smoothes traffic flow (Bose and Ioannou 1999).

The lateral and longitudinal functions of an automated vehicle are performed with the use of lateral and longitudinal controllers that work in conjunction with on-board sensors (Walker and Harris 1993). The longitudinal controller comprises two subsystems, namely throttle and brake controllers (Ioannou and Xu 1994). A switching logic dictates the switching from one controller to the other. The lateral controller uses a lateral control system (Peng and Tomizuka 1990) that uses a road referencing/sensing system that measures the position and orientation of the vehicle relative to the road (Hessburg et al. 1991).

This chapter begins with longitudinal and lateral controller designs for light and heavy-duty vehicles in Sections 7.2 and 7.3. These discussions are followed by issues and concerns with automated vehicle sensors in Section 7.4. Section 7.5 outlines vehicle-to-vehicle communication issues. Lastly, two benefits of automation, namely traffic flow characteristics and fuel consumption and pollution, are elaborated in Section 7.6. The chapter ends with conclusions in Section 7.7.

7.2   AUTOMATED LONGITUDINAL CONTROL

The control phase of automobile driving is concerned with actuation of steering wheel, accelerator and brakes in such a way that the vehicle follows its preceding vehicle or the desired path with a desired velocity and with acceptable precision. Longitudinal controllers automate the actuation of accelerator and brakes. Lateral controllers automate the actuation of the steering wheel.

Longitudinal Controller Design

Different longitudinal schemes have been proposed in the literature (Swaroop et al. 1994, Ioannou and Chien 1993). Ioannou and Xu (1994) proposed a linearized vehicle longitudinal controller design. They linearized a nonlinear vehicle model around different operating points (Kuo 1995 and Ogata 2001). Their design considers a vehicle system with two input variables: throttle angle command and brake command, and one output variable: vehicle speed. The other inputs, such as aerodynamic drag, road conditions and vehicle mass changes, are treated as disturbances. The throttle and brake subsystems are designed separately and are not allowed to operate simultaneously. A switching logic dictates switching between the two subsystems.

Other longitudinal controller designs include one by Hedrick et al. (1991), where a combined throttle/brake controller is outlined using a modified sliding control method (Utkin 1992). In Ioannou et al. (1992) an autonomous controller is designed for a constant time headway policy. In Raza et al. (1997), a model and a computer controller are developed for the brake subsystem for implementation in automatic vehicle following.

Heavy-duty Vehicles

The control algorithms mentioned above are applicable to light-duty passenger vehicles. For heavy-duty vehicles such as commercial trucks and buses, however, different vehicle dynamics modelling is necessary along with different control algorithms. Kanellakopoulos and Tomizuka (1997) have developed such analytical tools. The reasons put forward for using different controllers include: (1) because of increased weight, heavy-duty vehicles have a low actuation-to-weight ratio; (2) heavy-duty vehicles have roll and yaw instability modes that are insignificant in light-duty vehicles; (3) there is strong interaction between longitudinal and lateral dynamics in heavy-duty vehicles; (4) there are pronounced actuator delays and nonlinearities and (5) there is increased sensitivity to disturbances such as wind gusts. Kanellakopoulos and Tomizuka (1997) developed a model for truck–semitrailer vehicles and linearized the longitudinal model around different operating points determined by different fuel command/vehicle mass combinations. The resultant sixth order model is finally reduced to a first order by neglecting the fast mode dynamics associated with the angular velocity of the wheel, fuel systems, intake manifold pressure, engine speed and the turbocharged diesel engine rotor speed.

7.3   AUTOMATED LATERAL CONTROL

Lateral Controller Design

Lateral control of vehicles has been achieved using different types of systems. A vision-based control system with on-board camera is discussed in Jurie et al. (1993), where the position (state) of the vehicle is estimated using extended Kalman filtering. Other systems include navigation along a known road network using a priori information and low-level road detection (Zhang and Thomas 1993). Peng and Tomizuka (1990), used a magnetic road marker-based system for lateral control of vehicles, which integrates a feedback controller with a feedforward loop as shown in Figure 7.1. The roadway reference/sensing system is based on a series of magnetic markers placed in the centre of the roadway to be followed by the automated vehicle (Hessburg et al. 1991). Hall effect magnetometers mounted at the front in the centre of the vehicle sense the magnetic field from the markers.

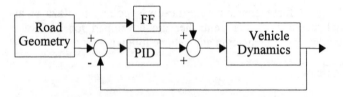

Source: Peng and Tomizuka 1990.

Figure 7.1   Block diagram of lateral controller

Heavy-duty Vehicles

Different techniques can be used for automated lateral control of single-unit heavy-duty vehicles. For constant longitudinal velocity, Kanellakopoulos and Tomizuka (1997), used techniques such as frequency-shaped linear quadratic (FSLQ) (Anderson and Moore 1991) and gain scheduling (Ioannou and Sun 1996) that have been used for light-duty passenger vehicles. However, in the case of varying longitudinal velocity, a different controller such as sliding mode control (SMC) (Utkin 1992) has to be used. A sliding variable is defined as the vehicle lateral displacement error and the rate of change of the error. The control law uses a sign function that moves the sliding variable to zero in finite time (Hingwe et al. 2000). However, the control law introduced chattering that is removed by using a saturation function in place of the sign function. Simulations demonstrate that low tracking error is obtained by using this method.

7.4   AUTOMATED VEHICLE SENSORS

Automated vehicle control necessitates the use of sensors. This section briefly describes some of the issues and options associated with the usage of sensors for vehicle automation.

Longitudinal Sensors

Automated vehicles are expected to be equipped with longitudinal sensors that measure the relative distance and relative speed of all vehicles in the immediate neighbourhood in the same lane. Naturally, vehicles ahead must be detected with the highest accuracy and precision. Relative speed readings need to be accurate and sensitive to small speed changes of less than 2 mph.

There are two types of longitudinal sensors on automated vehicles: forward looking and backward looking longitudinal sensors. The forward

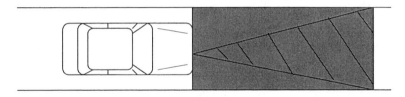

Source: Bose and Ioannou (1998).

*Figure 7.2   Frontal longitudinal ranging sensor: ideal sensor coverage
(shaded area) and actual coverage for single beam sensor
(crossed area)*

looking longitudinal sensors are placed in front of an automated vehicle and
are designed to sense objects in front of the automated vehicle. On the other
hand, the backward looking sensors are placed at the rear of an automated
vehicle and designed to sense objects behind the automated vehicle.

The forward-looking longitudinal sensors must have sufficient range to
allow the vehicle to come to a stop even under the assumption of a 'brick wall
scenario'. For example, a simple calculation shows that a vehicle travelling at
80 mph (128 kmph) that has a maximum deceleration ability of 0.65 g needs
100 metres to come to a complete stop. However, while deciding on the range
of the frontal longitudinal sensors, the degradation in braking capabilities due
to wet/icy road conditions must also be taken into consideration. Furthermore
the frontal sensors must be able to distinguish and resolve the position of all
the target vehicles in two dimensions, i.e. relative distance and relative angle.
The sensors must be able to track the target vehicle regardless of the presence
of other vehicles in adjacent lanes, in straight roadway segments and also
along curves. It is quite a task and may require the combined powers of
sophisticated radar systems and real-time image processing.

The frontal longitudinal ranging sensor may be chosen to be a single beam
sensor as depicted in Figure 7.2 (Ioannou et al. 1994). The primary reason is
that a single beam sensor has lower interference and hence less chance of
false alarms. However, the shaded region shows the ideal sensor coverage
needed to detect obstacles in the lane other than vehicles such as motorcycles,
animals, etc. and vehicles in cuting-in situations, while the crossed region in
Figure 7.2 shows actual sensor coverage. The single beam sensor may not be
able to detect vehicles suddenly cuting-in from adjacent lanes. Moreover,
with the increase in market penetration of automated vehicles, most vehicles
may have radar-type ranging sensors at similar frequencies, which means a
greater probability of interference and shorter radar ranges. In this case a
combination of a narrow beam radar with a video camera may provide the
desired properties of a ranging and obstacle detection sensor. Other
possibilities include multiple beam sensors like the one used by Bastian et al.
(1998) during field tests on the German autobahn.

The backward looking sensors have to measure the relative position and relative speed of the vehicle following and must be able to detect potential rear-end collision threats. They also need to evaluate the space available during lane changing and merging. They are similar to frontal longitudinal sensors and are subject to the same difficulties discussed above. However, backward looking sensors are not as essential as forward looking sensors and automated vehicles may or may not be equipped with them.

Lateral Sensors

The lateral/side sensors are needed mostly to assist an automated vehicle during lane changing (Figure 7.3). They detect if there is a vehicle in the target/destination lane, if a vehicle is merging from the other side or if a vehicle is approaching at a threatening speed in the target lane. They should be able to reliably detect all kinds of vehicles, even motorcycles.

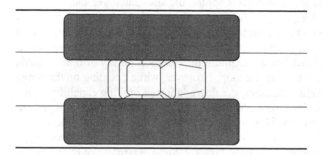

Figure 7.3   Coverage of lateral/side sensors on both sides of an automated vehicle

The demands on the lateral sensor systems for a fully automated vehicle are quite complex. Candidate technologies include ultrasound, radar and video systems (Hovanessian 1988). Ultrasound sensors detect target position and range by bouncing acoustic energy pulses off a target and estimating time of flight. Radar sensors measure range and relative speed using the echo from radio frequency pulses and measuring time of flight as well as the Doppler effect. Video based sensors rely on efficient real-time image processing for target recognition (Graefe and Kuhnert 1988, Smith and Brady 1993, Trassoudaine et al. 1993). They all have individual advantages and disadvantages and combinations of sensor types may offer the only reliable way of meeting all their complex requirements.

7.5   VEHICLE-TO-VEHICLE COMMUNICATION

Automated vehicles may be equipped with communication systems. Such vehicles can communicate with each other and exchange information about vehicle status and traffic flow conditions that help in the longitudinal control of the vehicles. For example, when an automated vehicle detects a stopped vehicle on the freeway it communicates to other similarly equipped automated vehicles about the obstacle. After receiving this information, the automated vehicles start slowing down, change lanes and propagate the message to other automated vehicles behind. As a consequence, the automated vehicles perform soft braking (i.e. braking at a comfortable rate), which slows down the whole traffic stream including any manually driven vehicles between the automated vehicles. Thus the disturbance caused by stopped vehicles is attenuated and the traffic flow is smoother.

The vehicle-to-vehicle communication system design may be based on two-way communication, with each vehicle simultaneously transmitting and receiving information. The transmitted signal is acknowledged by each receiving vehicle, thus allowing the automated vehicles to detect the surrounding vehicles.

The frequency of operation is an open issue. Frequencies as high as 64 GHz have been proposed (Kaltwasser and Kassubek 1994). Each automated vehicle has a 'zone of relevance' around it to which communication and data exchange is restricted (Figure 7.4). It is obvious that this zone may include automated vehicles with communication capability as well as manually driven vehicles. An appropriate strategy for dealing with this is the following: when a vehicle in the 'zone of relevance' does not acknowledge the transmission, it is automatically classified as a manually driven vehicle. This improves traffic co-ordination, as the automated vehicles know where other automated vehicles are in the immediate vicinity. Furthermore, it circumvents the potential danger due to failures of the communication system on an automated vehicle. An automated vehicle with a non-functional communication system is treated as a manually driven vehicle.

For each pair of automated vehicles, both the leader and the follower can exchange information like the 'Double Boomerang Transmission System' (Mitzui et al. 1994). Exchange of vehicle information like braking capability and tyre pressure in addition to traffic conditions reduces the minimum safe intervehicle spacing. The required information data transfer rate is over 1 Mbps, and the processing rate is between 1000 MIPS and 9000 MIPS (Milestone 2 Report 1996a). Contingencies exist for emergency measures (like hard braking) which will override any ongoing message and are given top priority.

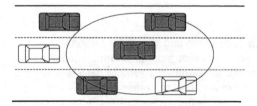

Figure 7.4   'Zone of relevance' of an automated (shaded) vehicle

7.6   TWO BENEFITS OF VEHICLE AUTOMATION

The gradual introduction of automated vehicles in today's traffic system gives rise to mixed manual/automated traffic. In this section, we present two potential benefits that can be expected with the market penetration of automated vehicles among manual traffic.

Traffic Flow Characteristics

The presence of automated vehicles improves traffic flow characteristics in manual traffic. Simulations demonstrate that automated vehicles accurately track the speed response of a smoothly accelerating lead vehicle and do not contribute to the 'slinky-type effect' that Sheikholeslam and Desoer (1991) and Swaroop and Hedrick (1996) observed in today's manual traffic. This is the phenomenon of error amplification as a traffic flow disturbance is propagated upstream. Consider ten vehicles following each other in a single lane with no passing and assume that the fourth vehicle v4 is automated. We use Pipes' (1953) model for manual vehicles that models slinky-type effects and the Ioannou and Xu (1994) model for the automated vehicle. The lead vehicle accelerates smoothly from 0 m/s to 24 m/s at 0.075 g and the rest follow suit. The velocity responses in Figure 7.5(a) show good tracking by the automated vehicle v4 which attenuates the position error and does not contribute to the slinky-effect phenomenon as shown in Figure 7.5(b).

Furthermore, simulations demonstrate that automated vehicles smooth traffic flow by filtering the transients caused by rapidly accelerating manual vehicles. Consider again ten vehicles in mixed manual/automated traffic in a single lane with no passing and assume that the fourth vehicle v4 is automated. The lead vehicle rapidly accelerates at 0.35 g from 0 m/s to 24.5 m/s, maintains a constant speed at 24.5 m/s, thereafter decelerates to 14.5 m/s at 0.3 g and finally accelerates to 24.5 m/s at 0.25 g.

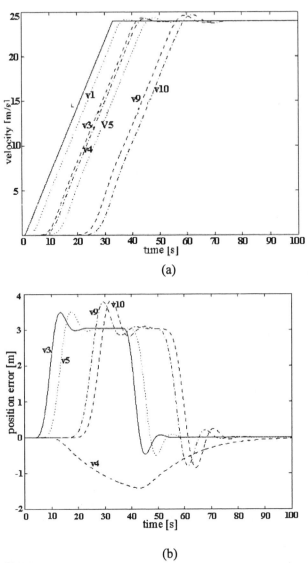

(a)

(b)

Source: Bose and Ioannou (2001).

Notes:
The fourth vehicle (v4) is automated. (a) Velocity response of leader (L), 1st vehicle
(v1) and vehicles 3 to 5 (v3–v5) and 9, 10 (v9, v10); (b) position error of vehicles 3 to
5 (v3–v5) and 9, 10 (v9, v10)

*Figure 7.5   Ten vehicles in mixed manual/automated traffic following a
            lead vehicle performing smooth acceleration manoeuvres*

The acceleration and deceleration values used are typical for many passenger cars (Consumer reports 1998). The velocity responses in Figure 7.6(a) show that the automated vehicle v4 filters the response of the rapidly accelerating vehicle v3 in an effort to maintain smooth driving. As a result the responses of vehicles v5, v9 and v10 are less oscillatory than those of v1 and v3. However, this is done at the expense of a sizeable position error in v4 (Figure 7.6(b)).

Fuel Consumption and Pollution

Barth (1997) lists vehicle parameters such as second-by-second velocity, acceleration and grade that determine emission levels and fuel consumption. Bose and Ioannou (2001) used the above stated parameters in simulations and experiments using actual vehicles to examine the environmental effect of automated vehicles among manual ones. The quantities measured are the tailpipe emissions of unburnt hydrocarbons (HC), carbon monoxide (CO), carbon dioxide (CO_2), oxides of nitrogen (NO, NO_2, denoted by NO_x in this chapter) and fuel consumption. The Comprehensive Modal Emissions Model (CMEM) version 1.00, developed at UC Riverside, is used to analyse the vehicle data and calculate air pollution and fuel consumption. It is a high fidelity model that is very sensitive to transients (Barth 1998). The model calculates vehicle emissions and fuel consumption as a function of the vehicle operating mode, i.e. idle, steady state cruise, various levels of acceleration/deceleration, among others.

During simulations, smooth and rapid acceleration scenarios described in this section were evaluated. It is seen that accurate speed and position tracking and the smoothing of traffic flow by the automated vehicle translates into lower air pollution and fuel savings that are significant during rapid acceleration transients, as shown in Table 7.1.

During experiments, three actual vehicles were used since it was not possible to use ten vehicles. Therefore, to see how the simulation results compare with the experimental results, we reran the simulations using two vehicles following a lead vehicle in manual traffic and mixed traffic. The lead vehicle speed profiles obtained during the experiments were used for these simulations.

The speed responses of the models were collected and analysed using CMEM. The estimated environmental benefits resulting from the presence of an automated vehicle during experiments and simulations are presented in Table 7.2.

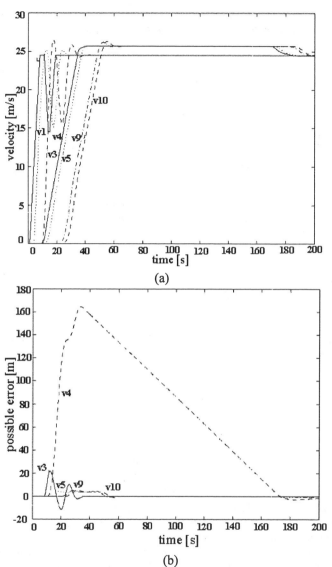

(a)

(b)

Notes:
The fourth vehicle (v4) is automated. (a) Velocity response of leader (L), 1st vehicle (v1) and vehicles 3 to 5 (v3–v5) and 9, 10 (v9, v10); (b) Position error of vehicles 3 to 5 (v3–v5) and 9, 10 (v9, v10).

Source: Bose and Ioannou (2001).

Figure 7.6 *Ten vehicles in mixed manual (Pipes model)/automated traffic following a rapidly accelerating lead vehicle*

Table 7.1   Percentage savings in pollution emission and fuel consumption for mixed traffic over manual traffic (simulation results)

	Smooth Acceleration	Rapid Acceleration
CO emission	18.4%	60.6%
CO_2 emission	8.1%	19.8%
NO_x emission	13.1%	1.5%
HC emission	15.5%	55.4%
Fuel consumption	8.5%	28.5%

Source: Bose and Ioannou (2001).

Table 7.2   Percentage savings in pollution emission and fuel consumption for mixed traffic over manual traffic (simulation and experiment results)

	Smooth Acceleration		Rapid Acceleration	
	Experiment	Simulation	Experiment	Simulation
CO emission	1.2%	0.8%	19.2%	12.3%
CO_2 emission	0.4%	0.2%	3.4%	3.3%
NO_x emission	1.6%	1.3%	25.7%	19.2%
HC emission	0.8%	0.4%	9.8%	6.6%
Fuel consumption	0.4%	0.2%	3.6%	3.4%

Source: Bose and Ioannou (2001).

7.7   CONCLUSIONS

Vehicles with automation in the longitudinal direction are already available in Japan, Europe and North America. Such vehicles have the capability to automatically follow another vehicle in the same lane as long as the latter is within range of the forward-looking ranging sensor. The introduction of such vehicles is an momentous step in automated vehicle control. In this chapter, we discuss some of the longitudinal and lateral controller designs for automated vehicle control. Furthermore, we briefly outline automated vehicle sensors and vehicle-to-vehicle communication issues associated with automated vehicle control.

In conclusion, we present two benefits to be expected with the introduction of automated vehicles in today's manual traffic. We observe that automated vehicles accurately track the speed response of smoothly accelerating vehicles. They also behave like a filter and smooth traffic flow characteristics during rapid acceleration transients when following fast accelerating vehicles. This smoothing out of traffic flow along with accurate speed response tracking are expected to reduce environmental pollution and decrease fuel consumption.

REFERENCES

Anderson, B.D.O. and J.B. Moore (1991), *Optimal Control: Linear Quadratic Methods*, New Jersey: Prentice Hall.

Barth, M.J. (1997), Integrating a Modal Emissions Model into Various Transportation Modeling Frameworks, *ASCE Conference Proceedings*.

Barth, M.J. (1998), *CMEM User's Manual*, UC Riverside.

Bastian, A., P. Andreas, R. Holze and R. Bergholz (1998), Autonomous Cruise Control: A First Step towards Automated Driving, *SAE Technical Paper Series* 981942.

Bose, A. and P.A. Ioannou (1998), Issues and Analysis of Mixed Semi-automated/Manual Traffic. *SAE Technical Paper Series* 981943.

Bose, A. and P.A. Ioannou (1999), Analysis of Traffic Flow with Mixed Manual and Semi-automated Vehicles, *Proceedings of American Control Conference*, pp. 2173–7.

Bose, A. and P.A. Ioannou (2001), Evaluation of the Environmental Effects of Intelligent Cruise Control Vehicles, *Journal of the Transportation Research Board*, Vol. 1774, pp. 90–7.

Consumer reports online (1998).

Graefe, V. and K.-D. Kuhnert (1988), Towards a Vision-based Robot with a Driver's License. *Proceedings, IEEE International Workshop on Intelligent Robots and Systems*, pp. 627–32.

Hall, R.W. (1997), System Configurations: Evolutionary Deployment Considerations, in P.A. Ioannou (ed.) *Automated Highway Systems*, New York: Plenum Press, pp. 49–71.

Hedrick, J.K., D. McMahon, V. Narendran and D. Swaroop (1991), Longitudinal Vehicle Controller Design for IVHS Systems, *Proceedings of American Control Conference*, pp. 3107–12.

Hessburg, T., H. Peng, M. Tomizuka and W.-B. Zhang (1991), An Experimental Study on Lateral Control of a Vehicle, *PATH Research Report* UCB-IT-PRR-91-17, UC Berkeley.

Hingwe, P., J.-Y. Wang, M. Tai and M. Tomizuka (2000), Lateral Control of Heavy Duty Vehicles for Automated Highway Systems: Experimental Study on a Tractor Semi-trailer, *PATH Working Paper* UCB-ITS-PWP-2000-1, UC Berkeley.

Hovanessian, S.A. (1988), Introduction to Sensor Systems, Artech House.

Ioannou, P.A. (1997), Control and Sensor Requirements and Issues in AHS, in P.A. Ioannou (ed.), *Automated Highway Systems*, New York: Plenum Press, pp. 195–212.

Ioannou, P.A., F. Ahmed-Zaid and D. Wuh (1992), A Time Headway Autonomous Intelligent Cruise Controller: Design and Simulation, *Technical Report*, USC-SCT 92-11-01, Los Angeles.

Ioannou, P.A. and C.C. Chien (1993), Autonomous Intelligent Cruise Control, *IEEE Trans. on Vehicular Tech.*, Vol. 42, no. 4, pp. 657–72.

Ioannou, P.A. and T. Xu (1994), Throttle and Brake Control, *IVHS Journal*, Vol. 1, no. 4, pp. 345–77.

Ioannou, P.A. and J. Sun (1996), *Robust Adaptive Control*, New Jersey: Prentice Hall.

Jurie, F., P. Rives, J. Gallice and J.L. Brame (1993), High Speed Vehicle Guidance Based on Vision. *Intelligent Autonomous Vehicles IFAC Workshop*, pp. 203–8.

Kaltwasser, J. and J. Kassubek (1994), A New Cooperative Optimized Access for Inter-vehicle Communication, *Vehicle Navigation & Information Systems Conference Proceedings*, pp. 144–8.

Kanellakopoulos, I. and I. Tomizuka (1997), Commercial Trucks and Buses in Automated Highway Systems, in P.A. Ioannou (ed.), *Automated Highway Systems*, New York: Plenum Press, pp. 213–46.

Kuo, B.C. (1995), *Automatic Control Systems*, seventh edition, New Jersey: Prentice Hall.

Milestone 2 Report (1996a), Cooperative Vehicle Concept Description, Appendix B, National Automated Highway System Consortium (NAHSC).

Milestone 2 Report (1996b), Hard-Braking Safety Analysis Method and Detailed Results, Appendix J, National Automated Highway System Consortium (NAHSC).

Mitzui, K., M. Uchida and M. Nakagawa (1994), Vehicle-to-vehicle 2-way Communication & Ranging System Using Spread Spectrum Technique, *Vehicle Navigation & Information Systems Conference Proceedings*, pp. 153–8.

Ogata, K. (2001), *Modern Control Engineering*, fourth edition, New Jersey: Prentice Hall.

Peng, H. and M. Tomizuka (1990), Vehicle Lateral Control for Highway Automation, *Proceedings of American Control Conference*, pp. 788–93.

Pipes, L.A. (1953), An Operational Analysis of Traffic Dynamics, *Journal of Applied Physics*, Vol. 24, pp. 271–81.

Raza, H., Z. Xu, B. Yang and P.A. Ioannou (1997), Modeling and Control Design for a Computer-controlled Brake System, *IEEE Transactions on Control Systems Technology*, Vol. 5, no. 3, pp. 279–96.

Sheikholeslam, S. and C.A. Desoer (1991), Longitudinal Control of a Platoon of Vehicles with no Communication of Lead Vehicle Information, *Proceedings of American Control Conference*, pp. 3102–6.

Smith, S.M. and J.M. Brady (1993), A Scene Segmenter: Visual Tracking of Moving Vehicles, *Intelligent Autonomous Vehicles, IFAC Workshop*, pp. 117–24.

Stevens, W.B. (1997), Evolution to an Automated Highway System, in P.A. Ioannou (ed.), *Automated Highway Systems*, New York: Plenum Press, pp. 109–24.

Swaroop, D. and J.K. Hedrick (1996), String Stability of Interconnected Systems, *IEEE Transactions on Automatic Control*, Vol. 41, no. 3, pp. 349–57.

Swaroop, D., J.K. Hedrick, C.C. Chien and P.A. Ioannou (1994), A Comparison of Spacing and Headway Control Laws for Automatically Controlled Vehicles, *Journal of Vehicle System Dynamics*, Vol. 23, pp. 597–625.

Trassoudaine, L., J. Alizon, F. Collange and J. Gallice (1993), Visual Tracking by a Multisensorial Approach, *Intelligent Autonomous Vehicles, IFAC Workshop,* pp. 111–16.

Utkin, V. (1992), *Sliding Modes in Control and Optimization*, Berlin: Springer and Verlag.

Walker, R.J. and C.J. Harris (1993), A Multi-Sensor Fusion System for a Laboratory Based Autonomous Vehicle, *Intelligent Autonomous Vehicles IFAC Workshop*, pp. 105–10.

Ward, J.D. (1997), Step by Step to an Automated Highway System and Beyond, in P.A. Ioannou (ed.), *Automated Highway Systems*, New York: Plenum Press, pp. 73–91.

Zhang, S. and B.T. Thomas (1993), Knowledge-based Vehicle Navigation in Complex Road Networks, *Intelligent Autonomous Vehicles IFAC Workshop*, pp. 209–14.

8. Automated traffic control for freight transport

Michiel Minderhoud and Ingo Hansen

8.1 INTRODUCTION

This chapter deals with the topic of automated traffic control for freight road transport, which has much in common with automated traffic control for passenger road transport. Although traffic control has been apparent since the automobile was introduced, its influence has been quite limited. Traffic signs and traffic regulations have been used to try to modify the behaviour of motorists to a certain desired pattern. By modifying the behaviour of the drivers, it was intended to create a safer and more efficient traffic situation for all traffic participants. Without traffic control measures, such as traffic lights, it would be hard to cross a busy road.

The application of modern electronics offered new opportunities to control traffic, for example, ramp-metering to control the number of cars entering a motorway, automated speed regulation on motorways, warning signs for queues, incidents, etc.

Nowadays, even more advanced technologies are available. In-vehicle navigation systems are already widespread, and may connect drivers to external sources to optimise trip lengths. Wireless communication between roadside traffic centres and cars will open a broad range of possibilities to apply a new range of control systems. In addition, communication between cars or trucks could also help to develop useful traffic control systems.

In this chapter some advanced systems, based on vehicle-to-vehicle or vehicle-to-road communication, with the objective of controlling traffic on motorways, are described. Although the systems described here can be applied to passenger cars as well as trucks, the focus is on trucks. Special attention is given to the impacts of one particular system, the platoon-driving concept for trucks.

State-of-the-art

Advanced, automated traffic control measures that focus especially on trucks systems do not distinguish between passenger cars and trucks.

Automated traffic control requires in-vehicle systems. These devices are mostly denoted as ADAS (Advanced Driver Assistance Systems).

It is useful to distinguish between those ADAS-systems that automate the driving task partially and those that do so fully. Vehicles with partial support systems, such as Autonomous Intelligent Cruise Control (AICC), can function alongside unequipped vehicles. Fully automated systems require a separate infrastructure or a dedicated lane. More on the integration of automated and manual driven freight transport can be found in Chapter 15 (van Binsbergen).

One concept of fully automated driving is platoon-driving. This is mostly denoted as AHS (Automated Highway System). The main objective of AHS is to change the sluggish, unpredictable and inefficient behaviour of the current traffic system through the use of automation. There is a common understanding that AHS will involve fully automated vehicles equipped with sophisticated sensors and computer-controlled systems, and the infrastructure will be actively involved in managing and controlling the flow of traffic by using sensor and communication techniques (Ioannou 1997, Marwitz 2001). Several experiments with speed control of automated heavy trucks have already been carried out (see e.g. Tan et al. 1999).

In the literature, many examples of platoon-driving can be found. Most activities evolved from the above mentioned 'Automated Highway' project that was carried out in the mid and late 1990s. The AHS research project focused mainly on passenger cars. Among other things, it was calculated that road capacity could increase significantly when applying the platoon concept, but only under certain assumed conditions. It was found that the main factor affecting the capacity gain of a platoon lane is the number of merging and diverging areas, and their traffic demand levels.

The platoon concept applied to trucks has attracted much less attention. One example of platoon-driving of trucks is the tow-bar concept, which has been demonstrated in the PROMOTE-CHAUFFEUR project (Promote-Chauffeur Consortium 1999). Other examples can be found in Chapter 2 (Shladover) and in Sandkühler et al. (2001). This concept uses existing road infrastructure, not a dedicated platoon lane. Advantages of this approach is the limited infrastructural adaptation required and comfort for driver(s) in the automated tow-bar trucks, but the concept will have limited impacts on capacity and safety, since the trucks are mixed with other (not automated) vehicles. Another example of a dual-mode truck operation, i.e. trucks with automated driving and manual driving capabilities, is given by Yamada et al. (1996).

Truck companies are considered to be an appropriate target group for the implementation of ADAS in trucks, with or without the need for separated lanes (Shladover 2001). A demonstration – on the same spot as the 1997 AHS Demo – was due to be given in August 2003 to show the possibilities and services of truck and bus automation (Misener and Miller 2002).

A concept with fully automated freight trucks on a dedicated lane would probably show more and larger benefits. In an ideal case, freight transport is carried out in a separate lane (safety benefit), is automated (safety and comfort benefit), with vehicles following at small distances (traffic efficiency and fuel efficiency gain), without congestion and travelling at reliable, constant speeds (fuel efficiency gain and transport cost benefit). This chapter focuses on such a fully automated platoon concept for trucks.

Traffic Control Approaches

Table 8.1 summarizes some possible traffic control approaches that focus on trucks.

Table 8.1   Overview traffic control approaches

Traffic control approach	*Intended impacts*
Lane change prohibition for trucks	Increase average car speed, Increase road capacity
Longitudinal support (autonomous intelligent cruise control, AICC)	Increase driver comfort, safety, road capacity
Longitudinal support (intelligent speed adaptor, ISA)	Increase safety
Lateral support (lane-keeping)	Increase safety
Fully automated control (platoon-driving)	Increase driver comfort, safety, lane capacity

The lane change prohibition for trucks is not an automated traffic control approach. Studies show increasing speeds of passenger cars, and a small decrease in truck speeds.

Several studies were performed after the impacts of AICC, were applied to cars and trucks (e.g. Minderhoud 1999). The impacts will be limited, since drivers overrule the system, especially near bottlenecks, while the system does not support the driving task at low speeds. A speed adaptor will mainly affect maximum driving speed; consequently, impacts on safety are expected. Lateral support, a lane-keeping system, is intended to reduce truck accidents. Impacts on efficiency are expected to be limited. As described in the previous section, platoon-driving affects driver comfort, safety and capacity.

8.2   TRAFFIC CONTROL CONCEPTS

Autonomous Intelligent Cruise Control (AICC)

Description
AICC is a system that is currently available on some more expensive cars. The vehicle measures the distance to the vehicle in front, and determines

relative speed. Based on these parameters, a safe distance is calculated and (if needed) a deceleration applied. The system uses only information available from the vehicle's own sensors, so it is called an autonomous system. The driver can (and sometimes must) overrule the system.

Benefits
Simulation studies, focused on passenger cars (Minderhoud 1999), show improved traffic performance (such as smoother accelerations, fewer disturbances and shock waves). Capacity increases are found; however, capacity gains are strongly related to desired distance setting.

Implementation
Trucks or cars with AICC can easily drive in traffic with vehicles not so equipped, so implementation is not a big issue.

Centralised Distance Control (CDC)

Description
One step further then AICC is CDC (Centralised Distance Control). It is not yet available. The system is able to receive commands from a roadside traffic centre. It may command the vehicle to drive at a certain distance. Using this approach, traffic is controlled externally by adapting gaps in the traffic flow. This may be useful at bottleneck locations, to create larger gaps for vehicles to merge more smoothly. The idea is that drivers cannot overrule the system when it is receiving a command, except when making a lane change. If the roadside centre is not active, the system can be used as an AICC.

Benefits
Simulation studies (Minderhoud and Hansen 2002) show improved traffic performance (smoother accelerations, fewer disturbances). Capacity increases are found. However, the capacity gains are strongly related to the desired distance setting, which is externally determined.

Implementation
Vehicles with CDC can drive in traffic with vehicles not so equipped, so implementation is not a big issue. However, near merging locations the centrally controlled vehicles cannot anticipate (overruling not allowed) merging vehicles, which may cause a safety hazard.

Platoon-driving

Description
In an Automated Highway System (AHS), vehicles will be required to maintain a safe speed and intervehicle spacing. Both vehicle speed and spacing affect safety and performance. Safety is one consideration in applying

the platoon-concept. Since safety is related to the relative impact speed (expressed as Δv^2) one could try to establish a safe intervehicle distance using this relationship. See Figure 8.1 for an illustration of the relation between relative speed and intervehicle distance. A high relative quadratic impact speed means a severe collision. One could conclude that either a very small distance or a very large distance is a relatively safe intervehicle distance.

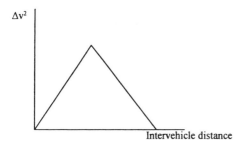

Source: Ioannou (1997).

Figure 8.1   Collision curve

Based on these considerations the platoon-driving concept has evolved over the last few decades. The concept can be described as follows. Groups of vehicles follow each other at small intervehicle distances (intraplatoon), and these groups follow at large (inter-platoon) intervals. See Figure 8.2 for an overview of the platoon notations.

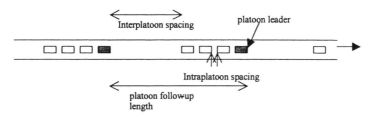

Figure 8.2   Platoon definitions

Benefits
For the ideal case of vehicles and platoons following at their predefined distances at a constant speed, the maximum throughput in a single lane can easily be calculated.

Let us denote:

s_{intra} intraplatoon spacing (m) (distance between vehicles in platoon)
s_{inter} interplatoon spacing (m) (distance between platoons)
L average length of vehicles (m)
N number of vehicles in a platoon
v_{plat} desired platoon speed (m/s)

Since capacity can be expressed as $C = 1/h_{average}$ (veh/sec) we are interested in the average headway and spacing of vehicles in the platoon. The average spacing is formulated by:

$$s_{average} = [s_{intra} \cdot (N-1) + L \cdot N + s_{inter}] / N$$

and the average headway by:

$$h_{average} = \frac{s_{average}}{v_{plat}}.$$

Note that the interplatoon spacing and intraplatoon spacing may be a function of actual speed. We assume speed-independent spacings since it is desired that platoons operate at a high constant speed.

Based on selected values different upper bound capacity values can be determined. Such an analysis is performed and shown in Figure 8.3. In the analysis the applied parameter values were:

s_{intra} 10 m
s_{inter} 150 m
L 5 m (cars)
N 20
v_{plat} 30 m/s = 108 km/h

In the analysis one parameter was changed while the other values remained equal to the given values.

Using the selected values a capacity of about 5000 veh/h can be expected under ideal conditions, which is much more than 3000 veh/h, the maximum flow rate found in practice on the left-hand lane of a motorway.

The next section will describe the platoon-driving approach implemented in the microscopic simulation model Simone, which is used for the analysis of truck-platoons.

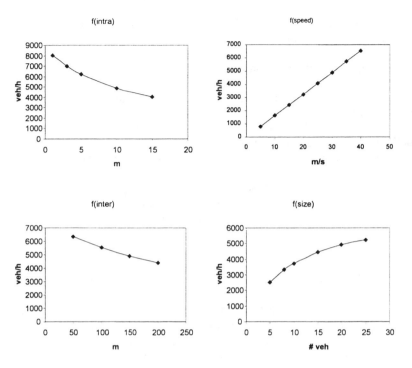

Notes:
Maximum attainable flows are as shown: (a) function of speed; (b) function of intra-spacing; (c) function of inter-spacing; and (d) function of platoon size.

Figure 8.3   Impact of parameter values on theoretical capacity platoon-lane

Implementation
The concept requires an absolute separation between platoon-driving vehicles and non-platoon-driving vehicles. A separate lane for trucks is only efficient if freight traffic volumes are sufficient.

8.3   ASSESSMENT OF PLATOON-DRIVING

Introduction

The study on platoon-driving for trucks was set up to give us more insight into the efficiency impacts of platoon-driving of trucks compared to the case without such an automated concept. To analyse these impacts, a bottleneck location (on- and off-ramp) is selected, and a microscopic simulation tool is used as an instrument for the assessment.

Microscopic Modelling of Platoon-driving

Simone is the microscopic model used for research questions related with vehicle automation (Minderhoud 2002).

In Simone the location of the platoon lane is specified in a platoon definition file together with the parameter values of the platoon characteristics. In a scenario, the use of a platoon definition file must be specified.

Vehicles that enter a platoon lane will turn into the platoon-mode, and will behave according to the rules specified for platoon-driving. When entering the platoon lane, vehicles will receive a platoon index which represents the vehicle's order in a platoon. The leader of a platoon has platoon index 1, the last vehicle in a platoon has a platoon index maxsize, which is a platoon parameter. In the simulation it is decided if a vehicle is a leader (and so receives platoon index 1) based on one of the following conditions:

- the vehicle that enters the platoon lane has no platoon leader within a range equal to the platoon follow-up length (see Figure 8.2);
- here was no vehicle directly in front observed within the platoon follow-up range, and the last generated platoon leader passed the entry longer ago than the platoon cycle-time (follow-up time in case of a full platoon), which is defined by:

$$T_{cyclus} = [s_{intra} \cdot (N-1) + L \cdot N + s_{inter}] / V_{platoon;}$$

- a vehicle in front (within the platoon follow-up range) is observed with platoon index equal to the desired initial size of a platoon.

In all other cases the platoon index is adjusted using the next vehicle's platoon index.

Where a vehicle enters the platoon lane before the platoon-cycle-time has elapsed, the platoon index is adjusted until initsize, a platoon parameter that indicates the desired initial size of a platoon, is reached.

Implementation of platoon-driving at platoon lane merging zones

The merging process for vehicles equipped with the platoon-driving system (referred to as the CPC (Centralized Platoon Control) system wanting to enter the platoon lane at a merging zone is similar to the merging process for normal vehicles. The rules for gap-searching and lane-change decisions can be used for automated vehicles also. However, there are some differences to be noted. These are described in the subsection 'Gap searching'.

Vehicles merging into a platoon lane will become platoon leader if:

- a leader index is observed within the platoon follow-up range; or
- a vehicle directly in front is observed.

Otherwise, the vehicle receives a platoon index based on the platoon index of the next vehicle.

Gap searching

The required rear margin, a parameter used for manual gap acceptance, is set equal to the intraplatoon spacing, so no lane change can be made in the desired 'safe' area of the platoon leader. This guarantees a certain level of flow stability for traffic in the platoon lane since no merging is allowed directly in front of the leader.

In addition, no lane change is allowed where the platoon index of the vehicle in front on the platoon lane is equal to maxsize. This requirement is introduced to restrict the number of vehicles in a platoon to the set limit. No new platoon leader is allowed to merge into the lane. However, in some cases it is possible that a new platoon leader will arise due to lane-changing vehicles (see next section).

The speed adaptation of gap searching vehicles is based on the platoon speed (platoon parameter) or actual speed if this is lower. The maximum deceleration for gap searching is limited to the platoon deceleration (platoon parameter).

Platoon-driving order check

Vehicles in a platoon can leave the platoon at merging zones to reach their destination. Also, new vehicles can merge into a platoon. Therefore it is necessary to update the platoon indices of the vehicles on the platoon lane, and possibly assign new platoon leaders.

For non-leaders the platoon index is checked to ensure it does not exceed maxsize. If it does, the vehicle will become a platoon leader. This change is not desired since it creates shockwaves in the platoon lane. It would be better to improve the initsize and maxsize parameters to limit the number of occasions in which such a situation occurs.

For platoon leaders a check is made to see if there is a vehicle in front within a range of $DC\_z0 + DC\_z1*v$ (CPC-parameters for supported driving). If this is so, the leader is deemed to be too close to the next vehicle and will no longer be leader. His platoon index changes to the correct one, but only where the next vehicle has a platoon index smaller then maxsize.

Platoon-driving
The implementation of car-following by vehicles with a CPC-system in platoon mode, is based on the normal procedures for driving, apart from some new rules which are added to different procedures. These adaptations are shown below.

Speed adaptation
All vehicles in a platoon receive a speed limit command that limits the maximum speed to the platoon speed parameter.

Followers in a platoon are allowed to drive faster (7 km/h) in order to catch up with the platoon-leader or followers in front. This is needed to create the platoons and make them as compact as possible. A maximum acceleration equal to the platoon acceleration parameter is allowed for followers.

Desired distance
The desired distance of platoon-leaders (index 1) is principally equal to the inter-platoon distance. This is controlled by the leader-generation routines described above. However, for car-following purposes and calculation of smooth acceleration responses a 'normal' desired distance is selected. The desired distance is set at $DC\_z0 + DC\_z1*v$ (CPC-parameters for supported driving).

All non-leaders in a platoon will follow at a desired distance equal to the intra-platoon distance parameter.

Car-following
The normal car-following routines within Simone are applied to all platoon-vehicles.

In addition, for the platoon-leader a check is made to see if the inter-platoon distance is maintained (this is speed-dependent: using the time headway of the inter-platoon distance). If the headway to the next vehicle is smaller than the desired inter-platoon headway, a deceleration of -0.2 m/s^2 will be applied.

Setup of Assessment Study

The study compares two cases. The first case assumes the presence of a dedicated lane in the right-hand lane on which trucks drive manually (see Figure 8.4).

The off- and on-ramp flows from/to the mainline (Lanes 1 and 2) cross the dedicated lane. Since all drivers control their vehicle manually, no additional traffic control measures are needed.

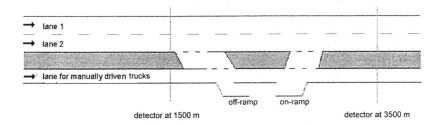

Figure 8.4   Layout case 1: manually driven trucks on dedicated lane

The other case assumes fully automated trucks that drive on a dedicated lane (see Figure 8.5). Both longitudinal and lateral control are automated. Car-following will be carried out in platoons. The layout is similar to the manual case, however, additional traffic control measures are needed to ensure safe crossing by the manually driven passenger cars from/to the mainline via the automated platoon-lane.

From a technical and legal point of view, manually driven vehicles are not allowed to merge into a flow of automated vehicles; this could result in dangerous situations.

Four traffic lights control the flows, with priority for trucks on the platoon lane. In order to regulate the traffic lights, there are measurement loops on the lanes.

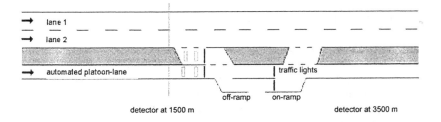

Figure 8.5   Layout case 2: automated trucks on dedicated platoon lane

Traffic demand
The traffic demand specification is similar in both cases.

The flow on the main line is on average 4000 veh/hr. Only passenger cars and vans are present in the flow. About 10% will leave the motorway at the off-ramp. The on-ramp flow is 1000 veh/h with 10% trucks (these trucks will enter the dedicated lane).

Traffic demand on the dedicated lane increases from 500 veh/h to 1500 veh/h. Only trucks are generated at its origin. As a result of increasing demand, congestion will probably occur near the ramps at a certain point in the simulation.

Platoon-driving settings
As described in the previous section, several parameters affect the performance of the platoon-lane:

- initial size; affects the time before one platoon is split into two. A value of 5 is selected after some preliminary experiments;
- maximum platoon size; affects among other things, the capacity of the platoon-lane. A maximum value of 10 is set;
- intra-platoon distance, the distance within the platoon; also affects capacity. A value of 10 m is selected;
- inter-platoon distance, distance between full platoons. Set at 150 m: according to the 'brick-wall braking strategy' a safe setting;
- platoon speed, the goal speed when driving on a platoon-lane, set to 85 km/h for trucks;
- maximum acceleration and deceleration in the platoon: set to +2 and -4 m/s^2.

These parameters can be changed in order to optimize throughput and safety. However, for a first impression of the impacts the selected values will be acceptable. The theoretical lane capacity, assuming a truck length of 15 m, is easily calculated from these parameter values:

average spacing: { 9*10 m + 10*15 m +150 m } / 10 = 39 m

average headway at 85 km/h: 39/23.6 m/s = 1.65 s

Consequently, the theoretical upper bound of the lane capacity is 3600/1.65 = 2180 trucks/hr, which is much higher than the maximum capacity of a dedicated lane with manually controlled trucks (estimated to be around 1400 trucks/hr using simulation tools).

Traffic control settings
With the introduction of automated trucks additional measures are needed to guarantee safe crossing for the manual vehicles. The easiest approach is the use of traffic lights, which has been assumed for the analysis. The automated trucks receive the traffic signal commands by means of road-side communication.
   The following traffic light regulations have been specified for the simulation:

- maximum 60 s green for traffic leaving the main line to the off-ramp;

- maximum 120 s green for the dedicated truck lane;
- clearance time is set to 3 seconds;
- on-ramp green time depends on available gaps (traffic dependent).

In conclusion, since the trucks may spend 66% of the available time at the crossing, the priority for the trucks is controlled by the maximum green setting. Introduction of a clearance time will automatically reduce total available capacity.

A simulation run of one hour is carried out for the 'manual' and 'platoon' case. As stated before, it is a preliminary analysis, since there are many parameters that may affect the outcome of the simulation run. However, the selected values are based on the expected 'best' settings, so the results give us an indication of the differences between the 'manual' and the 'platoon' case. The results are described in the next section.

Simulation Results

After running the simulation, the results – a wide range of traffic flow indicators – are available for further analysis. This chapter presents some of the outcomes. More specifically, efficiency, travel time and energy consumption are compared.

Efficiency is expressed as the number of vehicles that, during a simulation run, arrived at their destinations. This value is the same as 'capacity'. The capacity definition is less useful when the cross-section consists of separate lanes (a main line and a dedicated lane). For a true capacity estimate it is necessary to have sufficient traffic demand for all lanes.

The indicator values, established after a 1-hour simulation, are shown in Table 8.2. The numbers refer only to the vehicles that arrived at their destination.

Table 8.2   Efficiency comparison

	No. of cars	No. of vans	No. of trucks	Total
Manual case	3698	915	925	5538
Automated case	3297 (–10%)	836 (–9%)	739 (–20%)	4872 (–12%)

It is observed that the automated 'platoon' case did not perform as well as the 'manual' case.

How can the paper performance of the automated case be explained? This is due mainly to the application of the traffic lights which are required for safety reasons. During a red light the throughput of traffic on the off-/on-ramp or the dedicated lane is equal to zero. About 33% of the time the traffic light on the dedicated lane was red. Nevertheless, due to the use of automated truck platoons the efficiency loss is limited to 20%.

In Table 8.3 average travel time per vehicle type is presented. The reduction in throughput affects average travel time negatively. Consequently, the automated case shows higher travel times.

Table 8.3   Travel time comparison (in minutes)

	Cars	Vans	Trucks
Manual case	2.2	2.2	3.4
Automated case	2.7	2.7	4.8

Since it can be assumed that accelerations and decelerations have a negative impact on energy use and comfort level, an energy/comfort indicator is introduced that takes account of this. Ideally, all cars drive at a constant speed, without any distortions, resulting in an indicator value of zero. Table 8.4 shows the energy/comfort indicator (summation of acceleration and absolute deceleration rates per time step, averaged per vehicle type). Again, the automated case shows the worst performance. This can be explained by the stop-and-go conditions introduced by the traffic control measures needed to ensure a safe crossing of the dedicated lane.

Table 8.4   Energy/comfort comparison (in m/s)

	Cars	Vans	Trucks
Manual case	123	111	97
Automated case	169	153	84

The exception is the decrease in the indicator value for trucks in the automated case. The platoon-driving rules, together with the traffic control, have a small positive impact on stop-and-go driving in the dedicated lane.

8.4   CONCLUSIONS

The simulation results showed that employment of automated trucks on a dedicated lane using the platoon concept is possible, although additional traffic control measures are required to ensure safe crossing by manually driven vehicles of the dedicated lane with automated trucks. In addition, the selected scenarios assumed a sufficient (high) proportion of trucks in the traffic stream, which is a precondition operating a dedicated truck lane.

Unfortunately, due to the required safety measures by means of traffic lights, and the clearance time needed, the performance of the studied roadway section decreases with respect to efficiency (fewer cars and trucks can pass the bottleneck), travel time (increased for cars and trucks) and energy consumption (increased for cars and trucks). The increased capacity of the dedicated truck lane, by means of automated platoons, could not be used optimally since platoons were forced to stop at traffic lights.

From this preliminary assessment, it is concluded that the introduction of fully automated trucks on a dedicated lane in metropolitan areas with many on- and off-ramps is possible but that performance would be reduced compared to the case of manually driven trucks. It is questionable whether the beneficial impacts balance the negative impacts. It is therefore recommended that the dedicated lane should be separated from other traffic near on- and off-ramps in order to obtain maximum efficiency and safety benefits from platoon driving.

A further optimization of traffic control parameters, such as maximum red light time, platoon size, platoon speed, etc., may increase the performance indicators for the automated case.

REFERENCES

Ioannou, P. (ed.) (1997), *Automated Highway Systems*, New York: Plenum Press.

Marwitz, H. (2001), Status and Perspectives of Automatic Guidance-Systems (in German), in VDI-Gesellschaft Fahrzeug- und Verkehrstechnik, *Berichte 1617*, pp. 425–33.

Minderhoud, M.M. (1999), Supported Driving: Impacts on Motorway Traffic Flow, dissertation T99/4, Delft.

Minderhoud, M.M. (2002), *Technical Description of Simone*, Delft University of Technology, Transportation Planning and Traffic Engineering Section.

Minderhoud, M.M. and I.A. Hansen (2002), *Simulation Study after Traffic Flow Quality near Toll-Lane Merging Areas*, IEEE Fifth conference on ITS, Singapore.

Misener, J.A. and M.A. Miller (2002), *Show me the Benefits: A Truck and Bus Demonstration in 2003*, Proceedings of the Ninth World Congress on ITS, Chicago (CD-rom).

Promote-Chauffeur Consortium (1999), *Report on Results of Impact Evaluation Tests*, Deliverable D07.3.3.

Sandkühler, D, M. Laumans and N. Laumanns (2001), Roadtrain-Concept for the European Freight Transportation (in German), in VDI-Gesellschaft Fahrzeug- und Verkehrstechnik, *Berichte 1617*, pp. 25–42.

Shladover, S. (2001), *Opportunities in Truck Automation*, Proceedings of the Eight World Congress on ITS, Sydney (CD-rom).

Tan, Y, A. Robotis and I. Kanellakopoulos (1999), *Speed Control Experiments with an Automated Heavy Vehicle*, Proceedings of the Eight IEEE International Conference on Control Applications, Koala Coast, Hawaii, pp. 1353–58.

Yamada, M. et al. (1996), *Development of the Dual Mode Truck Control Technology for the New Freight Transport System*, Proceedings of the Third ITS Congress, Orlando, Florida, paper no. 3156.

9. Infrastructure and traffic flow issues: requirements and implications

Masoud Tabibi

9.1 INTRODUCTION

Demand for freight transport is ever increasing. Demand in the European Union (EU) countries has increased about three times during the last three decades (Eurostat 2003). Motorways have a more important role in road freight transport than other categories of roads. For instance, in the Netherlands, as one of the major centres of the global freight distribution network, motorways now carry about 40% of all vehicle-kilometres. International haulage of goods transport on Dutch motorways has increased by about 21% during the years 1995–1999, which indicates an annual growth of 4%. This haulage mostly takes place on motorways (CBS 2003).

This growing traffic on motorways might increase congestion, which is seen, commonly, by public opinion as a waste of time and money. Congestion should preferably be eliminated by means of increasing road capacity. However, the required high investment (in building motorways and acquisition of rights-of-way) and also the negative environmental impact can be considered as major drawbacks to developing motorways.

The idea proposed in this chapter to increase the efficiency of the freight transport system on existing motorways is to use the wasted (unused) capacity of existing motorways within off-peak periods and specially during night hours. Truck automation would provide this opportunity for trucks to be driven during night hours (or generally off-peak periods), since the driver has a limited role in driving Automatically Controlled Trucks (ACTs). Continuous traffic flow, high reliability and savings on personnel costs can be assumed as some major benefits of truck automation. However, in order to achieve these aims we need to provide the required facilities from different points of view. Chapter 2 addressed the major institutional and technical challenges of truck automation, while chapter 15 will describe the integration of automatically and manually controlled trucks in more detail.

The main aim of this chapter is to assess some major infrastructural requirements to facilitate and control the flow of ACTs on existing motorways. Since on a motorway network on-/off-ramps are the weakest sections, this chapter will focus on these sections of motorways.

Actually, a completely isolated network of dedicated freight lanes (DFLs) for transport of containers or other kinds of load-units seems infeasible in a larger network because of its extremely high costs and the risk of low expected utilization. Therefore, it would be necessary to use the existing space of motorways for the operation of both ordinary vehicles and automated trucks.

In such a case, one of the possible solution is to dedicate a lane of existing motorways, connecting major freight distribution centres, to trucks and operate ACTs on these DFLs. In the near future, a low proportion of trucks would be equipped with automatically controlled systems; therefore the dedication of a lane to the ACTs would take place only during limited time periods (e.g. night hours, or generally off-peak periods). In the long term, however, the DFL would actually be assigned to the operation of ACTs.

Through automatic control of trucks on DFLs and assigning one lane of the existing ordinary motorway to them, it is expected that the level of service of freight traffic would be different from that on ordinary motorways. This, however, might endanger the continuity of traffic flows and increase the risk of accidents at on-/off-ramps while the ACTs merging or diverging. Therefore, the main issues that will be addressed in this chapter are:

- to what extent the dedication of a lane of an existing motorway to the operation of trucks (either ordinary trucks or ACTs) would affect the flow of ordinary vehicles;
- which other infrastructural requirements would be needed to optimize the flow of ACTs while interacting with the flow of manually driven vehicles (MDVs) at on-/off-ramps of motorways?

9.2   KEY DESIGN AND CONTROL FACTORS FOR THE OPERATION OF ACTs ON EXISTING MOTOR WAYS

As traffic flow becomes less homogeneous, the probability of a decrease in efficiency becomes higher (Hoogendoorn and Minderhoud 2001). It means that increasing the number of ACTs on DFLs may result in much more congestion on motorways at merging areas while interacting with crossing MDVs. So, one of the proposed means for increasing the efficiency of existing motorways is to increase the level of homogeneity of the traffic flow. The creation of an exclusive lane for trucks and synchronizing the speed and density of ACTs based on the prevailing conditions of flow of MDVs at merging areas are two options which could improve homogeneity.

Creation of DFL: The First Key Factor

The dedication of special lane(s) along existing sections of motorways to specific user groups such as ACTs could be achieved by converting a lane of existing motorways. Figure 9.1 indicates a schematic layout for such a dedicated freight lane along an existing three-lane motorway where the shoulder lane is assigned to ACTs. In fact, a physically segregated truck lane is operated on the Rotterdam beltway (A16) in the Netherlands for the operation of ordinary trucks only. Such a dedicated lane could be assigned to the operation of ACTs in the future.

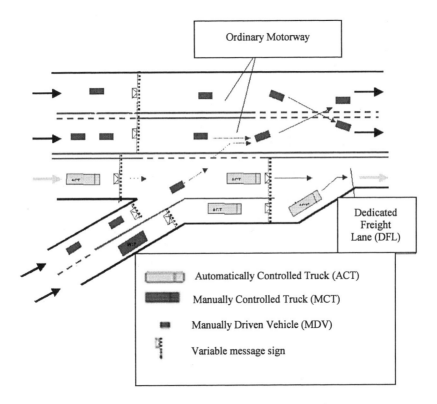

Figure 9.1   The general layout of the assumed motorway

It is clear that by converting one lane of an existing motorway to trucks only, the level of service for the traffic operation of other user classes would be worsened. In addition, since near bottlenecks (such as on-/off-ramps) traffic enters or exits, the other user classes may hinder or be hindered by trucks.

The processes differ for a dedicated lane on the left (truck must cross the mainline) or on the right (other user groups must cross the dedicated truck lane). Therefore, it would be necessary to assess to what extent performance, for instance total travel time of vehicles or total throughput, would be changed due to the assignment of one lane of motorway to the operation of ACTs. While assigning the right-hand lane to ACTs would facilitate the entering/exiting flow of ACTs to/from the dedicated lane, considering the left-hand lane as the dedicated freight lane may result in less interruption of flow of other user classes due to a smaller number of merging/diverging flows of ACTs in successive on-/off-ramps.

In the existing situation trucks are not allowed to drive on the left (median) lane because they may hinder the flow of other user groups considerably. However, it would be a matter of discussion to what extent such hindrance would be expected if trucks drive on dedicated lanes at the median lane and interrupt other user groups only at on-/off-ramps of motorways while entering/exiting from motorways. Moreover, if the speed of trucks could be harmonized with the other user groups upstream of on-/off-ramps, then it might improve the level of safety in scenarios where the dedicated freight lane is located in the median lane. It seems that operation of automatically controlled trucks would facilitate such an opportunity.

Research at Delft University of Technology states that a dedicated lane with flow control is the most promising approach to preventing future problems on motorways, as the share of trucks in traffic flow becomes higher (20%–30%) and the composition of traffic flow becomes more heterogeneous (Minderhoud and Hansen 2001).

The complementary research at Delft University of Technology compares the effectiveness of creating the DFL in the shoulder lane and the median lane of motorways with other options like lane change prohibition on trucks or normal situations in which a mixed traffic flow of cars and trucks on all lanes (with the exception of the speed lane) would be expected (Tabibi 2002, Tabibi and Minderhoud 2002). This analysis has been achieved by comparing different performance indicators like traffic operation indicators (such as capacity of bottlenecks, throughput, and average travel time of vehicles), energy consumption indicators, and safety and comfort indicators for the assumed scenarios of design and control. The results of simulations (Minderhoud and Bovy 1999, Minderhoud 2001) in this research also confirm the competitiveness of dedicating of a lane to trucks compared with certain other control strategies such as lane prohibition of trucks. In brief, it can be concluded that the dedication of the shoulder lane to trucks will be an effective solution to increasing the efficiency of freight transport considering all the respective performance indicators. Mainwhile, dedication of the left lane (median lane) to trucks would only be beneficial when there is a very low share of trucks on both mainline flow and the on-/off-ramp flow (< 10%). Figures 9.2 (a and b) and 9.3 (a and b) indicate the results of simulation concerning the capacity of on-/off-ramp areas in each of the proposed scenarios.

Taking all the findings together, the following remarks about the creation and location of DFLs, as one of the major infrastructures for the operation of ACTs, should be taken into account.

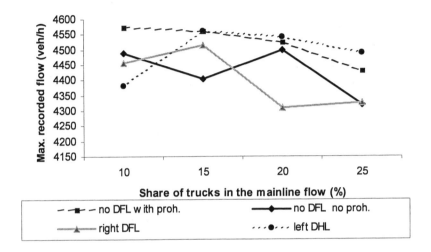

(a) Low share of trucks in the on-ramp flow (10%)

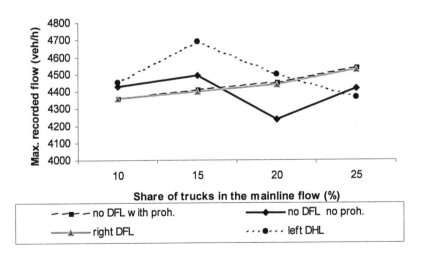

(b) High share of trucks in the on-ramp flow (30%)

Figure 9.2   Capacity at on-ramp area for all proposed scenarios

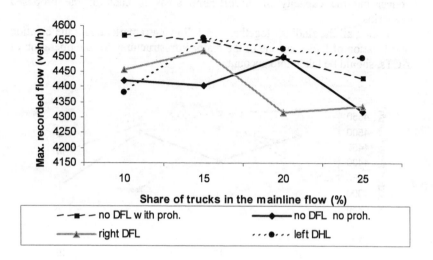

(a) Low share of off-ramp trucks (10%)

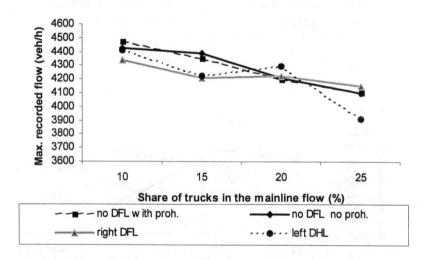

(b) High share of off-ramp trucks (30%)

Figure 9.3   Capacity at off-ramp area for all proposed scenarios

Regarding the creation of the DFL

- A DFL can prevent mixing a high proportion of trucks with other user classes on a major part of the motorways.
- A DFL could be justifiable when the share of the trucks in the traffic composition becomes about 20–30% (when the motorway includes at least three lanes).
- A DFL provides special kinds of control methods when the user of this lane has very different characteristics from the user classes in the other lanes.
- A DFL facilitates platooning and other car-following concepts that may increase throughput.

Regarding the location of the DFL

- Creation of a DFL on the median lane of the motorway cannot be considered an effective solution since (especially) at high rates of on- and/or off-ramp flow of trucks capacity will be decreased by up to 10 % and safety will be decreased considerably.
- Dedication of the median lane to trucks would only be suggested when both of the following conditions could be satisfied:
  - a low share of trucks is expected in the on-/off-ramp flow;
  - the safety issues have been satisfied by harmonizing the speed of the on-/off-ramp flow of trucks and the approaching flow of manually driven vehicles.
- Creation of the DFL on the shoulder lane of the motorway can be considered an effective solution, especially at high expected (rates of) flow of trucks on the mainline and/or the on-/off-ramp (> 20%). In such cases, dedication of a lane to ACTs would not affect the flow of MDVS significantly and might result in a better performance by the whole system.

The provision of a dedicated lane alone is not sufficient to control the flow of ACTs at merging areas (Smith and Noel, 1995, van Arem et al. 1997). Additional facilities are needed to minimize the hindrance caused by MDVs to the flow of ACT, approaching the merging areas. In such conditions, automation of trucks which can be centrally controlled could help control the flow of ACTs upstream of a merging area on both DFL and the on-ramp (Tabibi 2001).

Buffer Area: The Second Key Factor

Originally, the buffer area was a new physical element on Dutch motorways, designed to reduce congestion (Schuurman and Westland 1996,

Rijkswaterstaat 1997). A buffer is a section of motorway locally widened by one or more lanes in order to pack queues more compactly. The shortening of queue length stems not only from the additional lanes, but also from the higher density in the queue because of the lower speed in the queue, which is a result of the higher number of queuing lines relative to the number of discharge lanes.

However, on motorway networks including ACTs and MDVs, the buffer area refers to a calming area which regulates the traffic flow of ACTs and aims to minimize the delay of all traffic at on-/off-ramp areas (Tabibi and Hansen 2000).

While operating ACTs, trucks are under automatic control. This means that the distance an ACT maintains from the ACTs in front, its speed, and its route from entry onto a motorway until exit are all determined by the ACT's feedback control laws. One may therefore compare the effect on traffic of changes in vehicle control rules, and seek to calculate the 'optimum' control rules. By contrast, in non-automated (ordinary) trucks, the driver of a truck determines a truck's headway, its speed, its movement during a merge, etc. Driver behaviour is difficult to change significantly.

Similarly, the traffic control centre (TCC) for the operation of ACTs on DFLs can directly influence the flow by issuing orders to trucks regarding their speed and route. Those orders will be obeyed because the trucks (ACTs) are programmed to do so. The TCC can also make speed and route suggestions to an ordinary flow of vehicles, but drivers may ignore these suggestions or react to them in an unexpected manner. Thus the influence of TCC policies while operating ACTs is much stronger and more predictable than its influence on non-automated traffic; and so, one may again seek to determine the optimum TCC policies. Because it is possible to exercise much greater control over the movement of individual vehicles and the traffic as a whole, a theory of the dynamics of flow of ACTs will tend to be prescriptive. Non-automated traffic flow theory is more descriptive, by contrast.

Such a prescriptive structure, assumed for the flow of ACTs, could help effectively to minimize the flow hindrance of traffic flow of ACTs due to interaction with MDVs at merging/diverging areas.

It should be emphasized here that applying optimization methods has so far been mostly neglected in the literature of the traffic flow. This method has only been used for a ramp-metering strategy to control of flow at merging areas (Kotsialos et al. 2001). However, according to the above discussion, the application of optimization algorithms to the operation of ACTs would probably be widely used in the future.

Thus, the proposed approach is to create buffer areas for ACTs and try to find the optimal values of speed and density of ACTs which might result in the optimal situation for all vehicles (including ACTs and MDVs) at merging/diverging areas. It is clear that guidance of ACTs to these areas should be achieved in such a way as to create the optimal state for the operation of vehicles. In the following sections, different functions of buffer areas are addressed.

Optimizing the regulation of the traffic flow
This function would form the basic means for developing the concept of the buffer area. Since ACTs are fully automated, it would be possible to direct a proportion of the ACT upstream of merging areas to the buffer areas to control the total flow of ACTs and MDVs at merging areas based on the assumed level of service at merging areas. In such a case, the buffer area acts as an intermediate parking area for some of the ACTs. During off-peak hours when the volume of MDVs on the on-ramp is low, ACTs which have been parked in the buffer area would enter the DFL directly. Of course, these ACTs would experience some delays before entering the DFL (Figure 9.4).

Figure 9.5 indicates a similar design for the mainline buffer area situated upstream of an off-ramp. This buffer area would act similarly when there is a high volume of diverging MDVs which intend to exit the mainline and a high volume of ACTs which intend to pass the off-ramp and continue their journey on the DFL. In such a case, the traffic control centre could select a similar strategy for controlling the ACTs (namely splitting the existing ACTs into platoons and stopping the latter ones). By this method, the congestion at the off-ramp might be reduced. In order to quantify the effectiveness of the buffer area and its capacity to improve the quality of traffic, a simple case study is given in section 9.3.

Dynamic traffic management of DFLs
Buffer areas could also simplify traffic management of the ordinary motorway during peak hours. They might allow manually driven vehicles which intend to exit from the motorway to enter the DFL. In such a case, the ACTs upstream of the on-ramp (entrance point of the manually driven vehicles to the DFL) would be directed to the buffer area in order to avoid conflicts with the existing manually driven vehicles on the DFL. Moreover, the incident management of ACTs could be facilitated by using buffer areas.

Overruling the control mode of driving
Buffer areas could also be envisaged as major points of overruling the control mode of driving. For instance, in mainline buffers which are located just upstream of an off-ramp, ACTs which are intending to exit the mainline (go to the off-ramp) will be directed to the buffer area. In such a case, in the buffer area the control mode of driving will be changed from automatic to manual and the required checking will be provided. Conversely, when a manually controlled truck is intending to merge with the mainline, the control mode of driving will be changed in the on-ramp buffer from manual to automatic and the required inspections will be provided in these buffer areas.

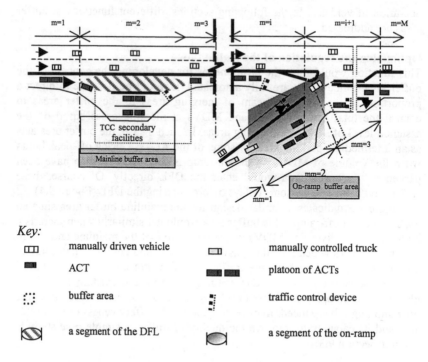

Key:

manually driven vehicle		manually controlled truck	
ACT		platoon of ACTs	
buffer area		traffic control device	
a segment of the DFL		a segment of the on-ramp	

Figure 9.4   Schematic layout of the mainline buffer combined with the on-ramp buffer

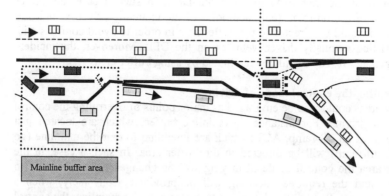

Key: see Figure 9.4.

Figure 9.5   Schematic layout of the mainline buffer combined with the off-ramp buffer

9.3   A NUMERICAL EXAMPLE

In order to assess the impact of buffer areas on the operation of ACTS, this section gives a numerical example. In this quantitative example the initial impact of the buffer area's capacity is analysed for different objective functions (for designing the system). It is assumed that ACTs are driving on the DFL and the only interaction between ACTs and MDVs takes place at on-/off-ramps. For reasons of simplicity, it is assumed that the layout only includes an on-ramp.

The preliminary analysis has been made for a period of 10 minutes, which has been divided into 10-second time intervals for each step of the analysis. This means that 61 time periods are taken into account, including the initial traffic flow conditions. It is assumed that the DFL is constituted by six segments, each with a length of 500 metres. Also the on-ramp includes three segments with a total length of 1500 metres where the third segment is connected to the DFL.

Moreover, it is assumed that there is a uniform traffic flow of 200 vehicles per hour for both ACTs and MDVs on the on-ramp. But in order to assess the impact of the creation of a buffer area on different levels of fluctuation of flow, in the first part of the analysis three levels of fluctuation of flow of ACTs are analysed as indicated in Table 9.1. In the second part, a more detailed analysis is made for one of the options (option 2 in Table 9.1). The feasibility of the problem for options both with and without the buffer will help us to compare the results in more detail. The main aim of the second part of the analysis is to evaluate the impact of the capacity of the buffer area.

Table 9.1   The assumed options indicating the fluctuation of flow of ACTs

Option	Fluctuation in traffic flow of ACT's (%)	Traffic flow of ACTs on the DFL (veh/h)	
		0–5 min.	6–10 min.
1	0% uniform traffic flow	700	700
2	20% moderate changes in flow	840	560
3	40% high changes in flow	980	420

In the case of the buffer area, it is assumed that there are three buffers in the layout, including two buffers in segments 2 and 3 of the DFL and one buffer on the on-ramp. These buffers control the traffic flow of ACTs on both the DFL and the on-ramp just upstream of the merging area. Different levels of capacity (0, 20, 50 and 100 ACT/h) are analysed to assess the impact of the capacity of the buffer areas on the proposed criteria of performance.

Model Formulation

For the purpose of formulation, the following categories of rules are taken into account:

- definition of the flow dynamics of ACTs on both the DFL and the on-ramp;
- definition of maximum allowable values of density and speed of ACTs;
- describing the gap acceptance at merging area;
- considering constraints related to the buffer areas;
- definition of the optimization function.

In order to determine the equations for each of the above categories, the DFL and the on-ramp are divided into different segments (cells). Then for each cell, equations with respect to each of the categories are developed.

The first category of rules contains the flow conservation of ACTs in each segment, the speed–density relationship, the description of the speed variation, and finally the output flow of each segment during each time step of analysis is computed (Gartner et al. 1992, Hoogendoorn and Bovy 2001, Papageorgiou 2001). The second category of rules limits the amount of speed and density of each segment to an upper bound like the free flow speed and jam density, respectively. The third category of rules defines the capacity at the merging area and will connect the individual flow of ACTs on the DFL and on the on-ramp to each other (Lertworawanich and Elefteriadou 2001, Shim and Kim 1998). This capacity could also be calculated based on results of simulations for running various combinations of the mainline flow versus on-/off-ramp flow. The fourth category takes into account the required equations for describing the function of the buffer area. Definition of the capacity of the buffer area; description of the allowable output flow of each buffer area during each time step of analysis; and finally the necessity to discharge all buffer areas at the end of the time analysis would be among the most important equations in the fourth category. The final category of rules specifies the proposed objective function for the design of the system. Since the main focus of this analysis is on ACTs, the following objectives are taken into account:

- minimization of total travel time of ACTs;
- minimization of average travel time of ACTs on the DFL;
- maximization of throughput of ACTs at merging area;
- minimization of variation of speed of ACTs on the motorway section.

Performance Indicators

In order to evaluate the performance of the buffer area and its capacity for different objectives of design, a broad range of indicators could be distinguished. Among all, the following criteria are selected:

(1) total travel time of ACTs;
(2) maximum waiting time of an ACT in buffer areas;
(3) percentage of capacity utilization of the buffer area by ACTS.

The first indicator compares the principal criteria for evaluating the impact of the proposed options on the efficiency of operation of ACTs. This indicator is introduced as the objective function of one of the assumed scenarios (objective functions), while in the other scenarios it could be computed based on the given results for the other effective variables. The second indicator reports the maximum waiting time of ACTs in buffer areas. The smaller the value of this indicator, the higher the efficiency of the respected scenario. These criteria could also be added to the structure of the model by defining an upper bound for describing the maximum feasible waiting time of each ACT in the buffer area. The last indicator verifies what percentage of the capacity provided by the buffer area is occupied by ACTs during the total time period of analysis. The higher the value of this indicator, the more effective the buffer area.

Solving the Model

The proposed optimization models, including all the proposed objective functions and constraints, are solved by using the GAMS software (Brooke et al. 1998). Each of the proposed models includes more than 3300 variables and 5000 constraints. The next section gives a summary of the results of solving the optimization models for each of the proposed scenarios of design (objective functions) and different capacities of buffer areas.

Results of the Analysis

Part 1 – The impact of the creation of a buffer area
Analysis of different levels of variation of flow of ACTs on the DFL indicates that the creation of a buffer area would help to handle those options (option 3) where in some time periods the demand by ACTs in both directions (DFL and on-ramp) is higher than the capacity provided. In such a case, when there is no buffer, solving the problem is infeasible. This means that one or more conditions (equations) are not satisfied. But, assuming a capacity of 100 ACT/h for the buffer areas leads to a solution of the problem. Therefore, it turns out that creation of a buffer area will help specially during critical intervals (threshold of congestion) when the interaction of the flow of ACTs

and MDVs, or the merging of ACTs from the on-ramp to the DFL reach capacity. In such situations, the rapid decrease of the speed of flow of ACTs (due to congestion) will justify an intermediate stop for some ACTs in the buffer areas. It can be concluded from this analysis that selection of the optimal capacity of the buffer area heavily depends on the upstream flow of ACTs and MDVs and the expected level of service at the merging/diverging area.

Part 2 – The impact of capacity of the buffer area
In order to assess the impact of the capacity of the buffer area, the second option of Table 9.1 is selected for further analysis. This option has been solved for all of the proposed capacities for the buffer areas (including no buffer option). Therefore, it has been selected as the basic option for detailed analysis in this subsection. Analysis of the proposed objective functions for the operation of ACTs with various capacities of the buffer areas (for option 2 of Table 9.1) reveals that generally the buffer area would improve the interaction of the ACTs and MDVs at merging areas. It would decrease the high rate of disturbance of ACTs and MDVs efficiently by holding back some ACTs in the buffer areas. In the following, some more detailed information about the comparison of the criteria introduced is discussed. It should be noted that the number of iterations for finding the optimal results for all scenarios lay between 1300–1500 iterations.

Indicator 1 – Total travel time of ACTs on the layout
Table 9.2 provides a summary overview of the results pertaining to this indicator. This table shows how total travel time changes through increasing the capacity of the buffer area. As is clear in the above table, for two objective functions, 'maximization of throughput at merging area' and 'minimization of buffer utilization', the capacity of the buffer area has no impact on this indicator. This is to be expected because these objectives work in the opposite direction to using the buffer area. Maximization of throughput at the merging area tries to maximize the number of ACTs at the merging area regardless of travel time. Also, 'minimization of buffer area' means using the buffer area at the minimum level. Therefore, increasing the capacity of the buffer areas makes no sense for these objectives.

For the rest of the objectives, the results indicate a negligible improvement of the total travel time by increasing the capacity of the buffer area. Moreover, comparing the changes also shows that these groups of objective functions nearly follow a trend. This means that these objectives are closely correlated with each other. Therefore, selection of the capacity of the buffer area basically depends on the prevailing conditions of traffic flow. This emphasizes once more on this rule that selection of the optimal capacity of the buffer area effectively depends on the level of the demand of ACTs compared with the provided capacity.

Table 9.2   Changes in total travel time for the assumed scenarios of analysis with regard to the 'no-buffer' scenario

Obj. no.	Objective function	Changes in total travel time for the respective capacity of the buffer area (%)		
		20	50	100
1	Min. total travel time of ACTs	−0.2	−0.5	−0.8
2	Min. ave. travel time of an ACT on the DFL	−0.2	−0.5	−0.8
3	Max. throughput at merging area	0	0	0
4	Min. variation of speed of ACTs on the layout	−0.2	−0.5	−0.8

Indicator 2 – Maximum waiting time of ACTs in the buffer areas
Figure 9.6 indicates the results of analysis concerning the maximum waiting time of ACTs on the mainline buffers located on segments 2 and 3 of the DFL. This figure illustrates that the maximum waiting time of ACTs in these buffers is limited to 3 minutes. For most of the objectives this indicator is limited to 2 minutes. Comparing the variation of graphs for different capacities emphasizes the selection of a capacity of 50 ACT/h for the mainline buffers. In such a case, the maximum expected waiting time for the ACTs in this buffer could be limited to 1.5 minutes. For each respective objective function, comparing the maximum waiting time of buffer area no. 2 with buffer area no. 3 indicates generally a higher value of this indicator for buffer no. 3. This can be explained by the fact that buffer area no. 3 is situated closer to the merging area and therefore it takes more time to achieve regulation of the flow.

This indicator specifies where percentage of the capacity provided is used while using the buffer area. The higher the value of the indicator, the higher the usage of the provided capacity and the less the flexibility of the assumed scenario of the analysis. Figure 9.7 (a) indicates the changes in this indicator for both mainline buffers and the on-ramp buffer.

The highest rate of using the provided capacity of the mainline buffers is related to the case where minimization of variation of speed of ACTs is the objective function of the analysis. This emphasizes the important role of buffer areas in regulating the flow of ACTs to achieve the minimum change in speed of ACTs on the DFL. Figure 9.7 (b) shows that about 90% of the capacity provided by mainline buffers is used. For the rest of the cases (objective functions) the index of use of the capacity provided varies between 45 and 65% depending on both the capacity of the buffer area and the assumed objective function.

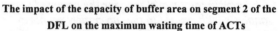

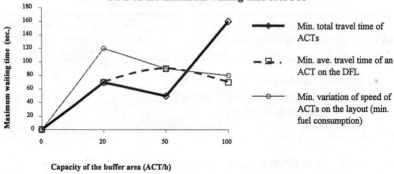

(a) Buffer area #2

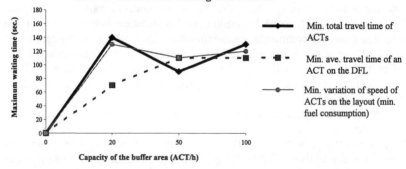

(b) Buffer area #3

Figure 9.6   The impact of the capacity of mainline buffers on the maximum waiting time of ACTs for the proposed objective functions, Indicator 3 – Capacity utilization of buffers

Capacity utilization of mainline buffers

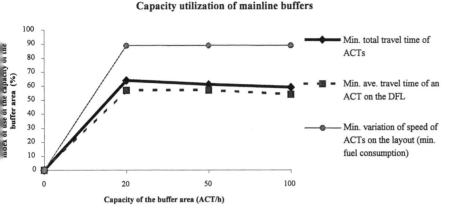

Capacity utilization of the on-ramp buffer

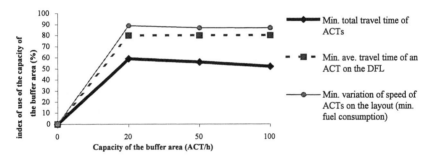

Figure 9.7   Capacity utilization (percentage of use of the provided capacity) of buffers on the mainline and the on-ramp

Similar to the mainline buffers, the highest rate of use of the capacity provided by the on-ramp buffer is related to the case when minimization of variation of speed of ACTs is the objective function of the analysis. It emphasizes the important role of buffer areas in regulating the flow of ACTs to ensure the minimum change in speed of ACTs on the DFL. The related graph in the above figure shows that about 90% of the capacity provided by the mainline buffers is occupied. It confirms once more the important impact of the on-ramp buffer on regulating the flow of ACTs in cases where the controller of the system gives priority to the flow of ACTs on the DFL. In such a case, more than 80% of the capacity provided by the on-ramp buffer is used by the ACTs. Increasing the capacity of the on-ramp buffer will decrease this indicator but the level of decrease is limited to 10%.

9.4   CONCLUSIONS

In brief, this chapter addressed two major infrastructure requirements for the operation of ACTs on existing motorways. The first requirement was the need to dedicate a lane of existing motorways to ACTs and the second requirement was the necessity to create a buffer area with the optimal capacity.

Dedication of a lane to ACTs would ensure the safety aspects in major parts of the motorways. Thus, it can be considered as an initial design requirement for the operation of automatically controlled trucks in which drivers on board will only take over control of a vehicle in emergency situations. This segregation of flow among ACTs and MDVs would improve safety and would not require high investment for the construction of completely isolated networks of ACTs. The preliminary results of our analysis indicate that if a high share of trucks in the traffic flow (> 20%) were expected then the dedication of a lane to ACTs would be a competitive solution in comparison with other proposed options such as the prohibition of overtaking of trucks. Therefore, the dedication of a lane would not hinder the ordinary traffic flow in the rest of the lanes significantly. The results of investigations also emphasize the creation of a dedicated freight lane on the shoulder lane of existing motorways. Meanwhile, creation of a DFL on the median lane would only be justified when a low share of trucks in the traffic flow was expected and where synchronization of flow of ACTs with the flow of MDVs had been provided upstream of on-/off-ramps.

A buffer area, as a complementary means, could provide the opportunity to regulate the flow of ACTs upstream of on-/off-ramps. This would facilitate synchronizing the speed and density of ACTs while approaching the on-/off-ramp areas. It could also function as an area for overruling the mode of driving (from automatic to manual and vice versa), dynamic traffic management of ACTs and MDVs and incident management of ACTs. Two major impacts that buffer areas might have on increasing the efficiency of operation of ACTs are:

(1) a meaningful impact on total travel time during time periods when the traffic demand of ACTs is higher than the provided capacity;
(2) a secondary impact on the operation of ACTs during off-peak periods by harmonizing the speed of ACTs in order to achieve the minimum fuel consumption.

Applying different control strategies such as ramp metering or platooning of ACTs on the DFL may have some major impacts on the results presented in this chapter. This would probably also improve the efficiency of operation of ACTs and the benefit of DFLs and buffer areas in combination with advanced traffic control measures. It is a matter of discussion which should be addressed in future research.

REFERENCES

Brooke, A., D. Kendrick, A. Meeraus and R. Raman (1998), *GAMS: A User's Guide*, Washington, DC: GAMS Development Corporation.

Centraal Bureau voor de Statistiek (CBS) (2003), http://www.cbs.nl.

Eurostat (2003), http://europa.eu.int/comm/energy_transport/etif/index.html.

Gartner, N., C.J. Messer and A.K. Rathi (1992), *Traffic Flow Theory: A State-of-the-Art Report*, Special Report 165, Transportation Research Board, TRB, National Research Council, Washington, DC.

Hoogendoorn, S.P. and P.H.L. Bovy (2001), State-of-the-Art of Vehicular Traffic Flow Modelling, *Proceeding of the Institute of Mechanical Engineering*, Vol. 215, no. 1, pp. 283–303.

Hoogendoorn, S.P. and M.M. Minderhoud (2001), ADAS Impact Assessment by Micro-simulation, *EJTIR*, Vol. 1, no. 3, pp. 255–275.

Kotsialos, A., M. Papageorgiou and F. Middelham (2001), *Optimal Co-ordinated Ramp Metering with AMOC*, Proceedings of the Seminar on Advanced Traffic Control, Delft, pp. 3–30.

Lertworawanich, P. and L. Elefteriadou (2001), *Capacity Estimations for Type B Weaving Areas Using Gap Acceptance*, Transportation Research Record 1776, Washington: National Academy Press, pp. 24–34.

Minderhoud, M.M. (2001), *Technical Specification of SiMoNe*, Delft: Delft University of Technology.

Minderhoud, M. and P.H.L Bovy (1999), *Modelling Driver Behavior on Motorways – Description of the SiMoNe model*, Report VK22206.302, Delft University of Technology, Transportation Planning and Traffic Engineering Section.

Minderhoud, M.M. and I.A. Hansen (2001), *A Microscopic Simulation Study after Freight Lanes near Merging Areas*, Proceedings of the Eighth Intelligent Transport Systems Conference (ITS), Sydney (CD-Rom).

Papageorgiou, M. (2001), *Short Course on Dynamic Traffic Flow Modelling and Control*, Technical University of Crete, pp. 3.1–3.51 and 5.1–5.64.

Rijkswaterstaat Adviesdienst Verkeer en Vervoer (1997), Handboek 'Buffers' – Deel 1: Beleid en planning, Rotterdam (in Dutch).

Schuurman, H. and D. Westland (1996), Buffers in Congested Motorway Networks, Proceedings of the Joint ARRB Transport Research Conference and Transit New Zealand Transport Symposium, Christchurch.

Shim, D.Y. and S.G. Kim (1998), *Improvement of the On-ramp Control Algorithm Considering the Merging Capacity Constraint*, Proceedings of the Fifth Intelligent Transport Systems Conference, Seoul (CD-Rom).

Shladover, S.E. (1998), Why We Should Develop a Truly Automated Highway System?, *Transportation Research Record*, Vol. 1651, pp. 66–73.

Shladover, S.E. (2001a), *Opportunities in Truck Automation*, Proceedings of the Eighth Intelligent Transport Systems Conference 2001, Sydney (CD-Rom).

Shladover, S.E. (2001b), *DEMO 2003: Showcasing the Benefits of Automated Driving of Transit Buses and Heavy Trucks*, Proceedings of the Eighth Intelligent Transport Systems Conference (ITS), Sydney (CD-Rom).

Smith, E.R. and E.C. Noel (1995), *Assessment of the Impact of an Automated Lane in Freeway Operations*, ITE 65th Annual Meeting, pp. 41–8.

Tabibi, M. (2001), *Buffer Area for Dedicated Lanes of Automated Freight Traffic*, Proceedings of the Ninth WCTR, Seoul (CD-Rom).

Tabibi, M. (2002), *The Impact of the On-/Off-Ramp Flow of Trucks on the Efficiency of the Dedicated Freight Lane*, Proceedings of the Seventh Trail Congress, Rotterdam (CD-Rom).

Tabibi, M. and I.A. Hansen (2000), *Dedicated Lanes for Automated Freight Traffic: A Solution for Rapid Increase of Freight Transport in the 21st Century*, Proceedings of the Fifth Conference of Traffic Engineering, Teheran (CD-Rom).

Tabibi, M. and M.M. Minderhoud (2002), *Decision Making about Creation and Location of Dedicated Freight Lane*, Proceedings of Third Conference on Decision Making in Urban and Civil Engineering (DMinUCE), London (CD-Rom).

van Arem, B., M.J.W.A. Vanderschuren and A.P. de Vos (1997), *The Effect of a Special Lane for Intelligent Vehicles on Traffic Flows*, an exploratory study using the microscopic traffic simulation model MIXIC, TNO Inro, Report INRO-VVG 1997-02a, Delft, The Netherlands.

PART II

Automated freight transport: design and
evaluation tools

10. Supporting the design of automated transport systems using innovative simulation

Corné Versteegt and Alexander Verbraeck

10.1 SIMULATION OF TRANSPORT SYSTEMS

Logistics systems and transportation systems are characterized by a high level of interaction and dynamics. These systems are difficult to design because of their dynamics, but also because the design involves at least three different aspects: the infrastructure of the transport system (e.g. the road infrastructure), the entities that are 'moving' within the transport systems (e.g. Automated Guided Vehicles), and the control system that is responsible for the logistic decisions (active control systems in the vehicles, and passive control in the traffic system). In addition, other aspects such as the involvement of different parties with different interests, economic aspects, and uncertainty around new technologies complicate the design process even further. In many projects, the multitude of alternatives and the amount of disciplines involved result in sub-optimal decisions during the design process. Simulation models can play an important role in the design process of automated transport systems, because they can offer a common frame of reference for all designers involved, and provide both quantitative and qualitative answers for many different aspects of the system. Simulation is inherently quantitative, but the often associated animation or visualization can provide qualitative insight as well (Vreede and Verbraeck 1996). Most of the modern discrete event simulation languages are especially focused on logistical and transport problems, where the infrastructure and entities using the infrastructure can be easily modelled (van Daalen et al. 1999, Banks 1998). Modelling of complex control activities, however, has always been more a software engineering activity and could not be easily incorporated in simulation models. Recent developments, however (Auinger et al. 1999), have changed this situation. Simulation models can now be extended or interfaced with complex control logic, enabling the holistic design of a transport system with all its aspects (Versteegt et al. 2001).

Introduction to Simulation

Within automated transport systems there are many possible courses of action, many design variables, and many external influences that determine the effectiveness of the design. The alternatives are often difficult to test in reality because of high costs of building prototypes and test environments. Many systems do not lend themselves at all to experimentation, as this may be expensive (e.g. wind tunnel experiments), dangerous (e.g. in nuclear power plants), impractical or impossible (e.g. social systems). The larger or more complex the system is, the harder it usually is to explore the solution space. In these situations, models may be developed in order to investigate the system.

To adequately design and analyse automated transport systems we advocate using simulation models that carefully 'mimic' the characteristics and dynamics of the system (Banks et al. 1996, Law and Kelton 1991). The methodology of simulation allows an organization to analyse the behaviour of complex systems in a flexible and detailed manner. Simulation also allows for a quick implementation of adjustments in the modelled system, making it possible to analyse different alternative solutions in a relatively short time. In our definition, simulation is (Shannon 1975):

> The process of designing a model of a real system and conducting experiments with this model for the purpose either of understanding the behaviour of the system or evaluating various strategies (within the limits imposed by a criterion or set of criteria) for the operation of the system.

We explicitly take models of the current situation into account in experimentation to act as a 'yardstick' for measuring the added value of logistics and transportation alternatives. For simulation studies in automated transport, we usually use so-called 'discrete event simulation' models. The models are built of discrete entities that model the infrastructure parts and the vehicles that use the infrastructure. When studying systems using discrete event simulation models, a discrete worldview has to be used when modelling the system. Therefore, discrete objects from the system are often chosen as the focus of attention. Take a freeway with cars as an example. When looking at this system from a continuous point of view, we could model the number of cars on a stretch of road, the properties of the road, and the continuous influence of these variables on the mean speed of the cars, which, in its turn, influences the number of cars per stretch of road. When looking at the system from a discrete point of view, we 'see' individual cars with their properties (speed, lane) and their behaviour (change speed, change lane) as a result of events (state changes from the environment, state changes of other cars, e.g. brake lights from the previous car). In other words, objects or entities within the system with attributes and behaviour are usually the main building blocks of discrete event simulation models.

Time is usually also advanced in a discrete way: instead of modelling an activity taking place in detail, only the start 'event' and the end 'event' of that activity are taken into account, as these mark the most important state changes in the model (Zeigler et al. 2000). When intermediate state changes take place (e.g. a vehicle moving from crossing to crossing, or a vehicle interacting with another vehicle), the activity is divided into a number of sub-activities, for which events are scheduled and state changes are carried out.

Computerized Support for Simulation Studies

Many commercial products are available to support and structure discrete event simulation studies. Some of these products can be characterized as 'flow-oriented' (Arena, ProModel), as they focus on the flow of moving entities through a stable infrastructure, and look at the state changes that occur at different places in the infrastructure. Other products can be characterized as being 'object-oriented' (eM-Plant, Enterprise Dynamics). In these simulation models, all entities of the model operate and interact at the same level. There is no clear distinction between infrastructure and moving entities. At first sight, flow oriented modelling looks ideal for modelling automated transportation systems, as the distinction between infrastructure and moving entities is clearly present. It turns out, however, that the control logic of the moving entities is very hard to implement and hard to recognize for transportation control experts. Furthermore, modern infrastructure is not completely passive: all kinds of decisions are taken in the infrastructure that influence the behaviour of the vehicles. Object oriented modelling has the advantage that the control logic can be implemented in separate objects that closely resemble the control systems in real systems. The main disadvantage, however, is that the flow is no longer visible to the modeller or to the design team. The flow is a result of many object–object interactions that take place in the model and are not explicitly visible any more.

Although simulation shows an enormous potential to bridge the gap between many disciplines and to function as a common reference model within large transportation projects, both of the two paradigms presented suffer from serious drawbacks. The challenge, therefore, is to augment simulation languages with possibilities to model infrastructure, flow, and control in a consistent and easy way. The next section will first introduce a futuristic transportation project for which this need was clearly present, the Underground Logistic System Schiphol. After that, some relevant recent developments within simulation are shown. Each development will be illustrated by examples from the Underground Logistic System Schiphol.

10.2 CASE STUDY: UNDERGROUND LOGISTIC SYSTEM SCHIPHOL

In the Netherlands the roads are heavily congested around Amsterdam Airport Schiphol and the Flower Auction Aalsmeer. This leads to long throughput times and unreliable transport delivery rates of time-critical and expensive airfreight (e.g. flowers, computer parts, newspapers) between Amsterdam Airport Schiphol, logistics centres near Schiphol, the Flower Auction Aalsmeer, and (a future) rail terminal near Schiphol. To solve this problem an underground logistic system has been proposed for the congestion-free transport of the expensive and time-critical air-cargo. The Underground Logistic System Schiphol (abbreviated to OLS Schiphol) makes a seamless connection possible between three different transport modes: air, rail, and road. The Underground Logistic System Schiphol will connect three geographical areas: Amsterdam Airport Schiphol, Flower Auction Aalsmeer and a rail terminal near Schiphol. At each location a number of terminals will be constructed where customers can deliver and pick up their cargo. Tunnel segments that may be one-directional or two-directional will connect the areas. The exact layout of the OLS has not yet been decided. One of the alternatives, with three variants for the tunnel between the Flower Auction Aalsmeer and Schiphol Airport, is shown in Figure 10.1. In this alternative two-directional tunnel segments are used to reduce construction costs.

As introduced in chapter 5, the OLS Schiphol is one of a number of projects by the Dutch Government to research the possibility of automated underground transport in The Netherlands. With projects like the OLS Schiphol, the Dutch Government hopes to offer fast and reliable cargo transport facilities in heavily populated and congested regions, without placing extra strain on the environment in these regions.

The Underground Logistic System is highly automated; it will use Automated Guided Vehicles (AGVs) and automated transshipment facilities (docks). Up to 400 AGVs and 30 docks – the final number of course depends on the final layout chosen – will be used when the system is completely operational. Control of equipment and management of the facilities will also be automated.

The OLS Schiphol project suffered from all the problems that were sketched in the first section of this chapter: high technological uncertainty, many alternatives, different disciplines, many actors with opposite goals, and no common reference model. For the feasibility study phase of the project, several traditional simulation models, both in object-oriented and in flow-oriented discrete event simulation languages, were constructed for the OLS Schiphol. The questions that were answered by these models covered both infrastructure variants (e.g. the effect of differences between layouts) and vehicle and dock alternatives (e.g. the number of vehicles needed, the

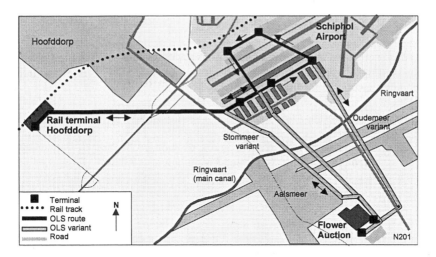

Figure 10.1   Three possible variants for the layout of the OLS Schiphol[1]

effects of increasing maximum vehicle speed, and the effects of shorter loading and unloading times). Although the simulation models provided good insight into the design options and the effects of choices at a higher systems level, these models were not suitable for more detailed options in the design. A clear example was the set of options for logistic control strategies that might be used to manage the OLS Schiphol system. Choices ranged from a completely centralized control system to decentralized variants where terminal operators have complete freedom over local priorities. The standard flow-oriented simulation environments we used for the high level simulations did not allow for an easy analysis of control algorithms. In most simulation languages, the algorithms for control are already built into the standard simulation components and cannot be changed. In addition, most flow-oriented simulation languages do not allow easy development of algorithms at all. Therefore, it proved to be difficult to test logistic control options for the OLS Schiphol project. Because it was clear to the project management that different options for the control system would have a huge effect on the transport system's performance, it was decided to look at advanced options for simulation use that surpassed the 'traditional' what-if simulation studies (Versteegt et al. 2001). The simulation options that were tested in the OLS Schiphol project and that proved to be useful in studying transport systems will be described in the next section.

10.3 RECENT DEVELOPMENTS

In this section we sketch out a number of recent developments in the field of simulation. All developments are illustrated by examples from simulation models constructed for the OLS Schiphol.

Flow-oriented versus Object-oriented Simulation

Within simulation two different schools of thought can be distinguished: flow-oriented and object-oriented simulation. Within flow-oriented simulation active entities 'flow' through the model, claiming resources on the way, and queuing for these resources when they are in use. For transport and logistic applications, this flow-oriented paradigm can easily be applied. Ships, trucks, and even containers or loads can be chosen as active entities that 'want' to be serviced and that 'flow' through the model. In combination with visual oriented simulation software like Arena, the model structure becomes a kind of flowchart that shows how the entities flow through the model. The great advantage of this type of simulation is that simulation models can be constructed relatively easy. Flow-oriented simulation can quickly be learned and the modelling process is usually fast and effective as long as the system that is modelled clearly displays the characteristics of flowing entities. On the other hand it is difficult, or even impossible, to model complex control structures in most flow-oriented languages.

In the simulation of automated transport systems complex control structures are needed, e.g. for modelling control options for a fleet of automated guided vehicles. To model such complex control structures the simulation software needs a programming-like interface instead of a visual programming environment. Object-oriented simulation software offers such programming environments and thus more possibilities to model complex control structures. Object-orientation simulation also offers advantages that originate from the field of object-oriented programming, like inheritance and polymorphism (Joines and Roberts 1998).

Within the OLS Schiphol Simple++[2] was used as the simulation environment. Simple++ is an object-oriented simulation package that offers a programming style interface in combination with a graphical user interface (Verbraeck and Versteegt 2000, Kalasky and Levasseur 1997). Within Simple++ inheritance is used to improve the maintainability of the simulation models and libraries that are created.

Libraries of Simulation Building Blocks

The strategy of building blocks is to start a simulation project by constructing a library of simulation building blocks. In later stages these building blocks are combined into simulation models. The idea is to re-use simulation building blocks in different models and even in different projects. This strategy of constructing simulation building blocks once and then re-using them should increase the efficiency of simulation projects.

The simulation project of the OLS Schiphol started with the construction of a library of simulation building blocks (Verbraeck et al. 2000). Each building block has a complete set of modelling dimensions, e.g. state, behaviour, structure, and interface. The building blocks for the OLS Schiphol were joined in a library of simulation components. Four categories of building blocks were distinguished in the OLS project (see Figure 10.2):

1. *Physical objects.* These represent physical components of a transport system such as automated guided vehicles, terminals, tracks, docks, crossings, and cargo.
2. *Information objects.* These represent information aspects that are used within transport systems, e.g. orders, acknowledgements, information requests, and event information.
3. *Control objects.* These represent control objects of transport systems, like customer order management, AGV management, traffic control, dock management, and infrastructure management.
4. *Simulation artefacts.* These building blocks are used to operate and control simulation models such as batch runs, communication with models, user interfaces, statistics, and log-files.

The simulation models that are constructed from building blocks and the building blocks themselves have a hierarchical structure. At the lowest level there are 'simple' building blocks for the basic elements of transport systems, e.g. tracks and transport equipment. These low-level building blocks are combined into higher-level building blocks for docking areas and parking as can be seen at the top of Figure 10.3. These higher-level building blocks are combined into building blocks of the terminals, as can be seen at the bottom of Figure 10.3. In the final stages high-level and low-level building blocks are joined into simulation models of the entire OLS Schiphol.

New simulation models can easily be made by just 'importing' the building blocks from the library into new models. Within the library for the OLS Schiphol the advantages that object-orientation offers are fully used, especially inheritance (Verbraeck and Versteegt 2000). Changes made in the parent library objects are automatically transferred to the children in the library and to the instances present in all available models. This makes the maintenance of simulation models very efficient and saves a lot of time in the later stages of simulation projects. The main disadvantage of the building blocks strategy is the huge effort that is needed at the beginning of a simulation project to construct the simulation building blocks.

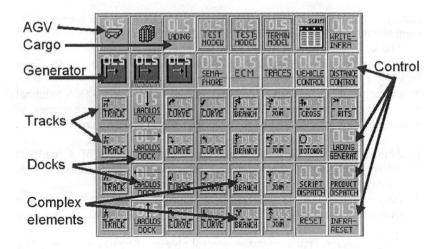

Figure 10.2   Library of simulation building blocks

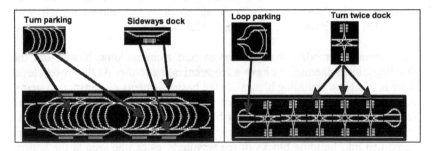

Figure 10.3   Hierarchical structure of simulation building blocks

Animation

In the early years of simulation only a few simulation software packages offered animation features. These features were often very simply squares and circles that changed colour during simulation runs. Today, animations are a standard feature of almost every simulation package. Automated transport systems are complex systems. Actors that are involved in the design of such systems, e.g. authorities, banks, insurance companies, often lack clear insight into how these systems function. Other actors with more knowledge of transport systems, e.g. mechanical and electrical engineers have detailed insight into how automated transport systems work, but do not share a common reference model. Animation, especially three-dimensional animation, can be used to show the external actors how automated transport systems function, and they can act as a common reference model for the engineers involved.

Source: Element B.V., Amsterdam.

Figure 10.4   Screen dumps of three-dimensional animations of AGV driving at a terminal (left) and transshipment of cargo units (right)

Within the OLS Schiphol project, both two- and three-dimensional animation was used, as can be seen in Figure 10.4. Animation was used as a communication tool for communication with different types of actors. Animation is used to show the operational aspects of the transport system to policy makers, both at national and regional levels, airport authorities, and people living near the airport.

The animations were also used for the verification and validation of the simulation models (Balci 1998). The simulation models were validated by showing them to experts in the field of logistics and transportation. By using animation, experts do not need to understand the simulation models or the simulation language itself or understand the underlying logic of models as long as they can follow the logic of the models displayed in the animation.

The major drawback of three-dimensional animation is that heavy computational power is needed. This is, however, becoming less of an issue. Computers and video cards are becoming increasingly powerful. Where computer power is still a problem, a solution is to run the simulation and the animation separately. In this case the simulation is carried out first. During the simulation run the information that is needed for the animations is recorded. The animations are constructed after the simulation has been carried out.

Distributed Simulation

Several reasons exist for distributing simulation models over a number of computers that jointly run the models. The first reason for distributing simulation models over several computers is computer performance. Models of complex automated transport systems are sometimes too large to run on one single computer system, or the type of computer on which it can run is too expensive or unavailable. Distributing models over more computers is a good way of running complex models at low cost. The second reason is that simulation models can be constructed by independent teams of modellers working at several geographic locations. Each team can work on parts of the model, which can be integrated into one model at a later stage. A third reason, which was important in the OLS Schiphol project, is that simulation models can be used for the control of real physical transport equipment. In this case the physical activities have to be separated from the control activities.

When a simulation is divided over several computer systems synchronization between the systems needs to take place. The most important one is synchronization of time (Verbraeck 2002). Each system or model has its own simulation clock, and it is of the utmost importance that no event takes place out of sequence as a result of non-synchronized clocks. Many different techniques are available, which can be divided into conservative techniques, – never do anything that should not yet take place – and optimistic techniques – just carry out an event, and make sure you can undo it when it turns out that the event should not have taken place (rollback). Although the optimistic techniques are much harder to implement, they can lead to faster distributed simulation models (Fujimoto 2000).

Real-time Control and Emulation

It is vital that both the automated transport systems and their control systems are tested under real-life circumstances before implementing them. Simulation can play an important role in such tests, but simulation models cannot adequately model the technical characteristics of transport systems. To study the technical aspects of transport and control systems, prototypes can be used.

In testing transport and control systems four combinations of reality and simulation can be identified (Versteegt and Verbraeck 2002, Auninger et al. 1999).

1. The *traditional way* to test control systems. A combination of a control system and logistic system both in reality. The control system is tested after commissioning, during the start-up phases of the transport system. This is an error-prone, expensive, and time-consuming way of testing control and transport. Any failures in the transport and control systems will disrupt operations.
2. *Soft commissioning (also called emulation).* A combination of a control system in reality and a simulated logistic system. Within emulation the real control system is connected to a simulation model that imitates the machines or production systems (McGregor 2002, Schiess 2001).

Emulation can reduce the developing time of control systems and shorten the time-to-market. Emulation allows testing of control systems faster than in real time and under safe conditions.

3. *Reality in the loop (also called simulation for real-time control).* A combination of a simulated control system and a real logistic system (Versteegt and Verbraeck 2002).

4. *Off-line simulation.* A combination of both a simulated control system and a simulated logistic system. Within a complete off-line simulation the transport and control systems can be tested in a safe environment and faster than real-time.

Each approach has its own advantages and disadvantages; we therefore suggest using a combination of approaches. In the OLS Schiphol project both control and transport systems were first tested in a full simulation environment (approach 4). By first using a fully simulated setting we can test transport and control systems in a safe environment, faster than real time, with better-controlled circumstances, in order to study many different scenarios like worst-case scenarios and machine breakdowns. After many failures were identified and solved, especially in the control systems, emulation and reality in the loop were used to study the technical aspects of both the control and the transport systems.

A specially equipped 1600 m^2 'TestSite' was built in Delft to perform tests with prototypes of Automated Guided Vehicles, vehicle software, loading and unloading equipment, and control strategies and software. Simulation is used as a real-time control system of prototypes at the TestSite (see step 3 in Figure 10.5). One of the main challenges is then of course how to construct the simulation models in such a way that they can be used to control both simulated and real transport systems without much adaptation. A lot of attention was paid to the interface between the simulated control systems and the simulated and prototype transport equipment. This interface is constructed in such a way that the control system does not see any differences between simulated and prototype transport systems. The simulated control system uses the same commands and the same protocols to control both simulated and prototype transport systems, and receives back the same event notifications.

This approach to constructing one interface to control both simulation and prototype transport systems lays extra demands on the simulation software. The simulation package has to have an open architecture. The software should be able easily to cooperate and communicate with other software packages and real equipment. The package should be able to deal with both standard communication protocols and user-defined communication protocols, e.g. DDE (Dynamic Data Exchange), DLL (Dynamic Link Library), TCP/IP socket connections, ActiveX, and OPC (OLE for Process Control).

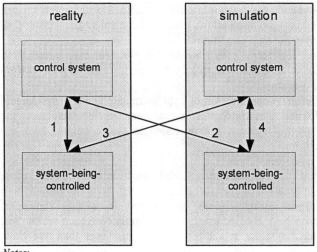

Notes:
1 = traditional testing;
2 = soft commissioning;
3 = reality in the loop;
4 = off-line simulation.

Figure 10.5   Approaches to test control and transport systems

Web-based Simulation

The term 'Web-based simulation' can have a number of different meanings. Examples are the joint development of simulation models using the Web, jointly running simulation models at different locations connected through the Web, or simulation environments that are fully embedded in the Web, e.g. as Java applications that can be remotely started and controlled.

In the simulation models of the OLS Schiphol, Web-based technology also plays an important role. The interactions between modellers/users and the simulation model are implemented in a set of Web pages, as can be seen in Figure 10.7.

The simulation environment functions as a Web server, where the simulation model generates Web pages. The interaction has two directions (see Figure 10.8). Firstly, modellers or users can send commands to the simulation model, like starting or stopping simulation models, but they can also send commands to the simulated transport system, like changing the direction of AGVs. Secondly, the simulation model can send information back to users on the state of the simulation model, and on the performance of the simulated transport system.

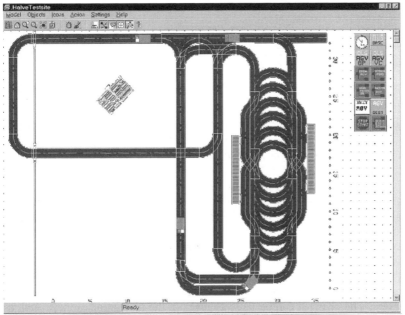

Top left: An AGV (scale 1:3) is unloading a Euro pallet.
Top right: An experiment with eight AGVs (scale 1:3) and two docks (scale 1:3).
Bottom: Screen dump of the animation model at the TestSite. The simulation model is controlling two automated material handling stations and four AGVs.

Figure 10.6   Simulation as real-time control system

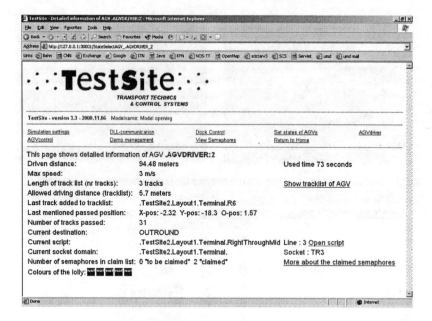

Figure 10.7   Web page as interface between user and simulation model

Using a Web page as interface between user and simulation model has a number of advantages. Web pages are easy to operate. People without any training or education in simulation are still able to operate the simulation models for the OLS Schiphol, as all commands are entered through the Web page. The simulation models themselves are hard to operate, even for people with a thorough understanding of simulation. Web pages are also highly dynamic in their content. Changes in simulation models were automatically implemented in the Web page, as the simulation models function as Web servers. The changes can be large changes in the simulation models, such as changes in the structure of the simulation model, or smaller changes like updating performance indicators during a simulation run.

10.4 CONCLUSIONS

Automated transport systems are complex systems as can be seen in the other chapters of this book. Simulation has been used many times in designing logistic and transport systems. Recent developments in simulation extend the lifecycle for simulation in the design process of future highly automated transport systems. Developments like object-oriented simulation, building blocks, (three-dimensional) animation, distributed simulation, Web-based simulation, and simulation for real-time control have strongly increased the innovative potential of simulation to adequately model complex automated transport systems.

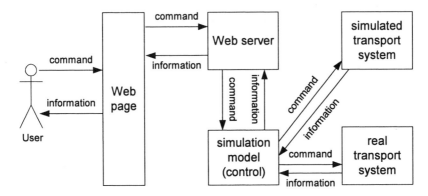

Figure 10.8   Two directions of communication using Web page as interface

NOTES

1. In the OLS Schiphol project many more variants have been evaluated.
2. Newer versions of the software are called eM-Plant.

REFERENCES

Auinger, F., M. Vorderwinkler and G. Buchtela (1999), Interface Driven Domain-independent Modelling Architecture for 'soft-commissioning' and 'reality in the loop', *Winter Simulation Conference 1999*, Phoenix: IEEE.

Balci, O. (1998), Verification, Validation, and Testing, in: Banks, J. (ed), *Handbook of simulation; Principles, methodology, advances, applications, and Practice*, New York: Wiley & Sons.

Banks, J. (ed.) (1998), *Handbook of Simulation; Principles, Methodology, Advances, Applications, and Practice*, New York: Wiley & Sons.

Banks, J., J.S. Carson and B.L. Nelson (1996), *Discrete-event System Simulation*, second edition, Englewood Cliffs, NJ: Prentice Hall.

Fujimoto, R.M. (2000), *Parallel and Distributed Simulation Systems*, New York: Wiley.

Joines, J.A. and S.D. Roberts (1998), Object-Oriented Simulation, in J. Banks (ed.), *Handbook of Simulation; Principles, Methodology, Advances, Applications, and Practice*, New York: Wiley & Sons.

Kalasky, D.R. and G.A. Levasseur (1997), Using SiMPLE++ for Improved Modeling Efficiencies and Extending Model Life Cycles, *Proceedings of the 1997 Winter Simulation Conference*, Atlanta: IEEE.

Law, A.M. and W.D. Kelton (1991), *Simulation Modeling and Analysis*, New York: McGraw-Hill.

McGregor, I. (2002), The Relationship between Simulation and Emulation, in E. Yücesan, C.H. Chen and J.M. Charnes (eds), *Proceedings of the 2002 Winter Simulation Conference*, pp. 1659–66, San Diego: IEEE.

Schiess, C. (2001), Emulation: Debug it in the Lab–Not on the Floor, *2001 Winter Simulation Conference*, Hawai: IEEE.

Shannon, R.E. (1975), *Systems Simulation; The Art and Science*, Englewood Cliffs, NJ: Prentice.

van Daalen, C., W.A.H. Thissen and A. Verbraeck (1999), Methods for the Modelling and Analysis of Alternatives. Chapter 26, in A.P. Sage and W.B. Rouse (eds), *Handbook of Systems Engineering and Management*, New York: Wiley.

Verbraeck, A. (2002), Simulation, in E. Ginters (ed.), *Logistic Information Systems, Part 2*, Riga, Latvia: Jumi, pp. 100–33.

Verbraeck, A., Y. Saanen and E. Valentin (2000), Designing Effective Terminals and their Control Systems for the Underground Logistic System Schiphol, *2nd International Symposium on Underground Freight Transportation by Capsule Pipelines and Other Tube/Tunnel Systems (ISUFT)*, Delft, The Netherlands.

Verbraeck, A. and C. Versteegt (2000), A Bridge between the Design and Implementation of Complex Transportation System; Linking Simulation Models and Physical Models, in D.P.F. Möller (ed.), *Simulation in*

Industry, Twelfth European Simulation Symposium, Hamburg, Germany, pp. 238–43.

Versteegt, C. and A. Verbraeck (2002), The Extended Use of Simulation in Evaluating Real-time Control Systems of AGVs and Automated Material Handling Systems, in E. Yücesan, C.H. Chen and J.M. Charnes (eds.), *Proceedings of the 2002 Winter Simulation Conference*, San Diego: IEEE.

Versteegt, C., A. Verbraeck and S. Geerdes (2001), Simulation as a Supporting Tool for Multidisciplinary Design of Underground Freight Transport Systems, in E. Taniguchi and R.G. Thompson (eds.), *City Logistics II, The Second International Conference on City Logistics*, Japan: Okinawa, pp. 83–97.

Vreede, G.J. and A. Verbraeck (1996), Animating Organizational Processes; Insight Eases Change, *Simulation Practice and Theory*, Vol. 4, pp. 245–63.

Zeigler, B.P., H. Praehofer and T.G. Kim (2000), *Theory of Modeling and Simulation: Integrating Discrete Event and Continuous Complex Dynamic Systems*, second edition, San Diego: Academic Press.

11. Multi-agent systems for planning and operational management

André Bos, Mathijs de Weerdt and Cees Witteveen

11.1 INTRODUCTION

Undoubtedly, information and communication technology (ICT) has a significant impact on the transportation sector. Within organizations ICT tools have been developed to support administrative and fairly complex planning processes. Between organizations, ICT enabled the automation of message passing activities such as transmitting bills of loading, invoices, manifests and the automation of financial transactions. Finally, recent developments in communication technology brought real-time tracing and tracking of cargo and vehicles, and greatly improved communication between transportation centres and drivers.

Although further developments have to be expected in all these areas, in this chapter we concentrate on the possible roles ICT can play in an area where, until now, its influence has been barely visible: ICT can also support complex inter-organizational processes and incident management processes.

We argue that in order to make significant progress in supporting these processes, we need another view on the modelling and development of software systems used to support automation in the transportation sector. Within such software systems the distributed nature of this sector should be reflected by explicitly representing organizations as autonomous decision making entities, called agents. In order to support these complex transportation processes, agents must be equipped with intelligent capabilities to (i) reason about multimodal transportation plans, and (ii) detect, isolate, and ideally predict, events that jeopardize normative plan execution.

To motivate this claim, we first present two situations in the transportation sector where these (inter-organizational and incident management) processes play a significant role. Then we discuss the current role of ICT in these situations. Thirdly, we outline a view on ICT development using multi-agent systems that is needed to achieve full support for the processes identified. Finally, we discuss some prototypes that use this view.

Current Challenges

One of the main problems in transportation is that it tends to be more and more a global activity, with requirements that no single transportation company can meet on its own. The transportation sector is confronted with the problem of how to integrate the services of different autonomous companies such that they (i) together are able to offer more complex services, but (ii) without losing their autonomy. We illustrate this problem with a generic example.

Example 1

In general, freight transport requires cooperation between companies. A single transportation request can often be realized only by splitting the task in to many sub-activities that must be executed by different parties, each having their own interest and responsibility.

The transportation process usually involves more than one mode of transportation and many interacting parties (see Figure 11.1). For example, where goods need to be transported from Europe to the US by ship, first, truck transport is required to move the goods from the shipper's location to a sea harbour. Then, the forwarder selects appropriate transportation companies. After the transportation has been planned, the different modes of transport must be coordinated. A shipbroker organizes the loading activities. The actual (un)loading is performed by a stevedore.

As can be seen, transportation of freight requires (i) administration by the different parties (often copying basic data), (ii) a high level of coordination (i.e., planning, scheduling), (iii) monitoring of the transport, and finally, in case things go wrong (iv) corrective actions.

To solve such inter-organizational coordination problems, first of all, mechanisms are required to carefully tune the individual planning processes. With the current state of technology this coordination problem can only be partially solved.[1]

Another real practical challenge is how to control the freight transportation chain in case an incident occurs. An incident affects the planned interaction between the different parties involved in the transportation process. Many different types of incident can jeopardize the planned interaction scheme.

For example, transportation resources (e.g., a truck) may break down during the process, or transportation equipment may experience serious delays (e.g., a traffic jam), or orders may change or get cancelled. The consequence of an incident is that one of the assumptions underlying the planned construction process is violated. This may render the coordination scheme invalid, e.g., due to a traffic jam a truck arrives too late at the airport.

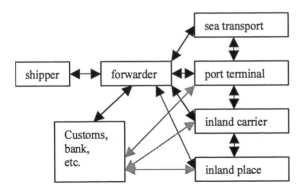

Figure 11.1   Example of party interactions

In such a case, all parties in the transportation chain affected by the incident must be promptly informed about the consequences. Not only must it quickly be recognized that the current plan does not meet the required objectives, but also corrective actions must be determined and communicated to the parties of interest. As it is mostly the case that remedial actions must be thought up under severe time constraints, transporters are forced to build a sufficient amount of slack into their plans to guarantee robust operations. Therefore, a second major challenge for the transportation community is to provide the operational flexibility to deal with these incidents.

As a second example where this need for robustness of operations and the support of ICT in incident management processes are essential, we focus on the management of Automated Guided Vehicles (AGVs).

Example 2

Nowadays, AGV systems are unmanned transportation systems executing a planned sequence of control actions. As the control actions are pre-computed, the process generating the actions (i.e., the planner) must make a number of simplifying assumptions about the AGV and its environment. For example, the planner must assume that the environment basically stays in the same (health) condition. Using current commercial off-the-shelf technology it is, however, almost impossible for the controller to account for all kinds of failures that might possibly happen in the infrastructure. This means that when something actually does go wrong (either in the infrastructure or in the AGV itself), the sequence of (pre-computed) control actions is no longer adequate, and manual interaction is required.

Where many AGVs are involved, this mode of manual interaction becomes very inefficient. Therefore, more autonomous control systems are required that take into account the actual state of AGV itself, the infrastructure, and other AGVs that may help to realize the transport objectives. That is, in order to reach these levels of autonomy, agents must be equipped with a capability that is able to detect, or ideally predict, failures, and isolate the root cause of failure such that correct remedial actions can be executed.

As we remarked in the beginning, the current state of the art of ICT in transportation is focusing mainly on the automation of controllable, transparent and relatively stable business and transportation processes. Undoubtedly, within an organization, tools such as EDI, ERP and workflow systems are suitable to support well-defined and routine tasks. These tools, however, are less suitable in frequently changing environments and environments where global controllability of processes is difficult or almost impossible to realize. It is not surprising, therefore, that the automation of inter-organizational coordination processes and incident management is still in its infancy and usually restricted to the automation of data sharing and exchange.

Before we present an overview of the approaches needed to solve the problems mentioned above, we first analyse some of the key problems that have to be solved in order to automate the initiation and maintenance of inter-organizational coordination and incident management processes.

11.2 ICT IN FREIGHT TRANSPORTATION

Referring to Examples 1 and 2 above, we distinguish four main processes that have to be supported in order to prepare and execute coordinated robust transportation services. ICT support for data handling and planning is already quite advanced. However, for managing incidents and coordinating inter-organizational transportation tasks, more advanced techniques are required.

Basic Data-handling Processes

Modern transportation requires multiple parties. Each of these parties requires a separate record of the transactions performed, and, as a consequence, information has to be copied from one form to another. So, first of all, support for administrative basic data-handling processes is needed.

Since manual copying of information is tedious and error prone, and to speed up the transportation process, the concept of Electronic Data Interchange (EDI) has been introduced. Although similar to electronic mail, an EDI message is highly structured. Using these structures, computer programs are able to interpret and 'understand' the message (to a certain extent, of course). For example, the supplier name on an invoice message can be automatically recognized and used for further processing in the administrative chain.

Universal standards for structured documents and data on the web such as XML and RDF are recent developments in EDI that add flexibility both to the data that can be exchanged and to the type of network required (e.g., enabling ad-hoc networking.

Other systems that have become popular are the so-called ERP (Enterprise Resource Planning) systems to coordinate the basic functions of an enterprise. An ERP system does not only maintain the actual status of, e.g., the inventory of an enterprise, but also allows a manager to project the effects of resource usage on the state of the enterprise. These kinds of analyses are prime prerequisites to realize robust control and coordination of the transportation process. In general, however, no mechanism exists that warns a planner about the possibly negative consequences of one of his decisions.

Planning and Scheduling

Many transportation problems can be modelled as well-understood combinatorial resource allocation problems, where a planner has to assign transportation means to tasks in order to realize an order in the most profitable way. Unfortunately, these planning and scheduling problems are notoriously difficult to solve optimally. Therefore, often (human) planners are content whenever they find a feasible solution; they cannot afford the time to find a best solution. Things become even worse if changing conditions during the planning process have to be recognized, such as in the case of no-shows: clients that have reserved a place on a freighter, but do not manage to deliver on time, causing the freighter to be loaded uneconomically.[2]

The role of ICT here is the construction and application of automated planners to generate and evaluate candidate solutions to logistic problems.

Typically, current automated planning systems are able to reduce transport costs by 10–20% and significantly reduce delivery lead times compared to manual transportation planning. But, even computers have difficulties solving these problems. The reason for this is that the number of possible candidates is so enormous for real-life applications that even the fastest computers will have serious difficulties solving realistic instances of these problems in a reasonable time.

Monitoring and Incident Management

Due to the advent of new electronics and communication equipment (satellite communication, mobile phone, chip cards), the process of tracing and tracking is becoming widely accepted. Many transportation companies now offer their clients the opportunity to monitor the status of their goods in the transportation process. Consequently, currently the various players are now given the sensory information needed to effectively control the transportation chain once something goes wrong. However, there is hardly any ICT-support available to actually derive the true root cause of the delay, and to construct remedial actions in case of an incident.

This is the result of a number of reasons. First, just like solving transportation problems under normal conditions, computing remedial actions is computationally a very hard problem, especially as one has to take additional operational constraints into account, e.g., transporters are reluctant to break a commitment made to a customer.

Secondly, often an integral model of the whole transportation process is lacking. This results in a situation where the various applications involved are not able to communicate the remedial actions efficiently.

Coordination and Cooperation

Usually, transportation companies cooperating and executing multimodal transportation tasks are independently operating organizations with their own private mission, policies and planning capabilities. These companies only want to cooperate because they cannot complete the accepted orders independently.

Consider for example the multimodal transportation case, mentioned in the first example. In the simplest set-up, the transportation order is split up into a number of parts that have to be dealt with by a simple chain of different transportation companies. As a result, each of the companies receives a transportation request it has to handle on its own and can make a plan for. But since each of these requests forms a part of a single transportation order, the companies are also dependent on each other. Now they face the following problem: as autonomous organizations they would like to propose an optimal plan for their part of the order. Due to the inter-dependencies, however, most of the time they have to compromise and choose a sub-optimal plan.

Clearly, the solution to these inter-organizational coordination problems requires a common set of agreements to start with and a fair negotiation scheme to reach a solution that is satisfactory for all the parties involved. Currently, there is little or no ICT support for this kind of process.

Note that, even if the companies are able to plan their part of the job independently, they might profit from support for inter-organizational processes. Since their plans are likely to contain overlap for different orders, they might profit from a process called plan merging. Here, the individual plans of each of the parties involved are inspected to see if overlap can be removed, in order to come up with a more profitable plan. However, the autonomy of the cooperating parties prevents other parties having access to all the details of individual transportation plans.

Although the state of the art in ICT allows a transportation company to perform a large number of analyses about the consequences of their decisions or changes in the environment, there is currently no facility that truly thinks ahead for the designer, so that potential problem areas can be identified as soon as possible. In short, what is needed is active support for a human planner by investigating the possible actions given the actual state of the environment.

11.3 MULTI-AGENT SOLUTIONS

In the previous section we concluded that especially with respect to inter-organizational coordination and incident management, ICT support is still in its infancy. In order to make progress here we argue that another view on systems and their software modelling is needed. From our analysis of the processes that are required for inter-organizational coordination, it turns out that we at least need to make a careful distinction between the distributive nature of the systems involved, the restrictions on the capabilities they have, and their autonomy, that is the ability of systems to recognize their own goals and means to realize them. It is the last feature especially that requires a new approach to constructing software systems.

Surely, in ICT there is experience in modelling and designing distributive systems. Additionally, the modelling of systems with diverse capabilities is dealt with in, e.g., the popular object-oriented approach. The autonomy of the systems (organizations), however, creates an additional layer of complexity. Although a system for a specific organization might act rationally and predictably with respect to its own goals and plans, i.e., locally, this rationality might not be directly visible to other systems (organizations). As a consequence, systems cannot predict each other's behaviour.

The traditional view on software systems does not take into account such careful distinctions as have been made between the autonomy and distributivity of systems. Multi-agent technology, however, does. The study and modelling of multi-agent systems is called Distributed Artificial Intelligence (DAI) (Bond and Gasser 1988). Multi-agent systems are 'systems in which several interacting, intelligent agents pursue some set of goals or perform some set of tasks' (Weiß 1999). An agent is an autonomous problem solver (Wooldridge and Jennings 1995), i.e., a transport company or sometimes a transportation unit.

Coordinating the actions of several autonomous transport companies requires several multi-agent techniques. First, changes should be dealt with quickly. The theory on reactive agents (Maes 1990) describes how to have a direct mapping from a specific situation to a course of action to be taken. For more elaborate decisions the beliefs, desires and intentions (BDI) of an agent may need to be modelled more explicitly (Bratman et al. 1988).

Secondly, an agent (i.e., a software program representing a company) needs to be able to communicate with other agents. For this purpose several agent languages have been developed, such as Speech Acts (Searle 1970), KQML (Finin and Fritzson 1994), and, more recently, the FIPA Agent Communication Language (FIPA 2001).

Finally, to coordinate the activities of several transport companies these activities need to be planned. The methods to support this process, called multi-agent planning, have a very high impact on the overall performance of these companies. In the remainder of this section we focus on these multi-agent planning techniques. First, a brief overview of multi-agent planning techniques is given. Then, one of these techniques that can be used to improve pre-existing plans is presented in more detail. At the end of this section we describe how these techniques might be used in the two examples given in the first section.

Multi-agent Planning

In this section, we concentrate on the application of multi-agent technology in coordination and operational control problems. In particular, we argue that these problems can be considered as aspects of multi-agent planning problems, where each agent represents a specific organization.

In coordination problems, complex orders are split into several subtasks handed over to different agents. Each agent is therefore confronted with the problem of organizing a particular phase of a transport request. This can be considered a planning problem as well: find a sequence of actions including the required resources that will bring a good from A to B.

Secondly, an incident management process uses information about the changed environment to adapt a pre-existing plan in order to avoid any potential conflicts that might otherwise occur. Therefore, we look at a number of multi-agent planning techniques to deal with both coordination and incident management problems.

Centralized planning for multiple agents
If companies agree to share all their knowledge and plans, planning problems can be solved in a traditional centralistic way. In this case, a trusted (third) party, using a centralized algorithm, constructs an overall plan for the organizations involved. On the one hand, in order to coordinate the individual parts of this plan, the trusted party must be free to use any of the agents' information. Hence, it is not possible for an agent to keep details of its plan secret from such a third party. On the other hand, the fact that all information is available allows for the use of specific optimization techniques. In principle it is possible to calculate the best solution, given enough time.

Implicit distributed planning

It is not always necessary, or even desirable, for agents actually to send their plans to a trusted third party to ensure that no conflicts arise upon the execution of these plans. Instead, we may also assume that an agent knows how to react whenever a conflict arises. That is, an agent is equipped with a set of so-called social laws that can be applied in a conflict situation.

Typical examples of social laws are traffic rules: as everyone drives on the right side of the road, virtually no coordination with oncoming cars is required.[3] Generally, solutions found using social laws are not optimal, but they may be found relatively fast.

Unfortunately, not all conflicts can be prevented by using laws and regulations. Auctions are a method to solve conflicting interests for, e.g., scarce resources. Also auctions and even complete market models can be used to coordinate agents' plans without (costly) explicit communication of parts of plans.

For a given resource each agent usually has a different use, and therefore attaches a different value to such a resource. An auction is a way to make sure that a resource is given (sold) to the agent that attaches the highest value to it (Walsh et al. 2000, Wellman et al. 2001). A Vickrey (1961) auction is an example of an auction protocol that is quite often used. In a Vickrey auction each agent can make one (closed) bid, and the resource is assigned to the highest bidder for the price of the second-highest bidder. This auction has some nice properties such as that bidding agents are stimulated to bid their true private value (i.e., they do not cheat).

Market simulations and economics can also be used to distribute large quantities of resources among agents (Wellman 1998). The basic principle of such markets is that with more demand the price increases, and with more supply the price decreases. For example, Clearwater (1996) showed how costs and money are turned into a coordination device. Auctions and markets can be used both to allocate resources and to assign tasks. Hoen et al. (2002) showed that in a dynamic environment much better results can sometimes be obtained if agents are allowed to change such allocations.

In the context of such value-oriented environments, game-theoretical approaches where agents also reason about the cost of their decision-making become more important. An overview of value-oriented methods to coordinating agents is given by Fischer et al. (1998).

Explicit distributed planning

Methods that explicitly coordinate the plans of agents without a trusted party are called explicit distributed planning methods (Mali and Kambhampati 1999). We distinguish three types of distributed planning methods: partial global planning (PGP) methods (Durfee 1988) describe how information on an agent's plan can be re-distributed over the other agents in such a way that the other agents are able to synchronize their actions with each other.

Hierarchical planning methods assume that plans can be represented as a hierarchy, and that this ordering can be used to determine and to resolve conflicts between agents. Plan-merging methods specify how independently created plans can be merged.

In the PGP-framework (Durfee and Lesser 1987), each agent has a partial picture of the plans. Coordination is achieved by a process of negotiation. When an agent informs another of a portion of its plan, the other agent merges this information into his own partial global plan. He then tries to improve the global plan by, for example, eliminating redundancy. Such an improved plan is shown to other agents, who can accept, reject or modify it. This process is assumed to run in parallel with the execution of the (first part of the) local plan. This method has been applied to a distributed vehicle monitoring test-bed (Decker and Lesser 1992).

An alternative approach to plan coordination uses a natural ordering in the form of a hierarchy to guide the distributed planning process (von Martial 1992). The construction of such a hierarchy by domain experts can take quite some time, but planning using such a structured database of rules turns out to work quite well for, e.g., the planning of military operations (Wilkins and Desimone 1994). If possible, relations are solved or exploited at the top level; if this is not possible, a plan is refined and the process is repeated. For applications where privacy is not really important, and where all the individual agents tend to have similar problems, these approaches are quite useful, since hierarchical plans are especially suited to re-using and exchanging parts of plans. However, these methods are not really suited to solving more general multi-agent planning problems where agents need to be autonomous and independent.

Plan Merging

The principal idea behind plan merging is that agents can improve the efficiency of their plan by using partial results (resources) from the plans of other agents (Ephrati and Rosenschein 1997, de Weerdt et al. 2003). For example, a company that has to transport freight to Italy can cooperate with another company that has to get freight from somewhere in Italy back to Holland.

The plan merging process consists of a series of exchanges of such resources in an auction-like process. One of the agents, or a trusted third party, acts as the auctioneer. All agents deposit requests with this auctioneer. Each request corresponds to the removal of an action a from an agent's plan and contains a set of resources, such as spare capacity in a truck, which the agent needs in order to remove the action a. Furthermore, the request contains a cost reduction value defined by the difference in costs between the old plan and the resulting plan if the exchange succeeds. The (greedy) auctioneer deals with the request with the highest potential cost reduction first.

Just before each auction round starts, the requesting agent a_i is asked for the specific set of resource facts that has to be replaced by resource facts of other agents – this set is called the request set *Rs*. If for each resource in *Rs* a replacement can be found, the auctioneer tells the requesting agent a_i that it may discard the corresponding action(s). The replacing resources *R'* are marked as goals for the providing agents, and become additional 'available' resources for agent a_i. The plan-merging algorithm we have developed is an any-time algorithm, because it can be stopped at any moment.[4] If the algorithm is stopped, it still produces an improved set of agent plans, because this algorithm used a greedy policy, i.e., dealing with the requests with the largest potential cost reduction first. This algorithm has a quadratic time complexity:

Plan-merging algorithm

1. Auctioneer broadcasts minimum allowed cost reduction.
2. Auctioneer retrieves requests with their cost reduction from all agents A.
3. While some requests left do
    3.1. Get the request with the highest cost reduction.
    3.2. Ask the requesting agent a_i for the required resource facts Rs.
    3.3. for each $a_j \in A \backslash \{a_i\}$
        3.3.1. Ask agent a_j for free resource facts compatible to resource facts in *Rs*.
        3.3.2. Add these resource facts to *R'*.
    3.4 if *R'* contains *Rs*
        3.4.1. Let *R''* be the cheapest subset of *R'* that satisfies *Rs*.
        3.4.2. Add for each $r \in Rs$ the corresponding dependency to *R''*.
        3.4.3. Remove as many actions as possible from a_i.
        3.4.4. For each agent involved, update the cost reduction of all requests.

We have implemented the algorithm and used a realistic data set to test its performance and usability. In this case, we used a data set of orders as executed by a taxi company, but the algorithm can be used in a similar way to deal with the planning of trucks instead of taxis.

In this domain we assume that the cost of a plan equals the distance driven by the taxis. Consequently, our goal is to reduce this distance by exchanging orders among taxis. For these tests we simulated the coordination of a set of companies, i.e., agents, that each have only one taxi. For each run we store the total distance driven by the taxis, before and after the plan-merging algorithm. In Figure 11.2 the difference between these values is plotted against the number of actions. As can be seen, more relaxed time constraints on the arrival time of the passengers (*t* minutes) lead to more improvement. Furthermore, the total improvement seems linear in the number of actions. The relative improvement in drive distance (as a percentage) is given in Table 11.1.

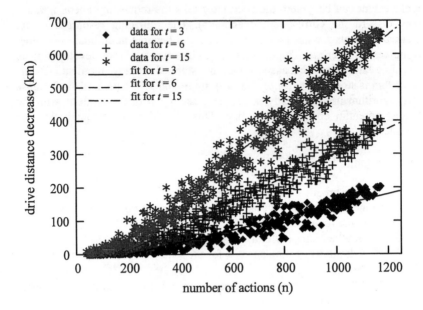

Figure 11.2   *The improvement in drive distance versus the number of actions*

As these results show, a 10% reduction in plan costs can be obtained by applying plan merging. We should mention that improving plan costs also results in an increase in travel time for the passengers. This increase, however, is acceptable.

Table 11.1   *The reduction of the drive distance, increase in passenger travel time and the standard deviations of these results for three values of t*

t	Reduction distance (%)	Standard deviation	Increase in travel time (%)	Standard deviation
3	2.97	1.75	5.53	3.85
6	6.77	3.10	10.36	5.77
15	13.01	4.46	22.56	10.31

Applying Multi-agent Technology

Some of these techniques can be used to solve the problems given in the previous section.

Inter-organizational coordination

For example, the coordination problem is about constructing joint plans to reach the goals of the companies. To tackle the coordination problem of the first example, we could use a plan-merging technique if each agent has already constructed its own plan. When the agents need to construct their plans cooperatively, we could use a market or an auction at each step of the planning algorithm.

To deal with incident management problems, however, a system of pure planning agents is not sufficient. At least, the agent system must be extended with monitoring capabilities that recognize plan execution failure, isolate the underlying problem, and find alternatives to keep the transportation chain going (Cox et al. 2001).

Incident handling of AGVs

In general, an incident affects the correct execution of a plan, and as a consequence remedial actions must be determined to guarantee satisfaction of the transport request. For example, we would prefer the control of highly autonomous (AGV) transportation systems to be without (or with limited) interference of a human operator. These AGV systems must remain active even in situations when part of the system breaks down. In order to fulfil this requirement, the control system must be able to reconfigure the internal structure of the AGV system to compensate for failure. As a consequence, the control system must infer the actual state of health of the components before a new plan can be generated that includes the reconfigured structure. Currently, this technology has been successfully applied in a flying demonstrator of a deep space probe (Muscettola et al. 1998).

The main problem in deriving the state of health is that the parameters (which the control agent is particularly interested in) cannot be observed directly. Especially with the advent of increasingly complex systems, estimating the state of health becomes very difficult. Therefore, an autonomous agent must in general be equipped with a so-called diagnosis system. A diagnosis system monitors how the system reacts to the inputs given to the system under scrutiny. In case of a failure, such a system tells the control agent which of the system components is at fault, based on the discrepancy between expected and observed behaviour.

Information about the root cause of failure is used to reconfigure, using inherent redundancy, the AGV system such that the transportation goals are satisfied as well as possible, although some loss in performance may be inevitable (e.g., the AGV must operate at reduced speed). It is possible to derive a reconfiguration using a process akin to planning and using the same physical model of the AGV used for the diagnosis process. An example of such a system can be found in Williams and Nayak (1996).

11.4 MULTI-AGENT TOOLS AND SYSTEMS

To apply the multi-agent solutions from the previous section to solve some of the coordination problems of transport companies, some additional support is welcome, because standard development tools lack support for developing multi-agent systems. Ideally, a developer should concentrate on the domain-specific problem solving abilities of the agents (e.g., planning or incident-handling), and not on problems that could be solved by generic means (e.g., distributed communication between agents). A multi-agent toolkit should support an open design to ensure extendibility, and standardized technology should be used whenever possible. Unfortunately, the penetration rate of the use of these tools is currently not very high, and although some standard protocols have been developed, often people tend to follow their own design. Therefore, in many situations, many different tools are used, or even developed on the spot. Currently, there are numerous tools, libraries and development environments, all for basically the same purpose.[5]

For the transportation domain, however, no tool is currently available that can help a software developer in all aspects. Two of the more well-known (multi-)agent general development tools and environments are ZEUS, and FIPA-OS (for a more detailed discussion see the report by Mangina (2002)).

The basic idea underlying the ZEUS (1997) project was to create a relatively general purpose and customizable, collaborative agent building toolkit that could be used by software engineers with only basic competence in agent technology to create functional multi-agent systems. The ZEUS toolkit consists of a set of components, written in the Java programming language, which can be categorized into three functional groups (or libraries). These are an agent component library, an agent building tool and a suite of utility agents comprising name server, facilitator and visualizing agents.

The FIPA-OS toolkit (FIPA 1997) by Nortel Networks is probably currently the most well-used set of components to construct a multi-agent system. FIPA-OS is named after the organization for standards for agents and agent protocols: the Foundation for Intelligent Physical Agents, and is based upon the specifications given by this foundation. The most important of these specifications concern the agent communication protocol and language, and the multi-agent infrastructure.

A prototype that is aimed at inter-organizational project management is the Cooperative Services Framework (Anderton et al. 1995). This tool supports Computer Supported Cooperative Work (CWCW) between organizations using agent technology. Currently, however, this framework does not support the planning of complex (transportation) tasks, and it still needs to be extended in order to perform incident management as well.

The Border Trade Facilititation System (BTFS) is a system specifically designed to support the information exchange and the monitoring of the transshipment of goods across the US–Mexico border (Goldsmith et al. 1998). Although this system does not support the planning of these tasks either, and the management of incidents is still limited to monitoring unexpected events, it still shows some of the advantages of using multi-agent technology to implement a system for inter-organizational coordination.

Finally, as another example of a prototype developed, we mention the Teletruck system (Funk et al. 1999, Bürckert et al. 1998) as a software system for intermodal transportation based on multi-agent technology. This system has been developed at DFKI in Germany as part of the Platform RTD project on intermodal transport. In Teletruck, haulage companies and their means of transportation are modelled as autonomous agents with local knowledge and abilities. Customer orders are assigned to agents by means of an (auction-like) negotiation process. Agents representing transportation resources place bids that take into account the vehicle's local cost function. The resulting assignment can be further improved at a later stage by the use of dynamic any-time algorithms thereby reducing empty rides and off-the-road time.

11.5 DISCUSSION

This chapter started with a number of requirements with respect to ICT support needed for the modern transportation problems. In particular, we discussed the issues of coordination of different transportation parties, monitoring and incident handling.

In our exposition, multi-agent systems and a plan representation of the behaviour of an agent played an important role. Many transportation problems can be reformulated as special planning problems whose solution requires complex operations on these plan representations.

Nowadays, automation of administration and planning has been introduced in most companies involved in transport. Recently, communication between companies is also being automated, due to EDI and the Internet. However, further automation can help to improve the efficiency of transport, by tackling two major issues. First, for the most part, the inter-organizational coordination and planning of transport is done manually, but people cannot usually cope with the complexity of this problem, and come up with feasible, but far from optimal, solutions. Secondly, on incidents, people often react far too slowly, and, again have trouble with complexity. We propose to introduce diagnosis and incident management systems capable of reacting immediately and adequately to incidents.

It must be admitted that, at the moment, this technology is still in its infancy and multi-agent systems cannot be used as a ready-made solution to real coordination problems. However, a couple of prototypes and tools show that, despite its infancy, multi-agent technology can play a significant role in solving modern transportation problems. Multi-agent systems help to implement incident management systems, and to support the coordinated planning of transport.

NOTES

1. For example, if all the parties involved are willing to share all their knowledge.
2. One way to improve the inefficiencies somewhat, is to better advertise that space is available on a certain route. The Internet is a very popular medium for publishing this kind of information, and a number of initiatives have recently been launched such as FreeCargo (1999), TimoCom (1999), Bid Freight Global (2000), and Trade-a-load (2002), to name a few.
3. Note that it is arbitrary on which side of the road one drives, as long as everyone does the same.
4. An any-time algorithm produces correct results even if it is interrupted during execution.
5. See http://www.agentlink.org/resources/agent-software.php for a list of agent tools by AgentLink.

REFERENCES

Anderton, M., J. Cunningham and J. Pitt (1995), A Framework for Multi-agent Inter-organizational Applications: A Position Paper, in Victor Lesser (ed.), *Proceedings of the First International Conference on Multi-Agent Systems*, San Francisco, CA: AAAI Press, p. 435.

Bid Freight Global (2000), Transportation Exchange, http://www.bidfreight.com/.

Bond, A.H. and L. Gasser (eds.) (1988), *Readings in Distributed Artificial Intelligence*, San Mateo, CA: Morgan Kaufmann Publishers.

Bratman, M.E., D.J. Israel and M.E. Pollack (1988), Plans and Resource-bound Practical Reasoning, *Computational Intelligence*, Vol. 4, no. 4, pp. 349–55.

British Telecom (1997), Zeus, http://www.labs.bt.com/projects/agents/zeus/.

Bürckert, H.-J., K. Fischer and G. Vierke (1998), Transportation Scheduling with Holonic MAS – The Teletruck Approach, in H.S. Nwana and D.T. Ndumu (eds.), *Proceedings of the Third International Conference on Practical Applications of Intelligent Agents and Multi-agents, London: The Practical Application Company Ltd.*

Clearwater, S. (1996), *Market-Base Control – A paradigm for distributed resource allocation*, Singapore: World Scientific Publishing Co.

Cox, J.S., B.C. Clement, P.M. Pappachan and E.H. Durfee (2001), Integrating Multi-agent Coordination with Reactive Plan Execution, *Proceedings of the ACM Conference on Autonomous Agents*, New York: ACM Press.

Decker, K.S. and V.R. Lesser (1992), Generalizing the Partial Global Planning Algorithm, *International Journal of Intelligent and Cooperative Information Systems*, Vol. 1, no. 2, pp. 319–46.

de Weerdt, M.M., A. Bos, J.F.M. Tonino and C. Witteveen (2003), A Resource Logic for Multi-agent Plan Merging, *Annals of Mathematics and Artificial Intelligence*, special issue on Computational Logic in Multi-agent Systems, Vol. 37, nos. 1–2, pp. 93–130.

Durfee, E.H. (1988), *Coordination of Distributed Problem Solvers*, Dordrecht, The Netherlands: Kluwer Academic Publishers.

Durfee, E.H. and V.R. Lesser (1987), Planning Coordinated Actions in Dynamic Domains, *Proceedings of the DARPA Knowledge-Based Planning Workshop*, Austin: University of Austin, pp. 18.1–18.10.

Ephrati, E. and J.S. Rosenschein (1997), A Heuristic Technique for Multi-agent Planning, *Annals of Mathematics and Artificial Intelligence*, Vol. 20, nos.1–4, Dordrecht: Kluwer Academic Publishers, pp. 13–67.

Finin, T. and R. Fritzson (1994), KQML – A Language and Protocol for Knowledge and Information Exchange, *Proceedings of the Thirteenth International Workshop on Distributed Artificial Intelligence*, Vol. 890 of Lecture Notes on Artificial Intelligence, Seattle, Washington USA: Springer Verlag, pp. 126–36.

FIPA (1997), Fipa-os. http://www.nortelnetworks.com/fipa-os.

FIPA (2001), FIPA Communicative Act Library Specification, Technical Report XC00037 and others, FIPA – Foundation for Intelligent Physical Agents. http://www.fipa.org.

Fischer, K., C. Ruß and G. Vierke (1998), Decision Theory and Coordination in Multi-Agent Systems, Technical Report RR-98-02, DFKI GmbH: German Research Center for Artificial Intelligence.

FreeCargo (1999), Road Haulage Freight Exchange for European Transport Companies. http://www.freecargo.co.uk/.

Funk, P., G. Vierke and H.-J. Bürckert (1999), A Multi-agent Systems Perspective on Intermodal Transport Chains, in E. Erkens (ed.), *Proceedings of the Conference on Logistik Management*, New York: Springer Verlag.

Goldsmith, S.Y., L.R. Phillips and S.V. Spiref (1998), A Multi-agent System for Coordinating International Shipping, *Agents '98 workshop on Agent Mediated Electronic Trading*.

Hoen, P.J. 't, D.D.B. van Bragt and J.A. La Poutré (2002), Bidding with Decommitment in a Multi-agent Transportation Model. Technical Report SEN-R0220, Centrum voor Wiskunde en Informatica, Amsterdam, The Netherlands.

Maes, P. (1990), *Designing Autonomous Agents*, Amsterdam, The Netherlands: Elsevier Science Publishers.

Mali, A.D. and S. Kambhampati (1999), Distributed Planning, in *The Encyclopaedia of Distributed Computing*, Dordrecht, The Netherlands: Kluwer Academic Publishers.

Mangina, E. (2002), Review of Software Products for Multi-Agent Systems, Technical Report, AgentLink.

Muscettola, N., P. Nayak, B. Pell and B. Williams (1998), Remote Agent: To Boldly Go Where No AI System has Gone Before, *Artificial Intelligence*, Vol. 103, nos.1–2, pp. 5–47.

Searle, J.R. (1970), *Speech Acts: An Essay in the Philosophy of Language*, Cambridge, UK: Cambridge University Press.

TimoCom (1999), Timocom Truck and Cargo, European-Wide Load Space and Freight Database, http://www.timocom.de/.

Trade-a-load (2002), Boat Load Exchange: Trade a Load and Save Money, http://www.absolutelynautical.com/tradeaload.html.

Vickrey, W. (1961), Computer Speculation, Auctions, and Competitive Sealed Tenders, *Journal of Finance*, Vol. 16, pp. 8–37.

von Martial, F. (1992), *Coordinating Plans of Autonomous Agents*, Vol. 610 of *Lecture Notes on Artificial Intelligence*, Berlin: Springer Verlag.

Walsh, W.E., M.P. Wellman and F. Ygge (2000), Combinatorial Auctions for Supply Chain Formation, *Second ACM Conference on Electronic Commerce*, New York: ACM, pp. 260–9.

Weiß, G. (ed.) (1999), *Multiagent Systems: A Modern Approach to Distributed Artificial Intelligence*, San Francisco, CA: The MIT Press.

Wellman, M.P. (1998), Market-aware Agents for a Multiagent World, *Robotics and Autonomous Systems*, Vol. 24, pp. 115–25.

Wellman, M.P., W.E. Walsh, P.R. Wurman and J.K. MacKie-Mason (2001), Auction Protocols for Decentralized Scheduling. *Games and Economic Behavior*, Vol. 35, nos. 1–2, pp. 271–303.

Wilkins, D.E. and R.V. Desimone (1994), Applying an AI Planner to Military Operations Planning, in M. Fox and M. Zweben (eds.), *Intelligent Scheduling*, San Mateo, CA: Morgan Kaufmann Publishers, pp. 685–709.

Williams, B. and P. Nayak (1996), A Model-based Approach to Reactive Self-configuring Systems, in *Proceedings of the Thirteenth National Conference on Artificial Intelligence*, Menlo Park, CA: AAAI Press, pp. 971-8.

Wooldridge, M.J. and N.R. Jennings (1995), Intelligent Agents: Theory and Practice, *The Knowledge Engineering Review*, Vol. 10, no. 2, pp. 115–52.

ZEUS (1997), see: British Telecom.

12. Evaluation of automated freight transport systems

Joy Dahlgren

12.1 INTRODUCTION

Some sort of evaluation precedes implementation of any transportation system. Some evaluations are careful analyses of all effects of the system, both intended and unintended. Some are cursory affairs based more on wishful thinking than hard fact. Some are designed to promote particular projects. A recent study found that many large public works projects are not objectively evaluated prior to being implemented – costs are underestimated and revenues and benefits overestimated (Flyvbjerg et al. 2002). Such evaluations may result in wasteful and ineffective projects that in the long run may reduce support for similar, more worthwhile, projects. People wishing to serve the public interest will want to perform fair and careful evaluations that take into account all of the effects of the new system on providers, users, and society in general, and that provide the most accurate information possible regarding the benefits and costs of the system.

Post-implementation evaluation is extremely useful as a means to provide information for future pre-implementation evaluations. But because the implementation of many new systems often does not go smoothly because of lack of experience with such systems and unforeseen problems and delays, the evaluation process must be somewhat long-term and open ended. The object is not to evaluate the skill of the implementers but to assess the potential benefits and costs of the system, to determine how best to deploy such systems, and to determine the physical and economic environment to which they are best suited. What costs were not foreseen? What intended benefits did not materialize? What unexpected benefits were realized? What are good implementation strategies? What characteristics of the environment in which it is implemented contribute to its success or failure? How do the post-implementation benefits and costs compare with the pre-implementation estimates? In what ways are they different, and why? Given the great value of the information gained from post-implementation evaluations, governments and other investors in automated freight systems should build post-implementation evaluation into project implementation plans and budgets.

Both pre- and post-implementation evaluations should be based on the extent to which the benefits of such investments exceed their costs. This is a simple concept. But there are a number of complexities in its application.

First, it is important to determine any unintended consequences of the investment and include them in the analysis. For example, will the operation of an underground transport system have a negative effect on underground utilities? Will vibrations or strong electrical currents affect underground water or electrical lines? Second, are some of the measures difficult to quantify or to value? What should be done if the effects are uncertain? What if people disagree about the importance of different effects? Also, how should alternative designs of an automated freight system be handled?

The purpose of this chapter is to examine these and other complexities and provide methods for addressing them. It will focus on a benefit–cost evaluation framework. The rationale for this is that although automated freight systems are complex and their effects are many, the criteria by which they should be evaluated are rather straightforward. The primary purpose is to reduce costs of transport, and these are relatively well known and methods have been developed for valuing most of the non-monetary costs, such as accidents. Sensitivity analyses can be used to deal with differences in valuation and uncertainty.

We begin by examining the nature of the most commonly discussed automated freight systems in order to understand their cost elements and how they interface with the existing freight system. This is followed by a discussion of the benefits and costs of transportation systems, a discussion of the purposes of evaluation, and then a listing of the components of the evaluation and methods for dealing with each.

Automated Freight Systems

The most common characteristic of automated freight systems is the absence of a human operator on the transport vehicle. Another characteristic common to most systems is increased computer control of routing and scheduling of vehicles once they are in the automated system.

The most mature automated system design is the pipeline. In widespread use for transporting fluid cargo, the pipeline concept for transporting packaged cargo has been used by the London mail since 1927, and for transporting small capsules within buildings using pneumatic pressure since the 19th century. Now, motivated by congested roads and streets in urban areas and the high cost and political infeasibility of expanding surface streets and roads, as well as improved tunnelling technology and electronic control, there is renewed interest in automated underground transportation. Most proposed designs involve a pipeline (tunnel), electronic control of vehicle movement within the pipeline, and electro-magnetic propulsion. But the pipeline diameters, vehicle speeds, methods for loading vehicles and terminal designs vary considerably. Tunnel construction is quite different from surface or elevated construction. Most urban areas have a complicated network of underground utilities and transportation facilities that must be either moved or avoided. The potential effects of the movement of freight through the tunnels on the existing utilities must be considered. Of course, as with any pipeline, it can be located above ground as well as below ground. Maintenance of tunnels is different than for surface or elevated pipelines because they are less accessible. Breakdowns within a tunnel pose more serious problems than on the surface, suggesting that a higher level of maintenance and sensing would be needed within a tunnel than on the surface.

The function of the terminals is the same as any terminal, but the form, and consequently the cost, will be highly dependent on the size of the vehicles and the proximity of terminals to destinations.

One proposed project is the OLS-ASH system, which would transport aircraft cargo containers and pallets and flower carts at a speed up to 6 metres/second (13 miles per hour) between the flower auction in Aalsmeer, the Schiphol airport and the Hoofddorp rail station in the Netherlands. Another is the proposed Tubexpress, which would move freight in 4 by 4 by 25 foot capsules through 6.5 foot diameter pipes at 18 miles per hour.

Another proposed system, Autran, would utilize elevated guideways to transport an automobile, a small passenger cabin, a medium-sized freight container or one large intermodal freight container. The CargoRail system would use elevated guideways over existing highway or rail rights of way to transport standard 20 to 40 foot land–sea containers or truck trailers, or loaded truck tractors at speeds of 75 miles per hour.

The TRAIL Research School has proposed a hybrid truck–rail system in the Rotterdam area (Evers 2001). Vehicles could operate on either rail or road. On the track they would operate automatically; on the road they would operate manually, automatically, or semi-automatically with a series of unmanned vehicles following a manned vehicle. An important feature is 'dynamic booking' whereby road space is reserved and paid for via a computerized allocation system that determines space availability, reserves space, and charges for space based on the level of demand and the user's adherence to the reserved time.

A system of self-propelled freight wagons operating on a rail network combined with driverless train operation has been proposed in Germany.

In the United States, PATH and the California Department of Transportation have been exploring automated truck operation on special truck-only lanes.

All automated modes promise reduced vehicle operator costs, reduced congestion on existing roadways, reduced vehicle emissions, and more reliable transport times. But they generally require increased control costs and terminal costs, at least relative to the existing truck mode. By concentrating traffic at the terminals they may introduce additional congestion and delay in the vicinity of the terminals. To accurately evaluate costs and benefits, the location, design, and operating characteristics of the terminal must be specified in considerable detail.

Benefits and Costs of Freight Transport

To provide a context for the discussion of the benefits and costs of automated freight transport systems, this section discusses the benefits and costs of freight transport in general and to whom they accrue.

Benefits

The benefit of shipping is the increase in value of goods that results from moving them from one location to another at which they have more value. Shipping allows producers to access more markets for raw materials, thus increasing the variety and complexity of products they can efficiently produce in a particular location. Shipping of finished goods expands producers' markets and consumers' choice. In both cases this leads to a more efficient allocation of resources and potentially increased production and wealth. Reduced shipping costs may result in lower costs for goods, which will result in more goods being sold and shipped.

Secondary benefits arise from the direct or indirect use of the goods transported. They are captured to some extent by what the users of the system pay to use the service, but the value of the service will usually exceed what the users must pay.

Costs

The shippers' costs are what is paid to the carrier[1] to cover carrier costs and profit, as well as the inventory cost of the goods during shipment. The inventory cost depends on the time elapsed during shipment and any damage to the goods during shipment. What the shippers pay the carriers represents a benefit to the carriers. If it is included as a shipper cost in the analysis, it should also be included as a carrier benefit. Its importance lies in how it affects the distribution of benefits and costs between shippers and carriers.

The private carriers' costs include the capital costs of facilities and vehicles, and operating and maintenance costs. Governments may participate in the provision of transportation infrastructure and services when these are shared by several carriers or when the infrastructure and services have significant external costs or benefits. There are capital, operating and maintenance costs associated with these facilities and services.

Freight transport imposes various costs on the community at large. These include the delay that freight transport vehicles impose on other vehicles, delay and damage caused by accidents related to transport vehicles or their cargo, emissions of pollutants and greenhouse gases, environmental damage due to cargo and fuel spills, wear on roads and bridges, and environmental damage caused by the construction, manufacture, and disposal of freight transport infrastructure, vehicles, and fuels. There may also be disruption of communities related to the construction of transport facilities.

12.2   PURPOSES OF EVALUATION

Evaluation is used to inform decisions, so the purposes of evaluation reflect the types of decisions that must be made. In developing an automated freight system there will be many decisions. Is it worth pursuing this type of automation? Where does such automation make sense? What type of automation would be best in a particular situation? Where should the automated system connect with the existing system? What types of vehicle would be best? Given the optimum design for a particular automated system, would it be better to shift to the automated system now or to continue with or improve the current system? Many of these decisions relate to system design and will not require an elaborate benefit–cost analysis, but they should be subject to the same kind of analytical process as the larger questions regarding which type of system to use or whether to implement an automated system at all. Post-implementation evaluation informs a broad range of future decisions on other projects including the types of benefits and costs that can be expected. These may differ from the benefits usually associated with conventional freight transportation. Travel times may be more reliable, requiring less buffer time and cargo storage. Costs for system control software maintenance will be higher because the control systems will be more complex.

12.3   ELEMENTS OF BENEFIT–COST ANALYSIS FOR EVALUATING PLANNED AUTOMATED FREIGHT TRANSPORT SYSTEMS

The tasks involved in benefit–cost analysis are listed below, roughly in the order in which they are first undertaken. The evaluation process does not occur in a strictly linear fashion, however, because new information or considerations may arise at each step of the evaluation. The decision to implement an automated freight system will involve multiple analyses of varying complexity. The elements listed below apply to the most complex analysis, the comparison of a particular automated freight system to other systems and the base case, but most also apply to the much less complex evaluations of various components of the systems. Each of the elements below will be discussed in detail later in this chapter.

1.   Identify the intended benefits and to whom they will accrue.
2.   Establish the point of view of the analysis. Will the decision be made on the basis of the benefits and costs to a private firm or on the basis of benefits and costs to society as a whole?
3.   Determine a base case against which alternatives will be compared.
4.   Specify the alternative automated system designs.
5.   Determine the scope of the systems.
6.   Select a discount rate for discounting future benefits and costs.
7.   Establish the time period for the analysis.
8.   Identify the costs and other effects of the alternatives (other than the benefits identified in 1) that are different from those of the base case.
9.   Determine the type of comparison to be made.
10.   Identify each organization and group of people who will be affected by the automated system and specify whose benefits and costs will be considered in the evaluation.
11.   Quantify and monetize the benefits, costs, and other effects of each alternative relative to the base case.
12.   Identify sources of uncertainty.
13.   Compare alternatives to the base case in terms of the type of comparison selected in 9.
14.   Assess the impacts on each group identified in 10.
15.   Conduct sensitivity analyses for various types of uncertainty and values of effects.
16.   Present the results of the evaluation.

1. Identify intended benefits of automated freight system
The primary benefit being sought by automation of freight transport is reduced transport costs. Transport costs that might be reduced by automation fall into the following categories:

- Government agency, private firm, or carrier costs for capital, operations, and maintenance of transport facilities including roads, tunnels, guideways, terminals, communications systems, and control systems;
- Carrier costs for capital, operations, and maintenance of transport vehicles;
- Carrier and shipper costs related to cargo damage;
- Shipper inventory costs during transport and at terminals;
- Costs of accidents involving freight;
- Costs of road delay to other users of the road system;

- Environmental costs, such as emissions, fuel or cargo spills, noise, and environmental damage due to the production or disposal of transport vehicles and facilities.

Another rationale for automated freight transport is economic development. To the extent that transport costs are reduced there may be secondary economic benefits, such as increased shipping and production due to lower shipping costs. However, these benefits are difficult to estimate; and since the system that results in the lowest transport cost also results in the most goods being shipped, this effect will not influence the ranking of alternatives in terms of net social benefits.

Even with the best possible analysis, the uncertainties related to implementing an automated freight transport system may be so significant that it is impossible to evaluate without some sort of field test. An additional benefit of implementation of a limited scale automated freight system is that knowledge is gained that can inform future system design and decisions regarding further deployment of such systems.

In comparing components of the automated system to achieve the best design, the evaluation will usually involve only a small subset of the above costs – only those that differ between alternate components.

Double counting of benefits should be avoided by checking all of the benefits to make sure that nothing in one category is also included in another. For example, if the reduction in road delay includes the reduction due to fewer truck accidents, then the savings from reduced truck accidents should not include the savings in delay.

2. Establish the point of view of the analysis

The benefits and costs to be considered will depend on the organization making the decision to implement an automated freight system. If the decision is being made by a private firm, it will be made primarily on the basis of the costs and benefits to the private firm. This does not mean that the costs and benefits to shippers or society as a whole will not matter. The benefits to shippers will be the basis for what they are willing to pay for the service. The benefits and costs to society as a whole will influence whether the necessary permits can be obtained and whether a government subsidy will be made available.

If the decision is being made by a government agency, then the decision should be made on the basis of all of the benefits and costs that accrue to firms and individuals governed by that agency.

3. Determine base case

Generally the base case is the current system, sometimes called the 'no build' alternative. But often underlying conditions, such as traffic congestion or demand for freight transport, are expected to change. Or new regulations may come into effect that would require a modification of current operations. In such cases a hypothetical base case that represents the manual system operating in these changed circumstances is often used. It is important that the assumptions regarding the underlying conditions are the same for the base case and all alternatives.

In comparing alternative components for an automated system one component alternative can be considered the base and the others compared to it. Any differences in their other effects or how they connect to the rest of the system must be accounted for in the analysis.

4.   Specify alternative automated system designs to be evaluated

The alternatives must be specified in sufficient detail that benefits and costs can be determined. Before the alternatives are compared to the base case, each should be refined so that it represents the optimum for that particular design alternative. The process for selecting designs and components should be a simpler version of the same evaluation process used for evaluating the entire system.

Alternative schedules for development of the various components of the automated system can also be compared. This might be a consideration if the system was being developed to serve an industrial area that was also under development, or if one component could be developed much faster than another. Here, the primary differences would be in the timing of the benefits and costs.

5.   Determine the scope of systems

The base case and alternatives to be evaluated should all have the same geographic scope. If two alternate automated systems meet the manual system at different locations, then the part of the manual system between the less extensive and more extensive automated system should be included in the less extensive automated system in order to obtain a valid comparison of the services. Also, costs related to the system interfaces must not be overlooked.

An extensive ultimate system may be envisioned, but with the idea that it would be deployed in stages. If the decision to be made is whether or not to build the whole system, then the scope of the evaluation should be the whole system. However, if the decision is only whether to build the first stage without a commitment to build the entire system, the scope could be only the first stage. Alternatively, a classic decision analysis approach might be used to estimate the expected cost of the first stage as a probability-weighted sum of the first stage alone and the first stage share of the costs of the whole system, should the whole system be built.

6. Select a discount rate

Because costs and benefits are compared based on their present value, they should be discounted to account for the ability of resources to produce wealth over time. This is an easy concept to grasp in terms of money. If one spends money now rather than in five years one loses the interest that would have been paid on that money during the five years as a result of its productive value. So a cost five years from now is less than a cost today. Similarly, a benefit in the future is worth less than a benefit today. The future costs and benefits to which the discount rate is applied should be expressed in constant dollars, euros or other currency, not including any future inflation. The discount rate will depend upon the point of view of the decision maker. If the decision is being made by a private firm, the discount rate should be the rate that could be obtained if the funds were invested elsewhere, but with no inflation component because it will be applied to benefits and costs expressed in constant dollars, euros, or other currency. If the decision is being made by a government, the rate should be the value of the funds if used for another government service, the true interest rate without the risk component. The US Office of Management and Budget (http://www.whitehouse.gov/omb/circulars/a094/a94_appx-c.html) recommended the following real interest rates in December 2002:

- 3 years   2.1
- 5 years   2.8
- 7 years   3.0
- 10 years   3.1
- 30 years   3.9

Of course, interest rates reflect the productive value of the funds. In a period of recession, there is less demand for funds, and so the interest rate is lower.

The present value of a dollar of cost or benefit n years in the future is $(1 + d)^{-n}$ where d is the discount rate.

7. Establish the time period for the analysis

The system is generally evaluated over the time during which it is expected to operate utilizing the initial capital investment. Benefits and costs too far in the future are very uncertain and are so heavily discounted that they have little effect on the outcome of the analysis. For example, a benefit worth 1 euro in 30 years is currently worth only 0.31 euros if the discount rate is 3.9%. If technologies were changing rapidly, the time period for analysis would be the time until obsolescence, rather than until replacement.

8.   Identify the costs and effects of the automated alternatives that differ from those of the base case

The only costs and other effects that need to be considered when alternate investments are compared are those that differ between alternatives. One approach to identifying these is to review the functions of the freight system and determine where they differ. Among these functions are:

- Booking and tracking of cargo;
- Sorting cargo;
- Loading cargo;
- Transporting cargo;
- Unloading cargo;
- Cargo storage;
- Facility construction;
- Operation of facilities;
- Operation of vehicles;
- Maintenance of facilities;
- Maintenance of vehicles.

In estimating the costs of these functions the following cost categories should be considered:

1.   Costs borne by the infrastructure provider, carriers, or shippers
   a.   Land and rights-of-way;
   b.   Materials;
   c.   Labour;
   d.   Purchased services;
   e.   Purchased components;
   f.   Energy;
   g.   Communications;
   h.   Interest;
   i.   Cargo inventory cost;
   j.   Risks of accidents to cargo or people employed by the infrastructure provider and carrier;
   k.   Taxes.[2]
2.   External costs borne by society at large
   a.   Emissions of air and water pollutants;
   b.   Greenhouse gas emissions;
   c.   Increased congestion;
   d.   Noise;
   e.   Risks of accidents to the public at large.

At the same time the organization or people who will bear these costs should be identified.

There may be other unintended effects that do not fit into the realm of costs. For example, continuous tracking of cargo might be a feature of an automated freight system but not the current system. This type of benefit should be taken into account.

9. Determine the type of comparison to be made

There are a number of ways to compare benefits to cost: the ratio of benefits to costs, benefits minus costs (net present value), the benefits that can be obtained for a particular cost or the cost required to achieve a particular benefit (cost-effectiveness), and the rate of return the benefits represent on the costs of the system (internal rate of return). The most appropriate way depends on the circumstances. For example, if a given amount of money is available, the benefits that can be achieved with that amount of money can be compared. On the other hand, if a given benefit is desired, the costs required to achieve that benefit can be compared. This approach is especially useful if the benefits are measurable but not easily monetized or valued. Most often the comparisons are between several alternatives with different costs and benefits, so the ratio of benefits to costs is most useful.

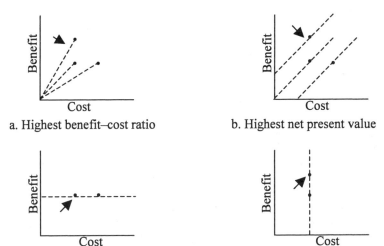

a. Highest benefit–cost ratio   b. Highest net present value

c. Lowest cost for a given benefit   d. Greatest benefit for a given cost

Figure 12.1   Graphs of benefit–cost comparisons

A useful tool for comparing projects is to plot the various projects on a graph with the benefits on the vertical axis and the costs on the horizontal axis. Figure 12.1 shows graphs of various types of benefit–cost comparisons.

Figure 12.1a. illustrates the use of the benefit–cost ratio. The slope of the line between the origin and the point representing the project is the benefit-cost ratio. The projects with the steepest slopes have the highest ratio of benefits to costs. All projects with slopes greater than 1 have benefits that exceed their costs. In this particular graph, only one project has benefits that exceed its cost.

Figure 12.1b. illustrates the use of the net present value, which is the y intercept of a 45° line drawn through the point. Only projects with a positive y intercept have benefits that exceed their costs; in this case only one project meets this standard, the one that also has the highest benefit–cost ratio. However, it is possible to have a set of alternate projects such that the one with the highest benefit–cost ratio does not have the highest net present value. This might result if projects being compared were of significantly different scale.

Of course, if funding is limited, projects with costs above the funding limit are not feasible even if their benefit–cost ratio or net present value is higher than those for other projects.

Figure 12.1c. illustrates the selection of the project with the lowest cost for a given benefit. The project furthest to the left on a horizontal line through the benefit value on the vertical axis has the lowest cost. Conversely, the project with the highest benefit for a given cost is the one located highest on a vertical line through the cost measure on the horizontal axis, as shown in Figure 12.1d. However, in either case only a project with benefits that exceed its costs should be pursued.

10. Identify organizations and groups of people who will be affected by the automated system and whose benefits and costs will be considered in the evaluation

The process of identification can begin with the benefits and costs. To whom does each accrue? There are the owners, operators and users of the automated freight infrastructure as well as the owners, operators and users of the current system. In addition, there are the other people who will be impacted by the automated system and are being impacted by the current system. If public funding is involved, there are taxpayers. If private funding is involved there are the people and organizations that provide the financing. Whose benefits and costs will be considered in the evaluation?

This process will show who may stand to lose by automation. These people and groups are likely to oppose the project. Finding a way to compensate them may be the key to gaining the necessary political and financial support for the project.

11. Quantify and monetize the benefits and costs of each alternative relative to the base case

A key benefit of an automated freight system would be the resulting reduction in total shipping costs. This cost reduction might result from lower charges by the carrier or from an improved service that reduced average travel time, travel time variation, or damage to freight. A second benefit would be the increase in value of the additional freight that would be shipped as a result of the lower costs. The provider(s) of the automated freight system would probably also enjoy a benefit.

To estimate these, the consumer surplus (in this case the shipper surplus)[3] can be estimated. First, one can begin by estimating the capital costs for each alternative and the per unit operating costs, including the required return on investment. This produces a total cost for each level of use, and from this the marginal cost of each additional unit can be derived. This marginal cost curve can be added (horizontally) to the existing supply curve to create a new supply curve. The relevant portion of the existing supply curve can be estimated from the current level of shipping and anything known about how freight volumes responded to changes in demand in the past. Similarly estimating the demand curve can begin with the current level of shipping and anything known about how the volume of shipping has responded to changes in the supply of shipping in the past. From these, the current demand curve, over the relevant shipping cost and demand range, can be estimated. The relevant portions of the demand and supply curves can be plotted, as shown in Figure 12.2. If freight volumes are expected to change over time because of exogenous economic factors unrelated to shipping costs, then the current demand curve can be shifted an appropriate distance to the right as shown in Figure 12.2. Here, the base case becomes the costs of the current system with the increased future demand. The same process can be used to estimate the benefits of adding conventional freight capacity.

The initial benefit of the automated freight system for existing shippers will be the reduction in price from P to P'. The benefit to the new shippers will be the area of the triangle formed by the demand D, the horizontal line from P' and the vertical line from Q. This represents the consumer surplus for the new shippers: the excess of their benefits over their costs. When the demand increases to D_{future} the price and quantity will both increase to the values at which future demand crosses the new supply, P'' and Q''. However, here the increase in consumer surplus is based on future demand. This construct can be used to estimate the current and future benefits of adding an automated freight system.

Inflation in future years can be ignored because both demand and supply are affected approximately equally by inflation.

Most of the effects of the automated freight system are cost savings, which are already in monetary terms. However, some of the effects are not measured in monetary terms and thus must be converted to monetary terms.

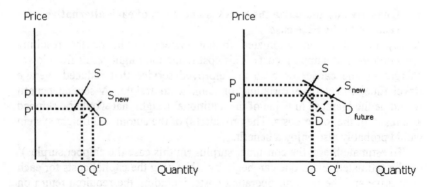

Figure 12.2   Benefits of reduced shipping costs

One such effect might be reduced accidents. Once the changes in the number of injuries or deaths, or the amount of property damage, have been estimated, they must be monetized. Fortunately, the monetary value of accidents has already been analysed. The 1997 publication Transportation Research Circular 477 gives the following range of values in 1996 dollars:

> Death $1.2–2.9 million.
> Injury $24–83 thousand.
> Property damage $2,000.

If there is environmental damage, it may be valued in terms of the cost of remediation or the extent to which it diminishes the value of property or a particular resource as determined by appraisals of similar cases. It can also be valued by what people would be willing to pay to prevent the damage. There is likely to be some difference of opinion regardless of how its value is estimated. Sensitivity analyses should also be used to account for differences in these values.

12. Identify sources of uncertainty
The most important uncertainty is the extent to which the system will be used. This depends on future economic conditions. Also, in implementing a new type of system there is no experience to guide people in identifying all the challenges that will be encountered and therefore it is likely that the cost and time required to implement the project will be underestimated. The developments in the non-automated system will also affect the cost differential. There may be environmental effects and social implications that cannot be foreseen. Thinking of these in terms of economic theory, the supply curve is uncertain, and the demand curve is uncertain, and these uncertainties interact.

Therefore, it is important to estimate demand in terms of a band rather than a curve. Supply, too, should be thought of in terms of a band. Figure 12.3 shows the possible range in outcomes given a particular set of uncertainties.

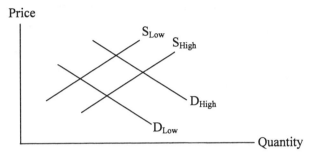

Figure 12.3   Range of outcomes under uncertainty

The space above the horizontal price line to the left of the demand curve represents the excess of benefits over costs, the consumer surplus. Of course, the entire demand curve will not be known, so the entire consumer surplus cannot be estimated. But this does not matter because only the difference in consumer surplus between the existing system and the automated system is being estimated, as was discussed in the previous section. This difference would be largest for the D_{High}, S_{High} case, in which there is high demand and low costs. Conversely, it would be smallest for the D_{Low}, S_{Low} case. The amount could fall anywhere between. This region can be broken into as many subregions as the analyst likes and each assigned a likelihood of occurring. Then the average benefit–cost ratio or net present value for each region can be calculated and then weighted by the probability of the outcome being in this region to yield an expected benefit–cost ratio or net present value.

13. Compare alternatives to the base case

The comparison of alternatives using any of the methods of comparison discussed in section 9 can be done with any spreadsheet software. Consider first the comparison of an automated freight system with the base system. These are the steps:

1. List all benefits and costs for the automated freight system that differ from the base system, the years in which they occur, their quantities and their unit monetary value if the units of benefit are not monetary. Use the most likely values. Later a sensitivity analysis can be used to determine how sensitive the outcome of the evaluation is to these values. If the base system differs from the current system, make sure that the costs and

benefits used represent the difference between the automated system and the base system, not the current system.

2. To calculate either the net present value or the benefit–cost ratio, set up a spreadsheet with the benefits and cost in each year, discount the benefits and costs using the selected discount rate and sum them over the period of analysis. Use the sums of benefits and costs to calculate the net present value or the benefit–cost ratio.

3. Alternatively, or in addition to these other types of comparisons, the internal rate of return can be calculated. Instead of using a pre-specified discount rate, the discount rate that results in the sum of the discounted benefits equalling the discounted costs is found. This can be easily done on a spreadsheet.

One way to set up the spreadsheet for calculating the net present value or benefit–cost ratio is to list the benefits and costs vertically on the sheet. Across the top of the sheet are the years included in the period of analysis with the amount of benefit, its monetary value per unit if it is not a monetary benefit, the discount to be applied for each year, and the discounted monetary value. In year n, the discount to be applied is $(1 + d)^{-n}$ for discount rate d. This discounted monetary value will be the product of the amount of benefit, the value per unit of benefit, and the discount. The discounted monetary value of benefits and costs for each year are summed horizontally. Then the benefits and costs are summed vertically.

The most worthwhile projects will have large positive net present values, benefit–cost ratios substantially greater than 1, or internal rates of return comparable with, or exceeding, other investments considered worthwhile.

The same setup can be used to compare the costs of achieving a particular benefit. In this case there would be no benefits columns. Similarly, to compare the benefits that can be achieved for a given cost, only the benefits need be considered.

The process for comparing system components is the same. One component considered is the base case. The costs and benefits of the alternate components are expressed in relation to the base component. Some components may not last for the entire period of analysis. In such cases their replacement must be accounted for.

14. Assess the impacts on organizations and groups of people who will be affected by the automated system

If the project appears to be worthwhile, repeat the analysis described above for each of the organizations and groups of people identified earlier, substituting the benefits and costs experienced by each for the total benefits and costs. This will yield the same comparison measure used above for each organization or group. If there are losers, measures can be considered to compensate them in some way.

15. Conduct sensitivity analyses to account for uncertainties and differences in valuing outcomes

Consider the types of uncertainties discussed above and set some bounds on the range of various benefits and costs. Also consider the values that different groups may place on the non-monetary benefits and costs. Then repeat the initial analysis using different values in the spreadsheet. This type of analysis will be simpler if the spreadsheet is set up so that the values are listed at the top of the sheet, and when changed, are automatically changed everywhere in the sheet.

16. Present the results of the evaluation

The presentation depends on the audience. In most cases there will be multiple audiences interested in varying levels of detail. The least detailed presentation should present the benefits and costs over the period of analysis, perhaps in graphical form. There should be some indication of the level of uncertainty, perhaps confidence bands on a graph or worst-case and best-case scenarios. The base case and alternate systems should be clearly described, including their geographic scope and the nature of the interface with the existing system. Some indication should be given of how different organizations and groups of people will be affected.

There should be a well-organized report describing each step of the analysis, how it was done, what assumptions were made, and why. The spreadsheets should be available in both paper and electronic form so that further analysis can easily be done if a decision should be made to evaluate an additional alternative.

12.4 EVALUATING IMPLEMENTED AUTOMATED FREIGHT SYSTEMS

The evaluation of implemented systems is similar to the evaluation of planned systems, except that actual benefits and costs are used and the period of analysis is shorter because the evaluation will probably be done several years before the system needs to be replaced or becomes obsolete, so it will not capture the benefits and costs in later years and may not reflect the performance for the entire period. However, these can be estimated based on performance to date.

Before implementation begins, the costs and benefits of the existing system should be measured to provide a base case for the evaluation. Methods should be devised and procedures set up to capture costs and benefits of the new system as it is implemented.

If a project was evaluated when it was being planned, then the benefits and costs for the period since its implementation began can be compared to those estimated in the planning phase. This should indicate how it will ultimately perform relative to the initial evaluation.

The object of post-implementation evaluation should not be primarily to judge the value of a particular implementation, but rather to provide information for evaluating systems planned in the future. The goal should be knowledge, and evaluations should have the widest distribution possible among people to whom they could be useful.

12.5 CONCLUSIONS

A well-planned and executed evaluation can be a vital tool in the decision whether or not to pursue an automated freight system. If the evaluation shows a substantial excess of benefits over costs it can be very useful in convincing decision makers of the value of the investment. If there are differences of opinion regarding the assumptions made in the analysis, these can be modified and the analysis easily repeated to see how changes in the assumptions affect the benefits and costs.

If the evaluation shows no or only a marginal excess, it can become a tool for looking for design modifications that would make the system more viable or for suggesting locations in which the system might be more cost-effective.

Any automated freight system involves a very substantial investment. The resources devoted to evaluation will pay substantial rewards either in gaining approval for a worthwhile project or in preventing an investment that is not worthwhile.

NOTES

1. The shipper and carrier are the same in cases where firms supply their own transportation.
2. Taxes will generally represent only a transfer from a private party to the government. If the analysis is being done from the point of view of the government, taxes could be ignored except for their effect on who bears the costs.
3. Because demand is summed horizontally, the consumer surplus represents the amount that consumers are willing to pay beyond what they actually pay.

REFERENCES

Print publications

Evers, J.J.M. (2001), *Intelligent Road-rail-hybrid Transport: Concepts and the Logistic Betuwe Corridor*, Delft: TRAIL Research School.

Flyvbjerg, B., M.S. Holm and S. Buhl (2002), Underestimating Costs in Public Works Projects: Error or Lie? *Journal of the American Planning Association*, Vol. 68, no. 3, pp. 279–96.

Friedman, L.S. (1984), *Microeconomic Policy Analysis*, New York: McGraw-Hill Book Company.

Gillen, D., J. Li, J. Dahlgren and E. Chang (1999), *Assessing the Benefits and Costs of ITS Projects: Volume 1 Methodology and Volume 2 An Application to Electronic Toll Collection*, California PATH Research Reports UCB-ITS-PRR-99-9 and 10, Berkeley: University of California.

Misener, J.A. and M.A. Miller (2002), Show Me the Benefits: A Truck and Bus Demonstration in 2003, in *Proceedings of the Ninth World Congress on ITS,* Chicago.

Siegmann, J. and S. Heidmeier (2002), New Quality of Service in Rail by Using self-propelled Freight Wagons.

Web Publications

Autran Automated Transport Systems , http://autrancorp.com
Capsule Pipelines, http://www.capsu.org
The CargoCap System, http://www.cargocap.de/html_en/system_01.html
Evacuated Tube Transport, http://www.et3.com/faq.htm
FROG Navigation Systems, http://www.frog.nl/end/cargo/menu.html
Magplane: Transportation for the Information Age,
    http://www.magplane.com/html/pipe.htm
MegaRail Transportation Systems,
    http://www.megarail.com/CagoRail_Heavy_Cargo
TUBEXPRESS, http://www.tubexpress.com/

PART III

Automated freight transport: implementation
issues

13. Financing and deploying automated freight systems

David Levinson and Xi Zou

13.1 INTRODUCTION

Efficient and flexible transport services advance economic growth and enhance competitiveness in the international market. Currently, however, traffic is growing faster than capacity (FHWA 2002). Increasing congestion prevents traditional transport modes from meeting the growing demand from shippers for reliable, inexpensive, fast, and flexible transport services. Moreover, heavily congested roadways are a major source of pollution. New technologies, such as advanced traffic management and traveler information systems, are developing slowly, and lag behind the pressing needs for transport improvements. Systematic innovation, developing new compatible but advanced transport modes, provides an alternative solution.

Typically, 15% to 25% of product cost reflects the expense of transport, inventory, warehousing, packaging, and material handling (Bowersox et al. 1999). Major automobile manufacturers, such as Ford and General Motors, spend more than $3 billion per year on freight transport (Coyle 1994).

Time compression, customer satisfaction, asset productivity, organizational re-engineering, and outsourcing all affect the demand for transport (Coyle 1994). Further, e-business has created new demand for freight transport. It has been said that more than 150,000 people are running their home-based business using the online auction site EBay (Reuter 2003). Transactions and the accompanying shipments are generated every second. These developments rely on timely shipment and delivery service. The increasing demand for effective freight transport is both a challenge and an opportunity for transport service providers. More and more small packages swarm to carriers, while the demand from conventional bulk shippers remains. The resolution of this challenge stems not only from the innovation of operating strategies, but also from the application of new technologies. Automated freight systems (AFS), which apply advanced technologies in computing, sensing, and communications to construct a highly efficient and safe transport system, include the following major components (FTAM 2002):

- New terminal technology for multi-modal freight transport;
- Modularized vehicle and traffic control;
- Intelligent vehicle and control system;
- Intelligent infrastructure;
- New logistic strategies for matching service and transport capacity.

Compared with conventional freight systems, the development of each of these components needs to change both hardware (the physical infrastructure and vehicles) and software (the policies, rules, and controls that govern transport). But the whole new system must remain compatible with existing networks because:

- The configuration of packages from shippers will not change significantly;
- The international standard container sizes that we input into the new AFS will remain, otherwise an increase in repackaging costs will be required;
- The conventional transport system will continue to exist.

Based on these constraints, the deployment of any AFS concept should be examined carefully to verify its feasibility and economic efficiency.

AFS heralds Intelligent Transport Systems. But compared to advanced passenger transport systems, AFS has some advantages. Passenger comfort is not an issue in freight transport. The allocation of travel time and delay in transport will not annoy package shippers in the same way that travelers get irritated. There are fewer safety issues among packages. Thus the carriers are freer to handle the system.

It is believed that, compared with conventional freight transport, AFS will improve cost effectiveness, enhance system reliability, reduce energy consumption, reduce delivery times, ensure all-weather delivery and around-the-clock service, ensure cargo security, reduce air and noise pollution, and consume less land (Roop et al. 2000). The issue is whether those benefits outweigh the costs, and who receives the benefits and costs. This chapter explores sources of financing for deploying AFS.

While there are many ideas about the future of the freight transport system, few of them are original. Many are just innovations or reinventions of old or even obsolete ideas. In this chapter we address three types of AFS: Pipeline, Rail, and Truck.

Automated Pipeline Systems (APS)

'I suppose so,' said Edith, 'but of course we have never known any other way. But, Mr. West, you must not fail to ask father to take you to the central warehouse some day, where they receive the orders from the different sample houses all over the city and parcel out and send the goods to their destinations. He took me there not long ago, and it was a wonderful sight. The system is certainly perfect; for example, over yonder in that sort of cage is the dispatching clerk. The orders, as they are taken by the different departments in the store, are sent by transmitters to him. His assistants sort them and enclose each class in a carrier-box by itself. The dispatching clerk has a dozen pneumatic transmitters before him answering to the general classes of goods, each communicating with the corresponding department at the warehouse. He drops the box of orders into the tube it calls for, and in a few moments later it drops on the proper desk in the warehouse, together with all the orders of the same sort from the other sample stores. The orders are read over, recorded, and sent to be filled, like lightning. The filling I thought the most interesting part. Bales of cloth are placed on spindles and turned by machinery, and the cutter, who also has a machine, works right through one bale after another till exhausted, when another man takes his place; and it is the same with those who fill the orders in any other staple. The packages are then delivered by larger tubes to the city districts, and thence distributed to the houses. You may understand how quickly it is all done when I tell you that my order will probably be at home sooner than I could have carried it from here.' (Edward Bellamy (1887), *Looking Backward: 2000–1887* (chapter 10, p. 106))

As suggested by Bellamy (1887), pipeline transport has long been the technology of the future. Each type of pipeline: slurry, pneumatic, and capsule pipeline, has a different history, characteristic, and status (Liu 2002). The slurry pipeline transmits liquefied oil, coal and other mining products; the pneumatic pipeline is mainly used to transport city waste; the pneumatic capsule pipeline is widely used in transporting parcel and bank documents over a short range (Liu 2002). APS originates with ideas dated from as early as the first century. Modern APS are still based on capsule pipelines. The major differences are in the propulsion system. Many advanced technologies have been proposed, from renovated pneumatic propulsion to the linear induction motor. Pipelines powered by linear-synchronous machines can carry freight capsules with higher efficiency and lower noise and pollution than trucking and rail systems. Meanwhile, tunneling technology has matured enough to build underground pipelines in an efficient and economical way. All these achievements make the automated pipeline systems technically feasible. Companies, such as Capsule Pipelines, CargoCap, Evacuated Tube Transport (ET3 Tube), Frog Cargo, Magplane Pipeline Transport, Pipenet, and TubeXpress have proposed or begun to implement initial systems.

Pipelines can be built underground in most places (at less cost than underground highways or railroads), which minimizes environmental impacts. The size of vehicles is physically limited by the diameter of the pipeline. Pipelines are a textbook example of economies of scale, because when the diameter of pipe increases, the pipe cost increases less than proportionally, the construction cost increases proportionally, and the capacity increases exponentially (Braeutigam 1999).

Automated Rail Systems (ARS)

Self-propelled rail cars have been around almost as long as the railroad itself, and are in wide use in passenger travel. Combining this with automation gives ARS. In automated rail systems, containers or vehicles are loaded onto carrier vehicles that, powered by their own electric motors, can move at high speed along a fixed guideway. Companies like Autran, MagneMotion's MagneTrak and MegaRail have proposed systems. While the AFS of this sort looks like a light rail system, unlike conventional rail where a fleet of trains operate according to schedule, ARS provides one vehicle for each load and can respond quickly to changing demands.

Automated Truck Systems (ATS)

> Nothing seems more certain than that many special highways will be constructed for motor trucking. (Editorial, *Roads and Streets*, 1928).

Automated truck systems can be seen as a special version of automated highway systems (AHS) for commercial vehicles. Separating trucks and cars is hardly a new idea, yet despite being suggested over 75 years ago, there must be difficulties or it would already have been done. An increasing number of trucks worsens traffic and generates serious accidents. Therefore screening trucks out of passenger traffic seems a reasonable solution. However, it is far easier to realize an automated system on rail tracks than roads, as control (steering) is simplified.

Trucking companies want to increase fleet safety and reliability of shipments. The cost of automated equipment is a smaller share of the cost of a truck than of a passenger vehicle. In this AFS concept, trucks operating in a dedicated lane are equipped with advanced control systems that cause trucks to follow the roadway and keep a safe spacing between each other, while running at high speed. The intelligence in the infrastructure communicates with the trucks to maintain the safe operation and implement control strategies.

Comparison

By comparing these concepts, it is obvious that the framework of Automated Freight Systems contains innovations in many transport modes. To study its deployment, we must not only investigate the characteristics of each single mode, but also understand their roles and impacts for intermodal transport systems. The rest of this chapter will concentrate on the financing and deployment issues of AFS. However, it should be noted that these two issues are highly correlated. Every deployment scheme can only be configured if financial resources are organized for capital and operating expenditures;

while every financing scheme depends on the relationship of actors responsible for deployment.

13.2 FINANCING

Current funding systems for general transport systems may serve as models for AHS and AFS, though there are differences in the proportion of contributions from public and private sectors.

Roadway systems are traditionally funded by general funds from federal and local government and the Highway Trust Fund. The revenue from tolls, user fees, and gas taxes are direct financing resources, as are the direct investment from private enterprises. For roadway improvement systems like ATS, automobile users' taxes and public transport subsidies could remain dominant sources for capital investment. However, funds from the private sector may become more and more important in that the operation of ATS entails higher expenses than traditional systems.

Funds for traditional freight railway systems are mainly private, though government often contributes right-of-way in the form of land, whose increase in value provides revenue to the railroad as land developer. Local government often contributes in urban railway improvements, especially for consolidation of rail yards in return for the redevelopment of the reclaimed area. For ARS, similar resources will be available, though cross-subsidies from automobile users' taxes contained in public subsidies for urban transit are less likely to be available. There is no fixed scheme that determines the allocation of the burdens of public and private financing resources in ATS and ARS. But private investment or private–public partnership for managing mixed financing resources are increasingly recognized as promising approaches in face of the constrained availability of public funding.

Current pipeline systems are mainly financed by the private sector because most of them are just for freight transport. This situation may make the transition to the APS smoother than for the other two AFS systems. For APS, the allocation of burdens will lean toward the private sector because less land is required. Subsides from federal and local government may be in the form of favorable tax policies and other indirect instruments.

Financing depends on beneficiaries. It is an accepted practice to associate costs with beneficiaries. It seems obvious that the companies who use AFS benefit from it; otherwise they would not use it. Users of conventional transport modes may benefit from reduced traffic. Society benefits from reduced negative externalities.

Rationales for Government Support

Garrison and Levinson (2005) summarized reasons for government intervention in the transport sector. Some of those reasons apply to financing AFS.

First, existing technologies have a large advantage in that they have already achieved economies of scale. A new technology may eventually be more cost effective, but isn't initially due to high fixed costs (network construction, new technology development) and low demand. A new industry requires maturation before the economies of scale are realized, and thus requires subsidy (from patient capitalists or the government) in its early years. While this argument is certainly true to some extent, the degree depends on circumstances, and the appropriate response depends on the confidence that one has in the industry. Further, government support here should be seen more as a loan than a grant.

Second, government support can be seen to fit the requirements of upfront investment of Social Overhead Capital (SOC). The government may act as a 'door-opener' to support the industrial development of the economy (Baum and Schulz 2000). The potential of AFS for increasing productivity in both the newly developed freight system and the conventional transport systems may justify government support. This economic development argument is often used in transportation, yet is even harder to quantify than the economies of scale argument.

Third, there is the externality argument of Pigou. Negative externalities should be internalized by taxes and positive externalities should be internalized by subsidies. Government subsidies, as instruments of intervention, can improve the optimal use of resources when there are market failures. To achieve the reduction in externalities, we have several options: (a) properly internalize those external costs everywhere in the transport sector, (b) subsidize the reduction of those negative externalities, or (c) some combination of the two. Ideally, in a first-best world, we would do (a). But since we haven't done (a), we can conclude that we live in a second-best world, and our next best option is (c), or failing that, (b). This justifies subsidies on an externality argument. But we must be careful not to double count and both tax the externality and subsidize its removal. We choose the subsidy only when the first best choice, taxing the externality, is politically infeasible.

We have a social demand curve higher than private demand (see Figure 13.1) because the new technologies will presumably reduce the negative externalities produced by conventional technology (Rothengatter 2001). Without subsidies, the social demand curve D^*, which is higher than the market demand curve D, is not achieved.

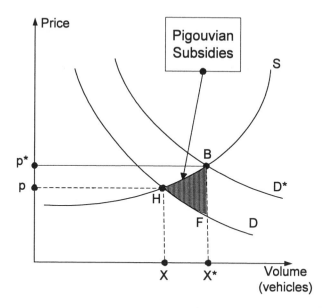

Figure 13.1   Transport subsidies

The tool to create incentives for the private sector is the subsidy BF. So a welfare increase is generated. Thus subsidies should go to the transport modes that produce positive external benefits or reduce negative external costs from other transport modes. Nevertheless, it would be better if the conventional transport modes that produced high negative external costs were taxed instead. We find this argument theoretically convincing, but question the magnitude of externalities that will be reduced through use of automated freight systems.

A fourth reason used to justify government support is that the involvement of private resources is not as large as required (i.e. the private sector can't build it alone, yet it 'must' be built). This failure of the private sector may be due to: (1) the limited resources of private capital; (2) the difficulties in obtaining credit from national and international banks by private investors; (3) the limited portion of cost coverage provided by bank credits (Burnewicz and Bak 2000); and (4) the perception that the government will provide support. When the market risks are very high, private investors will hesitate to enter the market. We don't find this rationale convincing; it simply explains why the private sector won't get involved, not why the public should.

The realization of AFS is such a complex issue that the market failures resulting from organizational and policy dysfunctions are almost inevitable. It is normally recognized as a function of government to remedy the failure when the process of technology evolution deviates too far from efficiency, equity, or environmental goals. The systematic intervention required for fixing the failures often can only be obtained from governments. Furthermore, the technology change embedded in AFS may need new institutional and societal arrangements that only governments can implement.

The Triad Structure

In general transportation systems can be divided into a triad structure: vehicles, track, and operations. In AFS, the ownership of vehicles may be conjoint with the ownership of infrastructure, which is not the case in general transport systems. A clarified understanding of this issue may help us allocate the financing burden.

(a) Vehicles
ATS highlights the intelligence of vehicles because the vehicles have fewer physical constraints imposed by the infrastructure (e.g. from pipeline, guideway and rail). Most dedicated truck lane systems require that vehicles can run on both intelligent roadways and conventional highways, i.e. they operate with a dual-mode operation. This means an additional cost for vehicle operators or truck-drivers, and vehicle owners.

In ATS, the cost of automated trucks should be separated from infrastructure investment and be covered by truck owners. Users, i.e. trucking companies, ideally cover the investment in automated trucks or truck modification. But in the initial stage, it will be difficult to prove to truckers that the investment in automated equipment is worthwhile and will be recouped from the use of ATS. Besides other instruments of promotion, the government can directly subsidize truck modification to ensure a minimum demand for ATS. Without this demand, the new system may not have a chance to survive. Also the benefit of participation should encourage more trucking companies to enter the system. As a stimulating tool, the need for this subsidy should decrease when demand increases and reaches the capacity of the system.

In APS, the design of the vehicle (or capsule) is a part of total system design, and the vehicles will be highly standardized and used exclusively within the APS. It is likely that the system operator owns every vehicle so it can manage operations effectively. Alternatively, it is possible that the system may be divided into vehicle (capsule) operators and pipeline operators, like the train–track separation in the British rail system. This can generate a totally different financing scenario, but it is more likely to happen when the pipeline-like systems become universal and are networked (as in Bellamy's *Looking Backward*). Standardized capsules that are designed to fit the international standard container will facilitate intermodal transport, reduce repackaging costs and thus mitigate the financing burden of vehicle owners.

ARS is a hybrid of the two; vehicles may or may not be owned separately from the track. Some intelligence lies in the vehicle, though tracks and switches minimize the need for this. When ARS vehicles operate on a mixed network, track costs have already been paid for. Thus in contrast with ATS and APS, the network itself may not need to be financed, rather only a small per-use charge will be paid.

In the APS and the ARS, the financing schemes differ because the ownership of vehicles (capsules, railcars) is different from ATS. If APS or ARS operators own the vehicles, their cost should be counted in the initial investment, though compared to the cost of construction and land use. If owners of vehicles are dedicated shipping companies, we find a similar case to the British railway system. The door of the new market is opened to the private sector. But to make the system run in the first place, the investment from them should be well organized before the system begins operation.

(b) Track
Track refers to the road, rails, or pipelines themselves. Track is characterized by a high fixed capital cost and relatively low variable maintenance cost. Because of this cost structure, it is often the case that competitive markets cannot recover the costs of the network backbone. (And the more competition, the harder it is to recover costs, which is why monopolies emerge so often in network businesses.) User fees charged to shippers and carriers, the groups that benefit most directly, likely will be unable to cover the total system cost of the new networks. It is here that subsidy is most likely needed if AFS are to emerge.

For the reasons described above, subsidies from central or local government are one of the major components of transport financing. Traditionally new transport infrastructure (highways, ports, railroads, airports) have been partially subsidized by government. There is a trend to transform transport financing to a situation in which private resources or private–public partnerships are encouraged to enter the business. In financing AFS, an innovative financing scheme may fit the characteristics of the new configuration of transport modes in which the private sector plays an important role. In these advanced systems, the capital investment may cover not only the cost of infrastructure but also the cost of the advanced equipment for both infrastructure and vehicles.

The instruments of subsidies vary. Subsidies are usually in the forms of direct financial supports, research incentives, tax reductions, or tax exemptions. The investment in the public transport infrastructure and other funding for regional and local public transport can also be seen as means of subsidies. Rothengatter (2001) suggested indirect subsidies could exist in (1) the overhead cost of public administration and political insurance and (2) the external costs of transport infrastructure and infrastructure use. In deploying AFS, both direct and indirect subsidies are necessary, though their realization is contingent on case particulars.

(c) Operations
The third component of transportation systems are operations, the management, communications, control, administration, and maintenance of the facility. Higher capital costs can be used to construct more automated facilities that have lower operating costs, so we would expect this to take place in AFS. Still there are ongoing costs of business after the network has been laid down. An important source for financing AFS infrastructure is the vehicle-related revenue from tolls. Collecting tolls is the transport economists' favorite because it represents the basic idea that users of the system should pay for it. There will not be argument on whether or not to collect fees in such an expensive system. The argument will concentrate on who should determine the level of fees and how much of the cost should be recouped.

An economically efficient AFS should yield enough revenue to cover the debt for construction and operating costs. Furthermore, it should generate funds for improving the system and for the construction of extensions. The general model is that the infrastructure owner invests in track and operations. These costs can be recovered in part or whole by user fees, the remainder from public subsidy (especially for the track). These sources may either pay for the costs directly, or may be used to pay back debt if the operator raised money from capital markets.

In the financing of AFS, though there are several possible financing resources available, government holds a vital role. Carefully organized and operated public–private partnerships will be necessary to dispatch financial resources, if such systems are to come to fruition in a widespread way.

13.3 DEPLOYMENT

Traffic in areas where AFS will be deployed should be significantly greater than in other areas. It is obvious that investors will try to find the market niche and route where the system will attract enough users to cover the capital and operating costs. However, this problem is not as simple as it appears at first sight. For instance, to maximize reduction in externalities, ATS should be located in places where truck volume affects traffic greatly and total traffic is large. There are also network effects, so that the link that is most valuable for future extensions may differ from the single most efficient link in an isolated system.

The foremost concern of investors should be how much demand will eventually emerge in the new system. We can imagine that both induced and diverted traffic will be there. Induced traffic refers to traffic that is generated only because of the new capacity (Lakshmanan and Anderson 2001, Levinson and Kanchi 2002). The diverted traffic refers to the traffic moving from the old system to the newly developed system. We expect the diverted traffic will dominate because the saving from the new network is only a small component of total cost.

The performance of dispatch in the intakes and outlets affects demand for AFS. This problem can be solved by advanced terminal and warehouse systems. The terminals and warehouses can act as buffer between the high capacity advanced system and low capacity conventional systems. In ATS, the buffer area may not function as well as expected, as shown in Figure 13.2(a). This is not only because of the limited space of the buffer area, but also because of the variability of the truck fleet. When a large number of trucks reaches the buffer area, the operator can make some of them wait for a while to limit the truck flow feeding into conventional transport systems – other freeway or highway systems. However, the buffering time suffered by truckers will reduce the total efficiency of the system and may eliminate the truckers' incentive to use the system. So there should be a special design of truck dispatching system and buffer areas, which provide enough exits for trucks and do not seriously affect the related transport systems. One possible answer is to mandate trucks to exit in a dispersed manner, as shown in Figure 13.2(b). This is possible because:

(1) The customers of the new system may differ in their destinations and can exit separately;
(2) The trucking fleets can be encouraged to cooperate by toll differentials;
(3) The truck fleets that use the system may be relatively static and few in number so that they can negotiate a mutually beneficial arrangement. This is analogous to an indefinitely repeated Prisoners' Dilemma (Fudenberg and Tirole 1995).

We have discussed various financing schemes that should be considered for different AFS modes. Although the spatial deployment of AFS should respond to demand, a national AFS deployment policy will direct the financial support and regulate market behavior. Government aid forms an important tool of regulation because it is vital for projects with large infrastructure construction to have controls imposed by their financiers.

Vance and Mills (1994) suggested three approaches to deploying APS, which may also apply to the deployment of other AFS. The first approach is 'to build the most needed and financially viable segments in congested areas'. Vance and Mills pointed out that its disadvantage is the requirement of standardization after some segments have already been built and in operation. However, the standardization process exists in every other technology deployment and can be accomplished in a step-by-step manner.

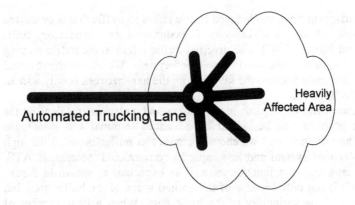

(a) One Major Dispatch Area

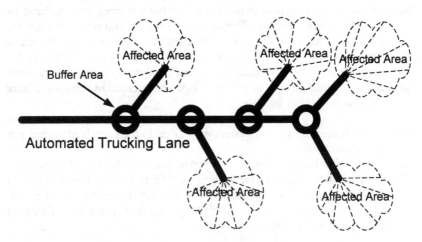

(b) Many Mandatory Dispatching Areas

Figure 13.2   Automated trucking lanes and dispatching areas

Yet many technologies have failed due to incompatibilities. AFS embraces innovations in both infrastructure and vehicle technologies, in both hardware and software (control and operation strategies). The standard for each of these aspects cannot be set up overnight. Fortunately, unlike other surface transport systems, the compatibility issue accompanied with the standard revision can be mitigated by the flexible multimodal terminal technology.

The second approach is like the development of the US interstate highway system, in which a national plan establishes standards in advance. It can be expected that the enactment process faces indifference from the legislature. The freight transport system draws limited public attention. The need for a renovated or additional freight system may not be seen as important as safety-related issues. The time taken to pass the related act may be long.

In facing these difficulties, a third approach assumes that APS would only provide niche services. This type of deployment will 'allow totally private planning with limited enabling legislation and, perhaps, access to federal right-of-way' (Vance and Mills 1994). This is an approach with minimal steps and reduces the danger of delaying the problem to the future. The niche-scale deployment does not necessarily lead to public recognition. It is an appropriate approach to supporting innovation when technologies are immature. Successful technologies in niche markets may then be extended, as happened with railroads in the 1830s.

For a location with a high probability of deploying AFS, there is still an issue of choosing among the AFS concepts. This choice-making process will be as complex as the problems we mentioned before, because of the conflict among interest groups with different opinions.

Environmentalists will likely object to ATS, which they view as like highway expansion. APS could be their favorite. Besides the merits we have discussed so far, like the innovation of the conventional pipeline system, APS can learn from the experience of conventional systems. Furthermore, it will benefit from the old system in the implementation because the new system can either take advantage of existing rights-of-way or even directly use a part of existing infrastructure. Though we will not go deeply into the technical issues, it should be noted that the propulsion mode would strongly affect the performance of the tube system. The energy efficiency, operating cost, maintenance cost, environmental impacts and system reliability of the system will largely depend on the propulsion technique used.

There is also a drawback for the APS and ARS: the size of vehicles is physically limited. As noted, some goods that fit conventional containers will face problems. The market share of the new system will be affected. For example, if the pipe is 1.83 m in diameter, some packages that currently fit the size of a standard container will be screened out of the APS shipment list.

13.4 CONCLUSIONS

Increasing traffic congestion argues for innovations that either enhance the capacity of current infrastructure or divert traffic to newly constructed infrastructure. The concern of the public for environmental conservation, community integrity and sustainable development makes the simple expansion of conventional highways more difficult than ever. Innovations in automated freight systems provide opportunities to mitigate congestion, enhance transport productivity, and reduce vehicle pollution without a large amount of land consumption. The number of alternatives for the technology of AFS is large and each results in different scenarios for their deployment and financing.

Financing strategies for the three concepts of AFS discussed in this chapter possess different characteristics in terms of monetary resources, private participation, cost sharing and management. Specific financing schemes should be designed according to these factors.

Government subsidies in the form of loans, grants, or tax breaks may be vital during the early years of AFS to construct infrastructure. The reduced negative externalities of AFS make them good candidates for public investments. However, the instruments of government subsidies vary according to the deployment scheme of AFS. A comprehensive AFS deployment strategy will prompt the market penetration process, but until a clearer picture of technology and financing emerges, the path of deployment remains murky.

The analysis we conducted above is mainly based on practice in developed countries. Developing countries, in which the government has relatively concentrated but limited economic power, may also have the ardor to deploy advanced transport systems, though most of them are still struggling to finance resources for general transport systems. For instance, the world's longest MAGLEV may be built in China between two of its biggest cities in the near future. It is common knowledge that the constrained financing resources from either public or private sectors in these countries will limit the demand for advanced transport systems and the capability to build them. The financing issue then becomes less important than the decision-making procedures, which may depend arbitrarily on non-market factors.

REFERENCES

Baum, H. and W.H. Schulz (2000), Transportation Policy, chapter 9 in *Analytical Transport Economics: An International Perspective*, J.B. Polak and A. Heertje (eds), Cheltenham: Edward Elgar Publishing Company.

Bowersox, D.J., D. Bowers and P.J. Daugherty (1999), *Logistical Excellence*, Burlington, VT: Digital Press.

Braeutigam, R.R. (1999), Learning about Transport Costs, chapter 3 in J.A. Gomez-Ibanez et al. (eds.), *Essays in Transport Economics and Policy*, Washington: Brookings Institution Press.

Burnewicz, J. and M. Bak (2000), Transportation in Economics in Transition, chapter 12 in J.B. Polak and A. Heertje (eds.), *Analytical Transport Economics: An International Perspective*, Cheltenham: Edward Elgar Publishing Company.

Coyle, M. (1994) *Future Manufacturing, Marketing, and Logistics Needs*, Conference Proceedings 3: International Symposium on Motor Carrier Transport, TRB, Washington: National Academy Press.

FHWA (2002), FHWA Administrator Testifies that Growing Traffic Congestion Threatens Nation's Economy, Quality of Life, http://www.fhwa.dot.gov/pressroom/fhwa0220.htm, accessed by Xi Zou in June 2003.

FTAM (2002), Envisaged Scientific Innovations Freight Transport Automation and Multimodality (FTAM), http://www.rstrail.nl/FTAM/index.html, accessed by Xi Zou in November.

Fudenberg, D. and J. Tirole (1995), *Game Theory*, Cambridge, MA: MIT Press.

Garrison, W.L. and D.M. Levinson (2005), *The Transportation Experience*, Oxford: Oxford University Press.

Lakshmanan, T.R. and W.P. Anderson (2001), Infrastructure Capacity, chapter 13 of K.J. Button and D.A. Hensher (eds.), *Handbook of Transport Systems and Traffic Control*, Amsterdam: Pergamon.

Levinson, D. and S. Kanchi (2002), Road Capacity and the Allocation of Time, *Journal of Transportation and Statistics*, Vol. 5, no. 1, pp. 25–46.

Liu, H. (2002), Freight Transport by Underground Pipelines: Past, Present and Future, http://www.ruhr-uni-bochum.de/isuft2002/abstracts/Liu_Henry_01.htl, accessed by Xi Zou in November.

Reuter, (2003), Ebay, U.S. Government Agency in Small Business Tie-Up, http://www.reuters.com/newsArticle.jhtml?type=topNews&storyID=3003 967, accessed by Xi Zou in June.

Roop, S.S., L. Olson, J. Warner, C. Morgan and O. Rediniotis (2000), *The Technical and Economic Feasibility of a Freight Pipeline System in Texas*, Year 1 Report, FHWA/TX-01/1519-1, http://tti.tamu.edu/product/catalog/reports/1519-1.pdf, accessed by Xi Zou in November.

Rothengatter, W. (2001), *Transport Subsidies*, chapter 11 of K.J. Button and D.A. Henscher (eds) *Handbook of Transport Systems and Traffic Control*, Amsterdam: Pergamon.

Vance, L. and M.K. Mills (1994), Public Roads On-line (Autumn 1994): Tube Freight Transport, http://www.tfhrc.gov/pubrds/fall94/p94au21.htm, accessed by Xi Zou in November.

14. Safety, a strategic aspect in transport systems design

John Stoop

14.1 INTRODUCTION

Over the past decade a major transition in transport policy-making has been called for, based on internal and external conditions. Internal factors focus on performance pressure within a system in order to control required growth, competition from other transport modes, intelligent operation and expansion of transport services. External factors should be integrated into any future systems development, dealing with land use, detrimental environmental effects, sustainability and safety.

Over the past decade, several major transport projects have been initiated in all modes of transportation, covering railway infrastructure, expansion of airports and ports, public transport networks, multiple land use and underground structures. Several major projects have been initiated in the freight transport market, such as the Betuwe Cargo Line railway, the Underground Logistic System near Schiphol Airport and the automated container transport system Combi-Road (Stoop 1993, OLS 1999, Combi-Road 1996a, 1996b).

During the first phase of the design of such transport systems, much attention has been devoted to a project-oriented approach, based on 'proven technology' and public–private partnership. Cooperation between partners has focused on practical and pragmatic modifications of existing technologies and concepts, foreseeing incremental change and evolutionary steps. In recent years, such systems have focused on accommodating freight markets with various degrees of automating freight transport processes. Such a project-oriented approach, however, has encountered numerous questions with respect to its innovative potential, construction costs and societal support, safety, environmental impacts and land use. Several of these projects have not been realized after a feasibility or pilot study phase or are still being criticized over their future performance and costs while under construction.

Technological Innovation

Recently, a more fundamental approach has been favoured. In reconsidering transport policy and system modification, a more strategic approach has been emerging, dealing with technological innovation, conceptual change and rearrangement of institutional conditions. Major issues in several modes of transportation have led to system pressure for major changes to be introduced. Such changes are so fundamental that only conceptual modifications may be satisfactory. A 'system leap' forward may be inevitable (Connekt 2001). Rather than applying proven technology and pragmatic improvements on a detailed level, technological innovation may be necessary to overcome constraints in system development. In the past, such technological innovation has had a tremendous impact on overall system performance and increased in achievable safety levels. Examples are to be found in shipping in the transformation from sailing to steam and diesel engine propulsion, in railways from steam engines to electrically powered locomotives or in aviation with the transformation from propeller driven commercial airplanes to jet engines with pressurized cabins. More recent developments are the implementation of ICT applications and telematics in all modes of transportation or the introduction of new hybrid construction materials in aviation.

Conceptual Change

In addition to technological innovation, a 'system' leap approach becomes necessary, introducing conceptual changes in the architecture of transport systems (Connekt 2001).

Examples are found in inland shipping, where the present concept of origin–destination leads to system pressure, shifting the focus to distri-shuttles in a network with fixed service points.

In the airfreight sector, system pressure within market partners requires a balancing between capacity and environmental constraints. In passenger aviation, 'free flight' logistic concepts might replace the hub-spoke and widebody concept.

In container logistics, system pressure leads to optimization and cooperation on dedicated terminals and reversed logistics. In public transport, system pressure exists in matching supply and demand and the organization of chain mobility.

In the north of the Randstad area, system pressure exists with respect to spatial planning, land use and urban development. Underground structures and multiple land use should cope with congestion, external safety and environmental constraints in densely populated areas and compact city concepts.

Integrating Safety

Historically, safety has been subject to a fragmented approach. In the past, every department has had its own responsibility for safety, focusing on either working conditions, or internal safety, external safety, rescue and emergency, public order or security. They each issued policy documents, which in their time were leading statements for elaboration and regulation such as Sustainable Safety, Integral Safety or quantitative risk assessment standards. Experiences over the past decade have demonstrated, however, that safety has not been integrated successfully in a series of major transport projects. The implementation of safety has presented a diverse and scattered picture, depending on accidental circumstances or project-specific conditions (Stoop and Beukenkamp 2003, Leeuwendaal 2001).

With the stated need for technological innovation and a 'system leap' in mind for all modes of transportation to fulfil internal and external demands, a 'conceptual leap' in the notion of safety may be required to fit in with these demands. A repositioning of safety into a more integrated framework may be necessary. It may become necessary to transform safety from an operational cost into a strategic policy-making issue (Stoop 2001). In particular during the development, design, construction and operation of innovative systems facilitating a 'systems leap', safety should be integrated in each phase during the life cycle of such systems.

As these developments, triggering several 'system leaps', become visible, the question arises how safety should be integrated in these developments in order to guarantee a pro-active and sustainable safe operation throughout their life cycles.

14.2 SAFETY SCHOOLS OF THOUGHT IN TRANSPORTATION

Four Schools of Thought

Safety in modern transportation systems has been an issue for about 150 years. It evolved as a discipline from several different domains and disciplines and has a strong practical bias. At present, safety and risk are also debated in the public domain due to a series of major accidents and disasters in various European countries and other parts of the world.

Consequently, various 'schools of thought' have been emerging, of which the most important can be categorized as the 'Tort Law School', the 'Reliability Engineering School' and the 'System Safety Engineering School' (McIntyre 2000). In addition a fourth school is defined as 'System Deficiency and Change' (Stoop 2002).

Each of these schools represents a different pattern of thinking and can be considered as consecutive, representing the societal and scientific safety concepts of their times. These schools are supported by extensive literature covering a wide variety of domains and scientific disciplines.

In general, four principal safety engineering design concepts can be derived from these schools of thought:

Deterministic engineering design

This concept is essentially reactive in its learning potential and focuses on failure modes, identification of failure causes and accident prevention strategies by developing technical design options. Failure modes are established from post-event investigations with a technical–analytical emphasis on the failure of hardware components and the acceptability of mechanical loads and margins (Carper 1989, Petroski 1992). Especially in aviation, railways and car design, these strategies have laid the basis for generic engineering design principles at a conceptual level such as fail-safe, safe life, crash worthiness, damage tolerance, situation awareness and graceful degradation. This school focuses on robustness and redundancy of the design product, identifying a performance 'envelope' and quantification of performance standards. An elaborated system has been developed at the detailed engineering design level to facilitate compliance with standards by testing, simulation and mathematical modelling of the performance. Undesirable deviations from operational standards are dealt with by enforcement and education strategies, focusing on the systems level of the vehicle operator.

Probabilistic engineering design

This engineering design school primarily focuses on the mathematical probability of failure and reliability of the system components performance during the system life cycle. Originally, this probabilistic concept was developed in non-transport sectors of industry such as hydraulic engineering, process industry and nuclear power supply, but has gained wide acceptance in the transportation industry over the past two decades. In particular the issue of transport of hazardous materials has spread the probabilistic engineering concept from the process industry onward. To prevent accidents and damage, potential deficiencies are identified during the design and manufacturing life phases of a product, related to maintenance, availability, reliability and safety of the system and its components. This approach relies on the availability of large amounts of reliable data and data registration systems. This design strategy has primarily been developed from a technical point of view, but has gradually evolved and at present incorporates ergonomics, human factor and organizational aspects. This school applies a wide diversity of techniques such as Reliability, Availability, Maintenance and Safety (RAMS), Probabilistic Risk Assessment (PRA), Failure Mode and

Effect Analysis (FMEA), human engineering and High Reliability Organizations (HRO). This engineering design concept does not discriminate between engineering design phases.

Systems engineering design
This engineering design school emerged from aerospace and defence applications and expanded into a wider area. Especially in the area of high risk, probabilistic attempts to evaluate operational mishaps by predictive analysis failed due to the lack of specific data needed to analyse such mishaps. Unpredictable interactions among an elaborated structure and intricate environmental influences characterize complex systems and modern technology. This school compensates for methodological shortcomings in deterministic and probabilistic concepts, in particular in the domain of low-probability/high-consequence events. This engineering design concept expands a strict technical intervention in objects and artefacts into incorporating environmental, organizational, social and societal conditions in a socio-technical systems design concept (Stoop 1997, Rasmussen and Svedung 2000). Interest in the safety performance of the systems components is supplemented by an interest in the overall systems safety performance by investigating mishaps and evaluating the quality of the programmed system safety performance (Rimson and Benner 1996). The methods and tools of this systems engineering design concept focus on modelling systems and dynamic interactions with their environment. In addition, an interest in disaster and emergency management occurs as a consequence, focusing on the safety performance of the overall system during all phases of its life cycle and the overall sequence of events such as before, during and after an accident or disaster. Consequently, technical–analytical approaches from the previous schools are supplemented by behavioural, sociological, managerial, decision-making and governance policy-making methodologies.

Safety deficiency identification and system change
This engineering design concept deals with the participative nature of major projects and systems change, taking into account safety requirements and interests from various groups of stakeholders during normal and deviant operation of transport systems. This concept transforms the closed nature of the engineering design process into a participative, open process in which stakeholders are able to express their requirements and new public–private partnership configurations are elaborated (Eisner and Stoop 1992). Such public–private partnership configurations are established under conditions of open European competition regarding tendering and contracting of major projects. In such a competitive environment, the pressure to innovate technologically and organizationally as well as methodologically, is clearly present. The conceptual integration of safety in such innovative configurations, methods and procedures has not, however, yet been fully

developed either practically or theoretically (Stoop 2003). This engineering design concept establishes a procedural relation between the design phase and the operational phase of socio-technical systems. A design process management procedure is applied, commonly known as the 'Safety Case' (Eurotunnel 1994). Such a procedure provides a safety assessment design document as a 'living' document for all system life phases, relating design decisions to operational safety management requirements. The concept assesses not only the performance of the design, but also the quality and consistency of the engineering design process itself (Stoop 1990). This engineering design concept identifies a specific role for single event investigation of major events. In order to provide feedback from disastrous events to the system's operational performance, timely transparency, credibility of findings and public confidence are required. To enhance system engineering design input, adequate understanding of failure and deficiencies is required. This approach is consistent with a more general trend in engineering design methodology to develop dedicated design methodologies focusing on integrating specific aspects in the design; the 'DFX' approach (Design For X, in which 'X' refers to the specific aspect).

Elaborating a Systems Safety Framework

Over the past decade, two major players have appeared as new stakeholders in the engineering design of new major transport systems: rescue and emergency management organizations and transportation safety boards. Their specific expertise, experience and requirements can be integrated in the engineering design of socio-technical systems.

Their expertise is based on reactive experiences with accidents and incidents.

Traditionally, safety boards have primarily focused on the pre-accident phase of events, identifying factors which caused accidents and disaster. Traditionally, rescue and emergency management organizations have focused on dealing with accidents and disaster during and after the occurrences. Combining both approaches will identify system deficiencies which have their origin before, during and after an occurrence. Such integration of an integral safety approach can be demonstrated in a systems safety model (Stoop 2001).

Consequently, the conventional risk model will have expanded its reactive definition of Risk equals Probability times Consequence focus with additional pro-active and systems oriented components. Traditionally available components such as data systems and quantitative risk assessment components are amplified with higher order components. Accident scenarios are no longer solely based on data systems or generic failure modes, but can be derived from an analysis of the overall systems structure, including specific characteristics and operational conditions. Such a systems analysis facilitates an object-, process- and system-specific decomposition. Safety interventions deal with the redesign and update of the system, modification of conditions and constraints in the operating envelope and organizational or institutional conditions. The main focus is on 'system deficiencies', replacing the conventional focus on deviation, liability or blame. Focusing on a multi-aspect approach, a variety of safety performance indicators become available, covering additional aspects beyond working conditions, internal and external safety such as rescue and emergency, public risk perception, incident handling or public order and security.

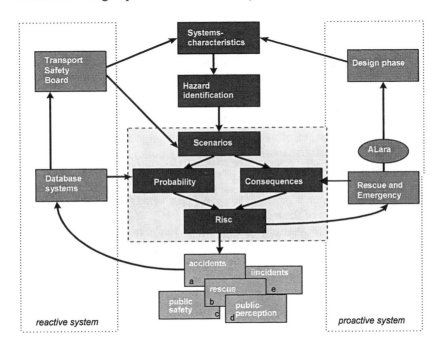

Figure 14.1   Systems safety model

Two principal new safety aspects and their actor groups are represented by the Transportation Safety Board component and the Rescue and Emergency component. They will both have a major impact on a new approach in engineering design of transportation systems from the point of view of innovation and a 'system's leap'. This requires a more specific focus on the Design Phase component in the systems safety approach scheme and changes in the design environment.

14.3   CHANGES IN THE DESIGN ENVIRONMENT

Several changes in the operating environment of railways have created the necessity to broaden the safety engineering design scope to other risk and safety issues.

1.   Changes in Safety Policy-making

From a railway safety policy-making perspective additional features have been introduced (Kadernota Railveiligheid 1999):

- a change in the role of national administration has taken place, privatizing the national railway company, creating private partners and admitting new entrants in the railway market. Since safety is an interfacing issue across systems, new boundaries within the former national railway company create a necessity to define new responsibilities among the parties involved;
- the development of new railway market segments such as light rail and urban rail transport requires a safety policy framework with new standards and procedures;
- redefining the railway market puts additional demands on certification and admittance procedures to enable new entrants to participate in the liberalization of the railway market;
- national administrations should define their policy framework in order to identify the responsibilities of private railway partners;
- a differentiation occurs with respect to the role of a national administration with respect to design, development and certification of new, innovative transport systems and the way safety is addressed, assessed and managed.

Consequently, the safety policy of the national administration has emphasized additional safety principles, dealing with:

- maintaining a standstill principle, despite increases in traffic volume and transport services diversity, in order to assure the safety of passengers, bystanders and staff;
- reduction of the number of accidents with injuries to generally accepted risk levels;
- reduction of risk and nuisance by applying the 'as low as reasonably achievable' principle.

To facilitate compliance with these safety policy goals, risk performance standards have been introduced for the safe performance of the railway system under considerations of cost-effectiveness and financial constraints of the railway safety policy.

2. A New Role for Accident Investigations

Owing to a series of major accidents and disasters, the focus of attention in public safety perception is shifting from complying with quantitative risk standards towards independent accident investigation of major events. In the Netherlands, the recognition of the importance of independent investigations has led to an expansion of the philosophy from the transport sector to other industrial and high-risk sectors. At a European level, mandatory investigation agencies are recognized as indispensable safety instruments for all modes of transportation, for which draft EU Directives are in progress (ETSC 2001).

The characteristics of modern, open, complex systems can be identified and analysed along the lines of:

- a preventive analysis of the primary processes and relevant actors during design and operation including safety-critical strategic decision-making issues. However, such a preventive encompassing analysis is not always feasible in practice due to the complexity and dynamic nature of transportation systems.

Therefore, a second reactive approach is indispensable:

- an in-depth and independent investigation into systemic incidents, accidents and disasters. Such independent investigations may provide a temporary transparency as a starting point for removing inherent deficiencies in such systems.

There is a growing consensus that such investigations may require separate institutions with formal and functional independence such as Transportation Safety Boards with their own specific methodology (van Vollenhoven 2002 and Stoop 2002). The concept of independent accident investigation has a generic potential, expanding its application to other sectors outside transportation, such as defence, other high-risk industry, natural disasters, threats to health and the environment, and major events such as explosions, major fires or the collapse of buildings and structures (IDAIP 2001). The concept deals with an integrated safety notion, addressing events throughout their sequence through a multidisciplinary investigation into all causes, before, during and after the event. Consequently, safety enhancement recommendations may cover issues of pro-action, prevention, preparation, repression and after care.

3.   A New Role for Rescue and Emergency

Over the past decade, several major accidents within the railway system have occurred, including a serious accident with an ICE high speed train in Germany due to derailment. Several major fires have occurred in road and rail tunnels, fuelling debates on rescue and emergency capabilities for dealing with the aftermath of such major accidents. A European Guideline for tunnel safety incorporates design and construction requirements for fire fighting, rescue and emergency handling.

During the design, development and construction of a series of major infrastructure projects in the Netherlands it became clear that the safety aspect lacked transparency and consistency across the major projects under design and construction (Leeuwendaal 2001). This awareness was fuelled by several factors:

- a wide variety of safety aspects exists, causing fragmentation of attention and procedural interference during various phases of the project developments and at the various levels of managerial responsibility;
- clear terms of reference were not yet developed for this type of project, while clarity about acceptable societal risk standards beyond quantitative individual risk levels was lacking;
- clarification was lacking regarding division of responsibilities across project phases and levels, in particular with reference to rescue and emergency tasks of fire fighting, medical support and trauma care in the public safety domain;
- there was an almost complete lack of understanding by lay stakeholders and the general public with regard to residual risks and safety responsibilities of stakeholders in the operational phase, combined with a reduced public risk acceptance.

Analysing these factors revealed three principal issues for the safety-integrated engineering design of major infrastructure projects.

First, adequate terms of reference were lacking, causing a lack of uniformity in risk and safety assessment across projects and state boundaries. In its turn, this revealed inconsistencies in licensing and consequence management during the operational phase. Second, there was no consistent procedure to organize the risk decision-making process among public and private partners during the various phases of the project. This deficiency in structuring collaboration and communication caused ad-hoc approaches and frustrated the continuity of projects given critical time and budget constraints. Third, a systematic acquisition of expertise and experience within the rescue and emergency sector was lacking. This not only caused vulnerabilities regarding a dependence on tacit knowledge within the rescue and emergency community but also created differences across stakeholders with respect to their negotiating and collaboration capabilities. This change is related to a fourth issue: designing the decision-making process among public and private stakeholders in the project management.

14.4 NEW NOTIONS IN TRANSPORT SYSTEMS ENGINEERING DESIGN

In order to integrate safety into the design and construction of major projects, a new notion of systems engineering design and system architecture should be defined. This notion consists of three principal elements, being Design, Control and Practice (DCP). They can be interrelated along three dimensions: a systems approach, a life cycle approach and a design approach. Together they constitute an integrated systems architecture prototype: the DCP diagram.

A systems dimension defines three levels: the micro level of the user/operator, the meso level of the organization and operational control and the macro level of institutional conditions. At this level the issue of integration of administrative and emergency organization across the various levels is crucial.

The life-cycle dimension defines a series of subsequent phases: design, development, construction, operation and modification. In this dimension, the coordination of decision-making among actors across the phases is crucial.

The design dimension identifies three principal phases in design: goal – expressed by a program of requirements, concepts and principles – function – expressed by design alternatives – and form – expressed by detailed design complying with standards and norms. In this dimension, the potential of technical innovation for new safety solutions is crucial.

Eventually, safety is visible only in practice and the actual consequences of accidents occur. At each of the other levels and phases, though separated in time or space, safety critical decisions have been made by different actors. Figure 14.2 demonstrates who can contribute to safety and risk assessment, how and at which moment.

Lessons learned in the development of major infrastructure projects can be put in a wider perspective. Common concerns and similarities in other infrastructure projects and technological innovation can be identified. Such concerns may be expected in view of theoretical considerations regarding a systems approach, the decision-making process and substantive aspects. Innovative solutions in aviation, railways and underground infrastructures have contributed to a significant increase in safety levels. Integrating safety into the technical design and construction process may be realized, but a different notion of safety is required. Also a link may be established with the control and management processes of the project. Proof of success is difficult, especially since safety performance parameters and supporting instruments are still under development (Stoop and Beukenkamp 2003).

Challenges in Safety Engineering Design

To manage the consequences of new technology and innovation in transport systems engineering design, two principal lines are available:

- the Design–Control line. Along this line, decision-making and safety assessment methods and standards should be elaborated, to facilitate coordination among the stakeholders and actors who are participating in major infrastructure and transportation project developments. Several initiatives have already been taken such as safety impact assessment techniques, harmonization of standards by draft EU Guidelines and national legislation regarding tunnel safety;
- the Design–Practice line. Engineering design methods for integration of safety in technological innovation are in their earliest phases of development. Historically, an impressive variety of design techniques is available. However, these instruments focus on the detailed level of engineering design and are not fully generically applicable across modes, disciplines or sectors.

The DCP diagram

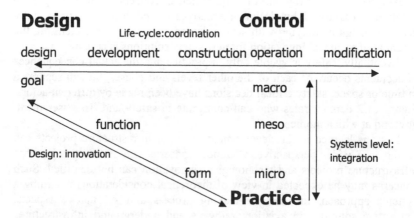

Source: Stoop (1996).

Figure 14.2   Systems architecture model

In order to design a coherent system and to maintain oversight over the system functioning, a system safety integrator role should be defined. During the design of complex transport systems, dedicated responsibility should be allocated to assure continuous monitoring of the safety aspects along both lines during its design. A safety expert should be a permanent member of the design team and should serve as a system safety integrator (Stoop and Beukenkamp 2003, Leeuwendaal 2001, Combi-Road 1996a, 1996b). Such a role of system safety integrator has existed in the past, when railway systems were designed as closed, integral and hierarchical systems, following prescriptive and normative design principles.

14.5 HISTORICAL OVERVIEW IN RAILWAY ENGINEERING DESIGN

The engineering design of railways has its roots in the first school in transport system engineering design as defined by McIntyre and emerged at the end of the 19th century. It may be considered the first design school focusing on the design of the most complex systems of its times: the design of integral railway systems. In contrast with other transport mode design approaches, such railway design covered all systems components and levels, including transport means, track and infrastructure, bridges and tunnels, traction, service logistics, timetables, operating instructions, signalling and training of drivers. Other transport systems approaches do not apply such an encompassing design approach and are restricted to a component level of infrastructure such as roads, airports, harbours, vehicles and traffic control systems or focus on isolated technological, economical or logistical aspects.

Due to their dedicated nature, most railway systems were developed as closed systems with specific, strictly defined interactions with their environment. Most track and infrastructure design was implemented in an undisturbed, mostly rural and scenic environment, avoiding interference with the spatial and urban congestion of their times, locating railway stations at the crossroads between old city centres and urban development areas.

Such integral system deals not only with technological components, but also refers to the conditions and constraints for its operational performance. The characteristics of such a closed, integral systems design are:

- Prescriptive. Dependencies are designed up to a detailed level and elaborated in international and – in particular after establishing national railway companies – national design guidelines, regulations and technical standards.
- Specific. The design is aimed at a well-defined set of operating requirements, market demands and specific use conditions in a

specific catchment area. In due course, major differences have evolved from such specific design, reducing the interoperability of connected railway systems.

- Normative. In order to achieve a proper functioning of the system, the behaviour of every individual driver had to be prescribed to a high extent. Since psychological support was not yet available, a strict normative, behavioural approach had to be developed, leading to elaborate and complicated driver manuals and prescriptions.

- Governmental involvement in design and construction. After nationalization of the railway sector, many national administrations became involved in the design and construction of their railway system. This approach resulted in a closed, hierarchical organized and tightly coupled design concept, controlled at national level, including legislation, inspection and enforcement functions.

Essentially, in the first engineering design school, three safety principles were applied in designing integral railway systems with respect to systems architecture:

The fail safe concept

Systems are fail safe if the failure of an internal function or component does not inflict further damage after the occurrence of the failure due to an unforeseen overload. Such a system contains provisions which may take over the load of the failing device and bring the system to a safe standstill. Emerging from this principle, more sophisticated equivalent principles have been developed over time, such as safe-life, damage tolerance or graceful degradation.

Interfacing with external hazards

This concept implies a protection against interfacing with and exposure to external hazards resulting from a failure in adjacent systems or the operating environment. The actual systems performance should not be affected by an external failure in order to avoid jeopardizing the system's performance. Design principles deal with physical aspects such as spatial zoning by separation from urban areas and industrial activities or controlled crossings with other transport systems. A procedural selectivity may be applied by exclusive admittance of qualified equipment and operators on the systems network to reduce the diversity of its user population.

Safety clearances

In any railway system, boundaries in its operating envelope and margins with respect to its optimal performance exist. The tightness of couplings, nature of interactions between systems functions and components impose restrictions on the operating envelope of a system. Differences between systems components may exist with respect to sizes, mass, speed ranges of vehicles or operating qualifications. Physical separations between system components may prevent disproportional damage to vulnerable components by dedicated lanes or networks. Procedural clearances are commonly applied in traffic control strategies in order to keep traffic processing within established operating limits. Legal clearances provide protection against interference with spatial or environmental claims regarding operational restrictions.

In general, three railway traffic control safety strategies were applied in order to assure safe railway operations:

- Separation of trains in time. Due to carefully designed service schedules and timetables, trains were not able to penetrate each other's separation zones. Strict adherence to the prescribed timetable by all train drivers would guarantee a safe performance.
- Separation by visual perception. After an early phase of direct visual perception, signalling systems separated trains. Drivers were assumed to drive safely by strictly obeying safety signals along the track, invariantly indicating the presence of any train in their operating environment.
- Separation in place. Trains may have a safe separation distance by prescribing the presence of one and only one train within a certain space zone. By identifying a block system, each block can be exclusively allocated to a train, prohibiting entrance of any other train to such a block. Block occupancy is provided and indicated by a traffic control function.

The role of a train driver is crucial to the safe operation of railway systems. A train driver should adhere strictly to the requirements of timetables, timely perception of signals and maintaining block discipline. In this respect, a disciplinary action against deficient driving performance is considered mandatory in order to correct deviations in the systems. Such an approach to the human factor differs from other modes in which the traffic control function is considered crucial. In shipping and aviation, the concept of 'good seamanship' or 'good airmanship' is an escape from deficiencies in rules and regulations which otherwise may jeopardize safety. In these modes, the responsibility for a safe performance is allocated to the pilot or captain, who has the responsibility to deviate from formal procedures in order to avoid an accident. Although not explicitly defined in road transport, such flexibility in behaviour and risk decision-making is present with road driver performance as well.

14.6 LIMITATIONS IN EXISTING RAILWAY ENGINEERING DESIGN CONCEPTS

Due to the changes in the design environment, limitations in the railway engineering design concept have become visible. These limitations deal with the aspects of designing normative behaviour and the transfer of design concepts across life-cycle phases of the engineering design process. In particular in designing automated transport systems with a high-volume performance demand and interoperability with adjacent systems, these limitations may prevent a desired 'system leap' improvement in the design.

Designing Normative Behaviour

Designing normative behaviour and enforcing such behaviour assumes the adequacy of the actions taken by the operator, based on the rules and regulations. Otherwise, accidents may occur if the operator strictly complies with deficient rules.

- In practice, accident investigations have revealed inadequacies and deficiencies in rule-bound behaviour of railway drivers. Deviations from role-bound behaviour however through adaptive decision-making and control strategies may compensate for deficiencies and unforeseen operational circumstances. Restricted flexibility in deviating from intended operations and actions may improve the efficiency of a system. Taking disciplinary actions against such deviations may satisfy liability demands for management, but does not necessarily enhance the safety performance of a system.
- Incremental changes during long-term operational practices may cause deviations from designed behavioural rules. Such deviations may be caused by changes in the system as a result of modifications, system updates, changes in specifications and technological changes in equipment. Adaptations of designed behaviour to systems changes during its life-cycle are required to identify changes in the operating envelope of a system to prevent a progressive and cumulative mismatch with initial design specifications.
- Adequacy of actions presumes feedback on performance by indicating operational margins before accidents occur. If such information is not available within a strict normative task description, it will eliminate feedback with learning potential. Additionally, incremental changes throughout the life-span of the system may erode these margins without a timely feedback on the actual safety margins which are available during critical operational conditions.

Tacit Design Knowledge Transfer

The length of the system's life-span may erode knowledge about engineering design decisions made in the early phases of the system's life cycle. Due to the long life-span of railway systems, design considerations and expertise may be lost due to their tacit nature. If a design philosophy, conceptual design considerations, intended and foreseen use, safety-critical decisions and allocation of operational responsibilities are not documented during the early phases of a design, this knowledge will be lost after a time. Within the first engineering design school, criteria and standards on a detailed engineering design have been preserved and documented in order to facilitate the testing and certification of systems components. Its tacit design knowledge about the architecture of railway designs has, however, been lost with the decease of the chief design engineer and principal members of his design team.

Loss of Tacit Knowledge may Reduce Learning from Accidents

After an accident it may become difficult to reconstruct such tacit design decisions due to the fact that designers and actors in the operational phase have different rationalities. It should be realized that actors involved in safety issues may have fundamentally different notions of risk and may apply completely different rationalities (Stoop 1996).

Different Rationalities

During the conceptual design phase, projects and products are defined by a systemic rationality derived from physics, mechanics, engineering design principles and construction. This phase is linear and confined to specialists. The results of these design decisions are firstly and only exposed to an outsider view and judgement after the detailed phase during testing or operation. The risk perception of operators and users is based on a political and societal rationality. Such rationality is defined by interactions with other actors, negotiating and defining social reality in which operators have to cope with the complex and dynamic operational environment. Decisions made by commissioner and designer have led to a product which can be perceived by its physical appearances without revealing the inherent decisions of the earlier phases. Its operational performance can only be reconstructed by its physical appearance and behaviour as exposed to operators and users. The technology which is applied is therefore 'to be discovered' by actors during the operational phase, taking the earlier design decisions as incontestable facts. Characteristics of the design may manifest themselves during the operational phase through incidents, accidents or disaster. The transparency of safety aspects in both rationalities is a crucial issue since safety may be outbalanced and obscured by other interests of a higher order. Such interests may manifest themselves only after an independent investigation into major accidents (van Vollenhoven 2002).

The rationality of a designer and engineer focuses on realization and consists of reasoning from goal and concept towards function and form. It follows a synthesizing and decision-oriented line of reasoning. The rationality of an operator and user focuses on perception and knowledge. It follows a line of reasoning from observation, perception, towards structure, function and goal. It is analytic and conclusion oriented.

To understand risks and safety issues two different lines of reasoning are available:

- An 'inside-out' vision of commissioners, designers, engineers and other actors who have oversight of the structure and contents of complex systems during their design, development and manufacturing. They are capable of defining complex interactions, couplings and causal relations within the system, risk management, mitigation and control included. They are less capable of dealing with the actual behaviour of the system in its dynamic social environment in terms of risk perception and risk acceptance issues.
- An 'outside-in' vision of operators, users, risk-bearers, regulators, administrators and other stakeholders who have to cope with the system characteristics in its operational environment. They are capable of dealing with global risk notions and causal relations at an aggregated level, but lack a profound insight into the functioning of complex systems. They may concentrate on perception and acceptance rather than on reconstructing event sequences and controlling risks.

An 'inside-out' vision is likely to define risk in terms of a program of requirements and standards, as a consensus document for the actual design and manufacturing. An 'outside-in' vision is likely to define risk in terms of a defined reality among actors, negotiating risk as a 'social construct' to achieve consensus on perception and acceptance between stakeholders. If such a consensus is lacking during events with a high social impact such as disasters, a 'battleground of subjective safety opinions' situation may occur (Rosenthal 1999).

14.7 ENGINEERING DESIGN CHALLENGES

A system Safety Integrator

During the operational phase of a complex system, an operator does not have oversight over the overall system performance. An encompassing set of rules, drills, skills and regulations is required to mould the actual behaviour of the operator to a normative behaviour. In order to comply with specific and conditional requirements, instructions should contain sufficient detail, producing voluminous rulebooks for operators and operating qualifications. Enforcement of rules is inadequate to gain insight into the system's functioning. Feedback, learning from deviating behaviour, is required to identify performance margins, system deficiencies and to change system characteristics before they have unacceptable consequences.

Systems eliminating the operator from strategic and tactical decision-making deprive the operator from interaction with the system beyond the level of mere execution of predefined tasks. The operator is limited 'to strike any key to continue' in his interactions with the system. In fully automated systems, the role of the operator as such is eliminated. To maintain oversight and insight in the system performance and to facilitate feedback learning, the monitoring function should be allocated within the hierarchy of the system. Pro-active testing and formal incident detection and diagnosis function within automated systems becomes a prerequisite, because a human operator capable of identifying failure and incident handling is absent.

Failure Mode Identification

Risk assessment and safety management of systems contain a deterministic and a probabilistic component. Assessing risk, managing safety and handling incidents do not only focus on the probability of events or the identification and categorization of accident causation factors. They also deal with controlling sequences of events with defined system operating parameters under specific conditions and operating environments. Current psychological approaches dealing with human error in classifying Generic Failure Modes or using Generic Error Modeling Systems remove failure from its specific context. Consequently, generic solutions related to these errors, dealing with obstructing error propagation by introducing 'barriers', are of a generic nature as well. Psychological models dealing with error are restricted to error propagation and do not deal with hazard elimination.

The aviation industry has developed specific accident scenarios dealing with human failure modes, based on pattern recognition within series of similar accidents and incidents. The design concept of 'situation awareness' and 'mode awareness' covers a specific range of system characteristics with respect to human performance and specific system interaction. In assessing the safety of automated systems, the identification of a systems mode and subsequent failure scenarios is a powerful tool and may replace a focus of keeping control over isolated accident causation factors (Combi-Road 1996a, 1996b).

In designing automated transport systems, the loss of two traffic control safety strategies should be taken into account:

- visual separation is lost due to the absence of a human operator in the vehicle;
- separation in time is abandoned for reasons of demand-controlled service provision. Automated transport systems apply dynamic slot allocation and maximize traffic density in the network.

The sole remaining separation principle is spatial separation by applying a moving separation block system around a single vehicle.

The Role of the Human Factor

By the middle of the previous century, a normative approach by the operator in his task performance was replaced by identifying the mental load on the driver. Cognitive modelling of his decision-making process during operations facilitated development of decision support systems to cope with the increase in complexity in the systems. Research on human performance and design of the operator environment however are subjected to modelling. In this respect the earlier normative and prescriptive approach has been replaced by a simplification of complexity in reality due to the modelling. Knowledge of the systems performance is acquired by training in simulators, which are a reduction of reality too. In addition, the rationality of a researcher is different from designers and accident investigators, making transfer of knowledge between these disciplines not self-evident. Research paradigms apply generic concepts and theories of human error and human behaviour, which may not necessarily deal in detail with specific operating conditions and context. In particular in complex and partially automated control systems, the operator has limited oversight and insight into the overall systems performance, reducing his capability for incident detection and recovery.

In order to cope with potential deficiencies in the representation of operator tasks by modelling, instructions and training, relative autonomy is allocated to the operator by defining a 'good operator ship' responsibility. A strategy of distributed and delegated control is introduced to deal with the complexity and capacity constraints of overall systems control, such as 'free flight' in aviation.

However, fully automated transport systems face the difficulty of the absence of operator flexibility and recovery capacity. The safety and operating performance of the single vehicle is fully dependent on the modelling and design of the operating software and hardware. Fully automated systems represent the ultimate transfer of responsibility for vehicle performance to a systems traffic control design concept. An incident diagnosis and recovery function should be implemented in the systems design to compensate for the loss of human diagnostic and recovery capability. The complexity and tight coupling of automated systems may leave the propagation of unforeseen events, fault and failure unnoticed until an accident occurs.

The interfacing of fully automated systems with their traffic environment should be carefully taken into account. In such an interface situation, two different rationalities exist; one rationality as designed into the automated system, another inherent to human operators in the surrounding system. Without adequate definition of their interfacing, these two rationalities will jeopardize the safety performance of both systems, in particular when the amount of interactions in the interfaces is voluminous due to dense traffic in a large network.

Allocation of Responsibilities

Allocation of responsibilities is not restricted to the operator level. In allocating responsibilities at a systems level, a hierarchy of goals and responsibilities is required in order to structure the interfacing between these responsibilities. Redundancy and flexibility to cope with hierarchical task performance are not restricted to the level of the operator in practice, but cover all phases of a system's life cycle and all levels of a system's performance. Such hierarchy may be required during design and construction in the area of new technologies, contracting, maintenance, cost charging of services, availability of capacity, accessibility and interoperability demands or public–private partnership arrangements.

Findings in accident investigations have shown that in operational practice the tension between economy and safety may manifest itself (van Vollenhoven 2002). In particular when a sector has to operate on a cost-marginal basis due to market pressure, a mismatch may occur between safety interests and other primary system interests. Public confidence in a transport system may erode due to a major event, when safety is outbalanced against policy interests such as technological image or environmental protection regulations such as strict noise abatement procedures. Finally, a mismatch may occur when for cost-efficiency reasons cost optimization takes place at the level of individual actors and stakeholders rather than on an integral systems level such as has been the case in several privatized national railway networks.

14.8 ASSESSING THE DESIGN OF TRANSPORT SYSTEMS

Assessing a design has traditionally emphasized type certification as the most common approach of the first engineering design school. Over the past decades, probabilistic risk standards from the second school have been introduced, migrating from stationary plant design in the process industry and energy sector. The influence of the third design school is reflected in introducing rescue and emergency aspects. Such issues are in their first phases of implementation in the certification process such as with tunnel fire design requirements. The influence of the fourth school is represented by the introduction of the Safety Case, which may take the form of a mandatory element in certification processes in almost any area of technological industrial activity. Legal procedures such as Safety Cases have their practical origin in major disasters encountered in the UK with Windscale (nuclear power supply), Piper Alpha (offshore), Flixborough (process industry) and Ladbroke Grove (railways). Independent investigations in each of these disasters drafted recommendations for dealing with structural deficiencies in the systems.

A Safety Case provides an independent assessment of the structure, transparency and maintenance of the evidence of a safe performance of the system throughout its life cycle, provided by the designer. The Safety Case identifies and defines the operating envelope and environment of a specific system and provides physical, procedural and process evidence of safe use of the system. The Safety Case Report serves as the documented certification of a design to protect the designer, supplier and user from legal liability.

Current certification processes are less appropriate for certifying the integral system safety performance. Such processes prove their value at the level of isolated components, are based on historical extrapolation of data, do not take into account specific conditions or the operating context, due to their generic nature, and are restricted to the design phase of a product design.

Present legislation in transport system certification is specifically developed for existing modes of transportation and are not easily converted to incorporate innovative, automated systems. A major issue in preventing an easy conversion deals with the central role of the human operator as the ultimately responsible system controller. Innovative systems may require specific safety-related legislation as has been indicated by underground structure projects and midlife-update tunnel modifications, which are based on European Directives and consecutive national Design Guidelines.

With respect to an integral safety assessment of automated systems, a component certification at the detailed level may be replaced by a functional certification. Such certification deals with an assessment of the primary system functions, processes, operating envelope, accident scenarios and their specific conditions and context (Akovuku 2002). Safety Integrity Levels express the safety performance in this functional certification.

Safety Cases provide transparency over the life cycle of a design and specify the operating envelope. By applying an integral safety concept, containing multiple performance indicators, an encompassing oversight is provided of the overall safety performance of a design. Safety Case Reports provide a relation between the design phase and other system life phases with similar instruments, such as Accident Reports after a system failure in practice and Audit Reports on the quality of performance of the safety management system. This type of reporting has a number of common characteristics. It is independent, documented, evidence-based, provides legal protection and comprises top-level commitment. Through these reports, feedback and feed forward learning loops are established, transferring evidence of actual and intended performance between design, control and operational practice. They provide input for identification of deficiencies and implementing changes in the system across its life-cycle phases.

14.9 PRINCIPAL DECISIONS IN AUTOMATED TRANSPORT DESIGN

Systems Characteristics

At the conceptual level of systems, engineering design, design principles and strategic choices define the integral system characteristics. In combination, they define the primary safety level of a system, which is ultimately achievable.

Strategic choices on the architecture of a system can be made, according to the TRAIL Layer scheme concept (Evers et al. 1994). These choices may be allocated at:

A freight and passenger market level:

- servicing a niche market with specific characteristics or a mass volume market with a variety of payload characteristics;
- technological and conceptual flexibility in the long term to accommodate change in market conditions;
- incorporation of cargo market segments regarding their specific hazardous nature;
- dedicated transport of goods or passengers or a combination of these.

A transport process level:

- centralized or distributed nature of the traffic control regime;
- allocation of responsibilities for safety critical functions to actors and stakeholders;
- the role of the human performer at any systems level of operation;
- coupling between payload and payload containment and the rate of flexibility and interchangeability between these components;
- limitations in accessibility to operators, vehicle types and quality of performance based on quality and equivalence criteria.

A transport means level:

- interoperability of vehicles and operators on interfaces in the network across different regions and operating conditions;
- identification of logistic coupling of services, movements and transfer of payload across the system and its adjacent transport systems;
- a hybrid nature of the system in its dedicated or generic nature regarding specific access to operators, application of technologies or transport concepts.

An infrastructure level:

- confined infrastructure for one mode of transportation or accommodating other modes of transportation simultaneously;
- embedment of the infrastructure in its spatial and operating environment;
- centralized or distributed nature of power supply and vehicle propulsion;
- incorporating supporting functionalities regarding incident handling, rescue and emergency.

The Roselawn Incident

If such safety critical decisions are not explicitly encountered in the conceptual design phase, systemic deficiencies may occur in practice with catastrophic consequences.

An ATR-72 American Eagle, flight 4184 departed from Indianapolis to Chicago anticipating bad weather on arrival. At 10,000 feet the de-icing was activated during descent and the airplane was put on hold. During descent to 8,000 feet, de-icing was initiated again and power was reduced. After a 'flap overspeed' warning, a roll manoeuvre was encountered and the plane crashed at Roselawn, nose down after a steep descent. The accident type was established as a 'rudder hardover' issue during holding of the aircraft in severe weather conditions.

The aircraft was put on extended hold, waiting for a delayed preferential landing of a connecting international flight. The 'rudder hardover' of the controls was caused by extended exposure to icing conditions in the holding pattern. The de-icing capacity equipment of the aircraft was insufficient to deal with the rate of icing, while the crew was not able to identify the extent of the icing on the control surfaces. During a debriefing in the investigation, a senior captain at the meeting clearly indicated the systemic deficiency by stating: 'What do you want if they put us on ice?'

REFERENCES

Akovuku, A. (2002), *Design of a Methodology for Failure Mode Identification in Complex Systems for FMECA. A Case of Automatically Guided Vehicles*, Faculty of Systems Engineering, Policy Analysis and Management, Delft University of Technology.

Carper, K.L. (1989), *Forensic Engineering*, First Edition, Boca Raton: CRC Press, 1989.

Combi-Road (1996a), *Combi-Road*, Eindrapport, CTT Publicatiereeks no. 12, Rotterdam: CTT Centrum Transport Technologie.

Combi-Road (1996b), *Combi-Road. Veiligheidsaspecten*, CTT Publicatiereeks no. 17, Rotterdam: CTT Centrum Transport Technologie.

Connekt (2001), *Ruimte voor Inhoud*, Connekt Kenniscentrum voor Verkeer en Vervoer, Amsterdam: Connekt Congres.

Eisner, H. and J.A. Stoop (1992), Incorporating Safety in the Channel Tunnel Design, *Safety Science*, Vol. 15, no. 2, July.

ETSC (2001), *Transport Accident and Incident Investigation in the European Union*, Brussels: European Transport Safety Council.

Eurotunnel (1994), *The Channel Tunnel, a Safety Case*, Langton Green, Tunbridge Wells, Kent, UK: Channel Tunnel Publications,

Evers, J., P. Bovy, J. De Kroes, R. Sommerhalder and W. Thissen (1994), *Transport, Infrastructuur en Logistiek: Een Proeve van een Integrerend Onderzoeksprogramma*, Onderzoeksschool voor Transport, Infrastructuur en Logistiek, Technische Universiteit Delft.

IDAIP (2001), *Main Points Memorandum on Independent Accident Investigation*, Independent Disaster and Accident Investigation Project, Ministry of the Interior and Kingdom Relations, the Netherlands.

Kadernota Railveiligheid (1999), *Directie Verkeersveiligheid en Voertuig*, Ministerie van Verkeer en Waterstaat.

Leeuwendaal (2001), *De Bochtige Weg naar Beheerst Risico. Naar een Evenwichtige Besluitvorming bij grote Infrastructurele Projecten*, Leeuwendaal Advies, the Netherlands.

McIntyre, G. (2000), *Patterns in Safety Thinking*, Hampshire: Ashgate.

OLS (1999), AMOLS. OLS *The Missing Link?* Stichting Initiatiefgroep Het Ondergronds Logistiek Systeem (OLS). Aalsmeer, Schiphol, Hoofddorp, Connekt, COB.

Petroski, H. (1992), *To Engineer is Human. The Role of Failure in Successful Design*, Vintage Books.

Rasmussen, J. and I. Svedung (2000), *Proactive Risk Management in a Dynamic Society*, Karlstad: Swedish Rescue Service Agency.

Rimson, I. and L. Benner (1996), *Mishaps Investigations: Tools for Evaluating the Quality of System Safety Program Performance*, in Proceedings Fourteenth International System Safety Conference, 12–17 August, Albuquerque, New Mexico, pp. 1C2-1–1C2-9.

Rosenthal, U. (1999), *Challenges of Crisis Management in Europe*, in International Conference on The Future of European Crisis Management, Crisis Research Center, Leiden University and The Swedish Agency for Civil Emergency Planning, November.

Stoop, J.A. (1990), *Safety and the Design Process*, Doctoral Thesis, Delft University of Technology, Delft University Press.

Stoop, J.A. (1993), *Veiligheids Effect Rapportage. Contouren van een Beleidsinstrument*, Faculteit Technische Bestuurskunde, Technische Universiteit Delft, September.

Stoop, J.A. (1996), Risicobeheersing bij Technisch-Complexe Projecten, in J.A. de Bruijn, P. de Jong and A.F.A. Korsten (eds.), *Grote Projecten, Besluitvorming & Management*, Alphen aan den Rijn: Samson H.D. Tjeenk Willink.

Stoop, J.A. (1997), Airport Growth and Safety; Improvement of the External and Internal Risks of Airports. Aviation Safety, in H.M. Soekkha (ed), Aviation Safety: Human Factors, System Engineering, Flight Operations, Economics, Strategies & Management, based on Netherlands International Aviation Safety Conference, Rotterdam, pp. 615-29.

Stoop, J.A. (2001), Veiligheid. Van Operationele Kostenpost naar Strategisch Beleidsissue, in *Zeven jaar transportbeleid en logistieke organisatie. Lessen voor de Toekomst*, Technische Universiteit Delft.

Stoop, J.A. (2002), Accident Investigations: Trends, Paradoxes and Opportunities, *International Journal of Emergency Management*, Vol. 1, no. 2, pp. 170–82.

Stoop, J.A. (2003), Critical Size Avents: A New Tool for Crisis Management Resource Allocation? *Safety Science*, Vol. 41, no. 3, pp. 465–80.

Stoop, J.A. and W. Beukenkamp (2003), *Monitoring Safety in Design and Construct; the HSL-South Case Study*, ITA World Tunneling Congress 2002, (Re)Claiming the Underground Space, 12–17 April, Amsterdam, the Netherlands.

van Vollenhoven, P. (2002), *Independent Accident Investigation: Every Citizen's Right, Society's Duty*, Chairman, Dutch Transportation Safety Board; Chairman, International Transport Safety Association; (Founding) Board Member, European Transport Safety Council, The Hague, the Netherlands.

15. Integration of automated and manned freight transport

Arjan van Binsbergen

15.1 AUTOMATED AND MANNED TRANSPORT: ASPECTS OF INTEGRATION

Part I of this book discusses a number of intriguing new perspectives and concepts on automated freight transport. All envisaged concepts have in common that they make up part of and should be embedded within the whole of a transport system that will largely consists of manned systems.

In particular the integration of manned and automated systems – both physically and from the point of operations – is a crucial element in the implementation process of automated systems. This chapter discusses the various infrastructural/technological and logistical aspects to take into consideration when implementing automated (sub-)systems for freight transportation.

Before we start discussing these aspects, we will categorise the various types of automated systems, because these various types of automation turn out to have quite different effects on the aspects as described above. Then we discuss the infrastructural provisions needed to support transportation. We conclude that, given the current and envisaged developments, fully automated systems will probably make use of dedicated infrastructures, and will rarely be involved in mixed (manned/automated) traffic conditions. Therefore, specific transfer facilities are needed to integrate the manned and automated systems.

From the logistics point of view, interesting parallels with combined or intermodal transport can be drawn. This enables us to draw conclusions with respect to the usability of the various automation concepts for specific niche markets in freight transport.

15.2 SYSTEMS DESCRIPTION

A systematic approach can be very helpful in analysing the consequences of transport automation.

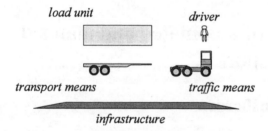

Figure 15.1   Physical elements of a transport system

Following the line of thought represented by the layer scheme of transportation (see Schaafsma et al. 2001– the physical elements of which are depicted in Figure 15.1), transport automation has direct impacts on 'transport means', on 'traffic means' and on 'infrastructures', and, as we will show in consecutive sections of this chapter, also on 'logistics organisation'.

Taking an articulated truck as an example, with respect to transport automation we have to distinguish:

- load and load unit – this layer will not be automated in itself; it however plays an important role in enabling specific types of transport automation (fully automated transport systems; see below);
- transport means – this layer represents the trailer that plays an important role when discussing specific automation types although a trailer in itself has no transport-functionality that can be automated;[1]
- traffic means – this layer represents the steering and propulsion part of a vehicle – the tractor in our example; this element of the system in particular will be automated;
- infrastructures – this layer represents line and node or terminal infrastructures providing means that enable automation.

Typology in Automation

With respect to transport automation and in the perspective of our later discussions, four main types of automation can be distinguished (for an extended categorisation see Marchau 2000):

A. Drivers' assistance and support systems and automated systems where the driver stays on board the vehicle and is ultimately responsible for vehicle behaviour;
B. 'Dual mode' manned–automated systems in which manned drive and (fully) automated drive can be alternated;
C. Fully automated tractor systems;
D. Fully automated vehicle systems.[2]

Note that the difference between types C and D lies with the vehicle type.

In C the tractor is automated (including the propulsion and guidance functions) whilst standard trailers can be used. This type of automation is proposed in the 'Combi-Road' (van der Heijden and Heere 1997, CTT 1996) initiative. In D the tractor and transport functions are combined into one rigid unit, a system such as applied in the Rotterdam ECT container terminals, and is proposed for several underground logistics systems (see van Binsbergen and Bovy 2000). Type B automation is in fact a combination of types A and D (hence the 'Dual Mode' reference; see Yamada et al. 1995).

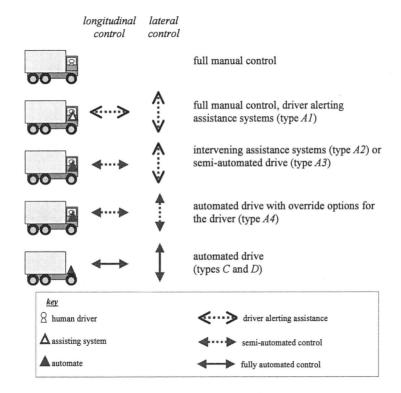

Figure 15.2   Different levels of automation

The first type A can be subdivided into:

A1. Non-intervening driver's assistance and support;
A2. Intervening systems in exceptional and emergency situations;
A3. Semi-automated drive;
A4. Automated drive with driver's overall control and override options.

Type A1 includes systems like speeding, mutual distance and lane warning systems that alert the driver to mistakes, but do not intervene, and systems to support driving tasks (power steering, power shift, cruise control etc.). Type A2 includes A1 systems and systems that take over specific drivers' actions in emergency or exceptional situations such as brake assist systems, anti-spin systems, airbags – especially in effect for longitudinal control (i.e. in the driving direction). Type A3 includes type A2 systems and systems like automated shifting, adaptive cruise control, automatic distance preservation – especially in effect for the longitudinal control. Type A4 takes over all controls. However, the driver may override the automate – in effect for both longitudinal and lateral (i.e. perpendicular to the driving direction) control. Examples of this system include the CHAUFFEUR and DistriRoad 'road–train' systems (see NDL 2002). For an overview of driver assist systems, see Rompe (1999), Hoedemaeker (1999), Heijden and Wiethoff (1999).

The various types of automation are illustrated by Figure 15.2 (adapted from van Binsbergen and Visser 2001, see also: AHSRA 1999).

15.3 AUTOMATING TRAFFIC VEHICLES

Drivers and Vehicles

Taking a tractor as an example, a traffic vehicle consists of main elements such as a propulsion system (engine, related machinery and fuel system), a steering mechanism and a cabin for the driver that contains the controls of the tractor.

The driver – of course – plays a crucial role in the driving process, loosely to be described in terms such as 'communicator', 'sensor', 'planner', 'decision taker', and 'actuator'. Various elements of these controlling and driving tasks can be automated (see also Figure 15.2).

The driver plans his trip and takes decisions (on a strategic or navigational level) and also 'plans' his way through a specific traffic condition on a tactical level: manoeuvring tasks – overtaking of not, taking a detour or not, etc. Also, the driver acts as a sensor and communicates with other drivers (visual 'communication' and incidentally via mobile telecommunication equipment) and often with the planners at the base. This communication is essential for the general planning of the trip – and especially where there are last minute changes in that planning. It is also essential for the actual driving task (for example: anticipating traffic conditions has to do with both sensoring and communicating). A human being is – in various ways – a highly efficient sensor, especially with respect to vision (pattern recognition, picture interpretation). Also sound and movements (vibrations) are important senses in the art of driving. Ultimately, the driver is also an actuator, as he or she turns the steering wheel and uses the pedals (operational level, elementary tasks). See Hoedemaeker (1999) for a fundamental analysis of drivers' tasks.

Now it is important to note that most of these tasks can be automated; however, not in a way that exactly mimics a driver. In some cases, automates perform 'better' (e.g. faster, more reliable, more accurate/precise); in other cases human drivers outperform automated systems (especially in relation to the interpretation of visual images, the possibility of anticipating, and the ability to find original solutions to unprecedented events).

15.4 INFRASTRUCTURES FOR AUTOMATED SYSTEMS

Main Functions of Infrastructures with respect to Transport Automation

Next to the function of 'carrying' vehicles, specific infrastructure provisions are necessary to support transport automation. First, infrastructure provisions can support automation in assessing and/or choosing a (lateral) position for the vehicle in the infrastructure (absolute positioning).

Second, infrastructure provisions may help to reduce or eliminate other traffic from interfering with automated operations, thus supporting the automated vehicle in choosing a position vis-à-vis other vehicles (relative positioning).

Infrastructure Provisions for Absolute Positioning

The main function of infrastructure provisions for absolute positioning is to help automated vehicles to stay on the right track. To this end, different infrastructure-related positioning technologies are available, each with their own advantages and disadvantages (see Figure 15.3). The first technology (a) refers to a system where the longitudinal positioning system is integrated in the propulsion system (chain or cable propulsion) and the lateral positioning is provided by rail (see (b)); an example of this system is the automated funicular people mover system in Montmartre, Paris.

In track guided systems (b) the vehicle is laterally guided by physical means, such as a rail system, and longitudinally by a system that makes use of odometers or transponders for positioning. Comparable to traditional railway transport, in systems (b1) and (b3) physical means prohibit the vehicle from leaving its track except under extreme conditions. Examples (in people mover systems) include the DLR, VAL, and Météor systems.

In contactless guided systems (c) positioning systems use active or passive transponders. The transponders do not directly control the vehicle, but only inform the vehicle of its position. The guidance system within the vehicle takes care of the actual positioning of the vehicle. An example of (c1) is the proposed Automated Transport System (Zelinkovsky et al. 1993 onwards); examples of a free-ranging system (c2) are the Rotterdam ECT container terminal AGV and Parkshuttle systems as developed by FROG Navigation Systems.

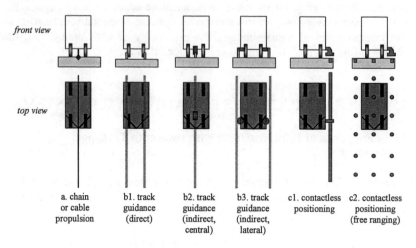

front view

top view

a. chain	b1. track	b2. track	b3. track	c1. contactless	c2. contactless
or cable	guidance	guidance	guidance	positioning	positioning
propulsion	(direct)	(indirect,	(indirect,		(free ranging)
		central)	lateral)		

Figure 15.3   Positioning technologies

The alternative positioning systems pose different challenges with respect to physical merger with other infrastructures, safety (especially related to preventing vehicles from leaving the track), and the complexity and versatility of the guidance system.

With respect to the physical merger with traditional infrastructures (taking road infrastructure as a reference), the contactless positioning systems (c) are easy to integrate, whilst lateral guidance systems (b3) are hardest to combine with existing infrastructures (especially with respect to level crossings). Experience with streetcar systems and harbour railway systems all over the world shows that rail systems (a, b1 and b2) can effectively be merged with road systems, although costs are higher than compared to contactless systems (c).

With respect to safety, contactless guided systems (c) and indirect central track guided systems (b2) cannot prevent vehicles from leaving the track. Because these systems are self-propelled, vehicles may by accident turn into unguided projectiles. Cable or chain propelled systems (a) and railway track guided systems (b1) may derail in (severe) accidents and may then pose danger because of the kinetic energy stored in the vehicle. In laterally guided systems (b3) the lateral track forms a physical barrier that will keep vehicles on the track, hence providing a high standard of external safety (see CTT 1996). Such a system is inherently safe.

With respect to the complexity of the positioning and thus the automation system, the physical guidance systems (types (a) through (b)) allow for a rather straightforward way of automation. The lateral position of vehicles is directly or indirectly fixed by the guidance system and only the longitudinal position has to be taken care of. This longitudinal position can be determined by using odometers, infrastructure tags, beacons or transponders. The guidance system for contactless positioning systems is somewhat more complex, especially in the case of free ranging systems. On the other hand, free ranging systems offer the highest degree of flexibility (versatility).

The above in fact means that with respect to provisions for absolute positioning, there is no single optimal solution when taking 'merging', 'safety', 'complexity' and 'versatility' into account. Some systems are very safe and don't require complicated control technologies, but are hard to (physically) merge with other infrastructures (lateral guidance – b3). Other systems are versatile and easy to (physically) merge with other systems, but are not inherently safe and need complex control systems (free ranging systems – c2). The other systems are 'in between' options that are relatively safe, don't require complex controls, are relatively easy to merge with road infrastructures, but are not very versatile.

Infrastructure Provisions for Relative Positioning

As indicated in the previous chapter, in some aspects of driving, human drivers outperform automated systems. This is especially the case with respect to interactions with other (non-controlled) events in the infrastructure. These events may include other traffic that is not controlled by the automated system, unforeseen/incidental obstacles and specific (bad) weather conditions.

The most important problem in relation to these occurrences is not so much detection, but interpretation and the consequential actions to take. A human mind can to a great extent anticipate the behaviour of other drivers and road users, can fairly accurately assess the danger of obstacles etc. Automated systems are not yet capable of mimicking these human functions in an efficient way. There are two related reasons for this.

First, automated systems are 'new' systems; thus high safety standards are applied (in certain respects, the new systems must comply to higher safety standards than existing systems). Second, this low societal acceptance of risks necessitates a strong risk-evading technology. This effectively means that automated systems cannot yet operate in mixed traffic conditions.

Therefore, most forms of automation are realised in either a 'restricted environment' or are eventually overseen by a human controller acting as a 'human interface' between an automated system and a non-adapted environment. Examples of the first type of implementation in the transportation sector are automated storage facilities, automated container terminals (Rotterdam), automated personal (rapid) transit systems such as the VAL Lille, Météor Paris, DLR London, Parkshuttles in Capelle aan den Yssel and Schiphol Airport, and various systems at airports, and automated shunting systems. All systems operate in an enclosed, dedicated environment, often using dedicated infrastructures. Examples of the second form of implementation are the various types of drivers' assistance systems such as are now available for trucks and passenger cars (braking assistance systems, cruise control, and distance control). Only by maintaining a 'human interface' are the automated systems able to cope with the complexity of the traffic environment.

For the time being, fully automated systems may only be expected to be used on separate, autonomous, dedicated infrastructures (either lanes or terminal areas), whilst partially automated systems (with human supervision) may be operated in 'restricted access' infrastructures, such as dedicated freight lanes on highways or pedestrian areas in cities.

Infrastructural provisions – such as elevated or underground infrastructures and signalised level crossings – are to be used to separate 'automated' from 'non-automated' operations. Such provisions are already widely applied to (underground) passenger transport systems. Further, various examples exist of 'dedicated freight lanes' along highways. Research on dedicated lanes suggests that such infrastructure adaptations can be effective (Tabibi and Minderhoud 2002, NDL 2002).

Intermediate Conclusion

From the above we may conclude that for operational reasons (see subsection on relative positioning) and in some cases also physical reasons (see subsection on absolute positioning) transport automation requires the use of dedicated, autonomous infrastructures.

The consequence is that fully automated transport cannot be seamlessly merged with manned freight transport. So in order to benefit from transport automation, automated systems should be integrated into the manned transportation system using 'interfaces'. The physical and operational forms of these interfaces are discussed in the next section ('Transition Alternatives'), the consequences for the logistics organisation in the section entitled 'Logistics Organisation'.

15.5 TRANSITION ALTERNATIVES

Transition Provisions

Bearing in mind that there are different types of transport automation (types A–D) and the fact that transport automation needs dedicated infrastructures and that making use of transport automation thus necessitates the use of transfers, we can define the following types of transitions:

- 'transition on the run';
- 'transition during stop';
- 'change of driver';
- 'change of tractor';
- 'transshipment of cargo'.

For these types of transitions, different types of infrastructure provisions ('terminals' or 'nodes') are necessary:

I. Intermediate zone on traffic lane;
II. Drivers' exchange facility/buffers;
III. Tractor interchange facility;
IV. Load transfer facility.

Table 15.1 shows the interrelations between transition type, automation type and required infrastructure provisions.

Table 15.1   Interrelations between transition type, automation type and required infrastructure provisions

Transition type	Automation type	Infrastructure provision
transition on the run	driver assistance (type A)	intermediate zone on traffic lane (type I)
transition during stop	driver assistance (type A)	drivers' exchange facility (type II)
change of driver	driver replacement with dual mode system (type B)	drivers' exchange facility (type II)
change of tractor	fully automated tractor (type C)	tractor exchange facility (type III)
transhipment of cargo	fully automated rigid vehicle (type D)	load transfer facility (type IV)

Transition on the Run

In the intermediate zone alternative (infrastructure type I), the switch between 'manual drive' and 'fully automated drive' is made 'on the move', in a specially designated area of the infrastructure (lane). Because system hiccups and disruptions in continuity can occur in the switch, it should be made in an area that is free of other (non-automated) traffic. This requires minimal adaptations to the existing infrastructures, and still puts very high demands on the reliability and safety of the switching process.

When a driver stays aboard whilst automated functions engage, theoretically, the transition can take place on the move, in a 'transition zone' in which drivers' tasks are taken over by automated systems or reversed.

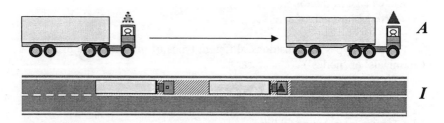

Figure 15.4   Transition 'on the move' (automation type A, infrastructure type I)

In principle, this can be performed either running in a straight line (longitudinal) or by merging operations (lateral). For various reasons, the transition process will take some time and thus some distance, because:

- speeds and mutual vehicle distances must be adjusted;
- capacity differences must be smoothed;
- in the engaging process, security checks for the performance of the automated system must be performed (and there must be space for alternative, manual, actions to override malfunctions);
- in the disengaging process, certainty about the alertness of the driver must be ascertained.

Even in the case of a 'transition on the move' some time delays may occur. However, these delays will be fairly limited (see Figure 15.5).

Although a 'transition on the run' is most flexible and thus preferable from the operational point of view, safety aspects, capacity aspects and risks of technological malfunction make this a difficult method to implement. One can imagine that only when transport automation has become 'proven technology' will transition on the move become fully acceptable.

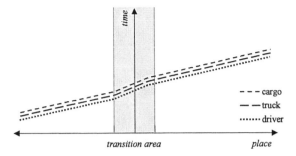

*Figure 15.5   Limited delays in switch 'on the run' (automation type A,
infrastructure type I)*

Transition during Full Stop/Change of Driver

Alternatively, for safety and reliability reasons, a switch between 'manual drive' and 'automated drive' can take place at a specific area in which the vehicle comes to a (short) full stop, for example in a buffer (see also Tabibi, chapter 9 in this volume). This also enables a driver to leave or enter a vehicle. This type of switch does require specific infrastructure provisions: a 'parking area' or buffer for the vehicle must be made (type II).

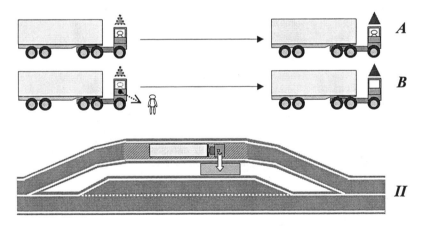

*Figure 15.6   Transition during a full stop/change of driver (automation
types A and B, infrastructure type II)*

A slow speed or a full stop by the vehicle presents sufficient time for all the safety and alertness checks required.

An important drawback of this method is that a special (physical) transition facility between the 'manned' and 'automated' system is needed.

This implies that transitions can only take place at discrete locations, a fact that significantly reduces the flexibility of the system.

The required infrastructural provisions also add to the costs of transition (compared to transition on the move).

In a driver's exchange facility, a driver can either leave a vehicle (when engaging automated drive) or enter a vehicle (when disengaging automated drive). This of course implies that the vehicle has to come to a full stop and that people have to walk at the facility. Further, additional facilities for drivers have to be added (waiting spaces, parking facilities for cars to move drivers without trucks proceeding).

In both cases, some delays will occur during the transition (see Figure 15.7).

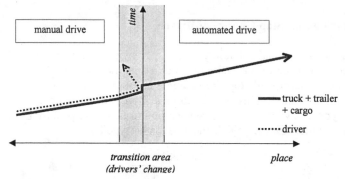

Figure 15.7   Some time delays in the full-stop switch (automation types A and B, infrastructure type II)

Change of Tractor

It is also possible to change a 'manned' tractor for an 'automated' tractor (or vice versa). In a tractor interchange facility (infrastructure type III), a manned tractor is replaced by an automated tractor (when engaging automated drive) or the reverse when disengaging an automated drive.

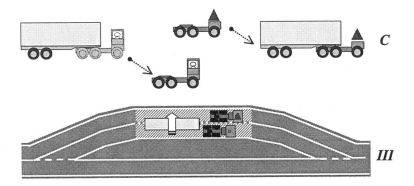

Figure 15.8   *Tractor switch (automation type C, infrastructure type III)*

This has significant consequences for the size and layout of the facility, because provisions should be available for:

- parking space for manned tractors waiting for a new load;
- parking space for automated tractors waiting for a new load ('buffer');
- separate lanes for automated and manned trucks, both with and without trailers attached;
- ample space for the actual interchange of vehicles.

There is also an important practical issue to be solved: driving with automated vehicles on a route is almost 'proven technology'; however, this is certainly not the case where automated tractors are coupled with trailers. Coupling trailers is quite a complex process that probably cannot be automated at short notice: personal assistance will probably be necessary for the coupling process itself. This will be carried out by specially trained people, so a tractor interchange facility will probably have its own staff.

Therefore, a tractor interchange facility must be regarded as being a 'terminal'.

The manoeuvring of the different tractors will require some (considerable) time, so during the switch, significant delays will occur (see Figure 15.9).

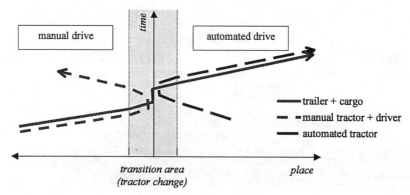

Figure 15.9   Important time delays during a tractor switch (automation type C, infrastructure type III)

Transfer of Load

Also, the cargo – or preferably a load unit – can be transferred from a manually operated vehicle to an automated vehicle. This switch requires a transhipment facility very similar to an intermodal (road–rail) transfer facility in which load units are either horizontally or vertically transferred between vehicles (infrastructure type IV). This facility requires both infrastructural provisions and transhipment equipment (gantry crane, fork lift trucks or reach-stackers).

From an operational point of view, this is a time consuming and thus costly step, however, it can be performed by proven technologies. Especially when load is transferred using load units (such as containers or swap bodies) efficiency gains can be achieved (see also Figure 15.11).

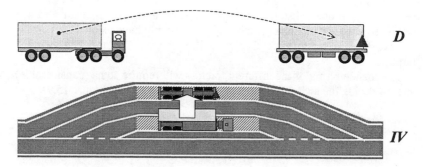

Figure 15.10 Switch of vehicle by transferring cargo (units) (automation type D, infrastructure type IV)

An important issue is whether the manned and automated systems have the same load capacity. If this is not the case, consolidation or deconsolidation has to take place, changing the facility in effect into a depot or distribution centre-like provision.

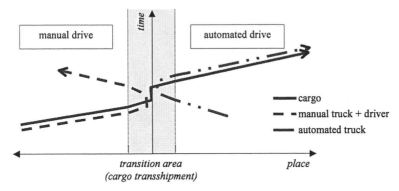

Figure 15.11 Important time delays during load transfer (automation type D, infrastructure type IV)

15.6 LOGISTICS ORGANISATION

From the logistics organisation point of view, the various types of automation have quite different effects.

With respect to (the costs of) logistics organisation, the following aspects play a role:

- the costs of drivers and aspects related to driving time regulations;
- the operational costs of equipment (manned and automated) and the costs of keeping the vehicles available (also waiting times and their costs should be included);
- the costs and times related to the transhipment of cargo or the transfer of trailers;
- the required organisational and planning activities and related costs.

Automated Transport and Intermodal Transport – An Analogy

To a certain extent, the logistics organisational effects of applying transport automation can be compared to the various forms of combined or intermodal transport – enabling us to draw tentative conclusions about the ideal niche for the different types of transport automation (see Merz 1995) for an overview of alternative intermodal concepts). Figure 15.12 gives an impression of the cost build-up comparison between unimodal and intermodal transport (see also Rutten 1995, van Binsbergen and Visser 2001).

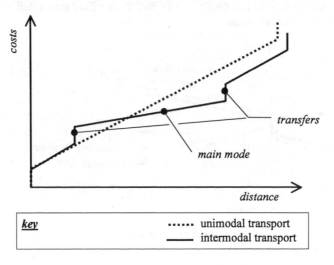

Figure 15.12 Typical cost structure of unimodal and multimodal transportation

The costs of unimodal transport can be – in a simplified form – related to the loading and unloading costs for cargo and the variable costs for the actual transportation. The costs of intermodal transport (and as an analogy, also a combination of manned and automated transport) consist of the costs of loading, first leg transport (manned), transfer, main leg transport (automated), transfer, last leg transport (manned), and unloading. Even though simplified, Figure 15.12 clearly shows that the additional costs of transfers should be compensated by the lower running costs of automated transport to ensure a competitive edge for automated transport. In fact, the ratio between 'fixed' transfer costs and 'variable' main leg transport costs for a specific type of transport automation determines which transport distance is most suitable for that type of transport automation.

Logistics Organisational Consequences of Automated Transport

With respect to drivers' assistance and support systems (automation type A), the driver stays aboard the vehicle during the automated drive. This has positive consequences for the continuity of the process (no delays in transition) and for all kinds of security and reliability aspects (see also under 'safety' and 'legal aspects'). Because the driver still bears responsibility, he or she has to stay aboard and should stay 'alert', probably a difficult task (from the perspective of concentration) because most driving tasks are automated.

With respect to 'dual mode automated systems' (automation type B) the logistics operators have the choice of either letting the driver aboard the vehicle or letting the driver leave the vehicle.

An important disadvantage of the first option is that during the automated drive the driver is redundant. The spare time may be used as resting time, and possibly some other (administrative) activities may be performed. In an operational sense, this type of automation can be compared with an intermodal variant where truck drivers travel together with their vehicles in or onto another mode ('rolling road/Rollende Landstrasse' and ferries).

The second option has the effect that savings can be achieved with respect to drivers' costs. However, the logistics organisation tends to become more complex as at the disengagement point (and moment) of the automated drive another driver must be available. An intermodal analogy for this type of automated transport is a ferry transporting truck-combinations without their drivers.

With respect to the use of specialised 'fully automated tractor systems' (automation type C), the logistics organisation can save both manned tractor time and driver's time (and costs) because during the automated drive specialised automatic tractors are in use. A disadvantage of this system is that the logistics organisation becomes even more complex, because at the disengagement point (place and time) a driver and an appropriate tractor must be available. This type of automation bears resemblances to bi-modal intermodal systems such as CODA-E. Another disadvantage is that important time delays and costs may be inflicted by the propulsion system switching process. These delays and costs should be recovered during the 'automated drive' section of the chain. Therefore, this type of automation is especially suitable for longer-distance transportation.

With respect to the 'fully automated vehicle systems' (automation type D), the logistics organisation in fact becomes intermodal: different transport systems are used sequentially to transport cargo. This has important consequences for logistics organisation, because during the automated drive, the manned vehicle and its driver become available for other transport tasks.

Of course, at the disengagement point (again: place and time), a vehicle and driver must be available to collect the cargo. This has profound organisational consequences, very much like the consequences of other intermodal transports.

Here again, an additional disadvantage is that important time delays and costs may be inflicted by transferring cargo. These delays and costs should be recovered during the 'automated drive' section of the chain. Therefore, this type of automation is also especially suitable for longer-distance transportation.

15.7 CONCLUSIONS

Thus far, automated freight transport is only applied in specific niches in the logistics system, for example within production facilities, distribution centres, and (container) terminals. Various research initiatives and pilots have been developed for larger scale or larger distance automated transportation, such as for underground logistics systems and above-ground dedicated systems in Japan and the Netherlands, and in relation to automated highway systems in the USA.

Further development of automated transport is only possible if automated systems can be integrated into the existing, expansive system of traditional freight transport activities. To that end, this chapter defines different types of freight transport automation, ranging from drivers' assistance systems to fully automated systems, and different variants of these fully automated systems. This distinction is used to further analyse the possibilities of integrating automated and manned freight transport.

A first conclusion is that for operational and in some cases also physical reasons transport automation requires the use of dedicated, autonomous infrastructures. This means that automated systems can only function as a part of the total transportation system when 'interfaces' are created.

It turns out that the transitions between manned transport and the various types of automated transport each require different types of interfaces, as is summarized in Table 15.2.

These advantages and disadvantages make the different types of freight transport automation especially suitable for specific transport market niches, a conclusion that can be derived by comparing the various types of transport automation with different types of intermodal transportation. This results in the following conclusions:

- both the driver's assistance and support system (automation type A) and the dual manned-automated system (automation type B) are especially suitable for short distances;
- the fully automated vehicle system (automation type D) is either suitable for quite long distances or for transport functions at the beginning or the end of the logistics chain (intermodal transhipment terminals, destination areas);
- the fully automated tractor system (automation type C) is suitable for the intermediate and long distances.

Other Implementation Aspects

Although not discussed in-depth in this chapter, we would like to draw attention to other, non-technological or logistical implementation aspects that will also turn out to be important when considering the implementation of automated systems. These aspects include:

- legal aspects: responsibility and liability with respect to traffic safety (accidents with automated vehicles) and with respect to cargo integrity (liability in case of theft or damage, related to unaccompanied transport);
- policy aspects: are automated systems 'public' or 'private' systems, so who is accountable/responsible for investment costs, land-use plans etc.?
- governance aspects: which party will – under what conditions – operate the (dedicated) line infrastructures, terminals, traffic/capacity control systems, automated propulsion systems (tractors)/transport systems?

Table 15.2   *Summary of various types of automation and their advantages and disadvantages*

Automation type	Infrastructure type	Advantages	Disadvantages
A driver's assistance	I transition on the move	Higher safety Higher capacity Driver must stay (alert) aboard vehicle Accompanied transport	Driver and manned vehicle not available for other jobs Driver's job is boring
A driver's assistance	II transition during full stop	Higher safety Higher capacity Driver must stay (alert) aboard vehicle 'Accompanied' transport	Redundant driver; automated functions Driver and vehicle not available for other jobs Driver's job is boring Facility costs Time delays
B driver's replacement	II transition during full stop	Driver available for other jobs	Vehicle not available for other jobs Logistics organisation Facility costs Time delays
		Driver stays aboard (for a rest or other activities)	Vehicle and driver not available for other jobs Logistics organisation Facility costs Time delays
C tractor replacement	III tractor interchange facility	Driver and (manned) tractor available for other jobs	Automated truck necessary Logistics organisation Facility costs Time delays
D vehicle replacement	IV cargo/load unit transhipment facility	Driver and (manned) vehicle available for other jobs	Automated vehicle necessary Logistics organisation Facility costs Equipment costs Time delays

NOTES

1. Except, possibly, for the coupling system; this aspect is however left on one side in our discussion.
2. Widely referred to as 'Automated Guided Vehicle' systems – AGV.

REFERENCES

AHSRA (1999), *Basic Research for Automated Highway Systems Requirements* (in Japanese, selections translated by K. Meguro, Mitsubishi Research Institute), Tokyo: AHSRA.

CTT (1996), *Combiroad eindrapport* (in Dutch), CTT Publicatiereeks no. 12, Krimpen a.d. Yssel: Centrum Transporttechnologie/Projectbureau Combi-Road.

Hoedemaeker, M. (1999), *Driving with Intelligent Vehicles, Driving Behaviour with Adaptive Cruise Control and the Acceptance by Individual Drivers*, TRAIL Thesis Series T99/6, Delft: Delft University Press.

Marchau, V. (2000), *Technology Assessment of Automated Vehicle Guidance, Prospects for Automated Driving Implementation*, TRAIL Thesis Series T2001/1, Delft: Delft University Press.

Merz, P. (1995), Large Communication Project, Switzerland – A Transit Country, *Japan Railway and Transport Review*, July, Tokyo: EJRCF, pp. 20–2.

NDL (2002), *DistriRoad – vrij baan voor personen en goederen*, NDL, Zoetermeer (CD-ROM).

Rompe, K. (1999), Driver Assist Systems for Motor Vehicles and Road Traffic Safety, in F. Karamitsos (ed.), *Transport Telematics Session*, Brussels: European Commission.

Rutten, B.J.C.M. (1995), *On Medium Distance Rail Transport*, Delft: Delft University of Technology.

Schaafsma, A.M., P.H.L. Bovy and A.J. van Binsbergen (2001), *Het lagenmodel voor Verkeer en Vervoer: een model voor een functionele systeembeschrijving* (in Dutch), TRAIL Report in Transportation Planning R 2001/05, Delft: TRAIL Onderzoekschool.

Tabibi, M. (2000), Ultra Long Trucks and Automatically Controlled Trucks as Two Options for Future Freight Transport, in P.H.L. Bovy (ed.), *Conference Proceedings TRAIL 6th Annual Congress – Part 3*, Delft: University Press.

Tabibi, M. and M.M. Minderhoud (2002), *Decision Making about Creation and Location of Dedicated Freight Lane*, Proceedings of Third Conference on Decision Making in Urban and Civil Engineering, London.

van Binsbergen, A.J. and P.H.L. Bovy (2000), Underground Urban Goods Distribution Networks. In: *Innovation*, Vol. 13, no. 1, Interdisciplinary Centre for Comparative Research in the Social Sciences.

van Binsbergen, A.J. and J.G.S.N. Visser (2001), Innovation Steps towards Efficient Goods Distribution Systems for Urban Areas, Thesis, T2001/5, Delft: DUP Science.

van der Heijden, R.E.C.M. and E. Heere (1997), Combiroad is on the Move, *Proceedings of the Fourth World Congress on Intelligent Transport Systems*, Berlin.

van der Heijden, R.E.C.M. and M. Wiethoff (eds) (1999), *Automation of Car Driving, Exploring Societal Impacts and Conditions*, TRAIL Studies in Transportation Science, Delft: Delft University Press.

Yamada, H., S. Ueda, T. Kono and Y. Tanaka (1995), *Development of the Dual Mode Truck Control Technology for the New Freight Transport System*, Tokyo: Public Works Research Institute, Ministry of Construction. Also published in *Proceedings of the Third World Congress on Intelligent Transport Systems* (1996), Orlando, Florida (paper no. 3156).

Zelinkovsky, R. and J. Zaphir (1993 onwards), *Automated Transport System* – www.global-transportation.com. The site refers to 'The Intelligent Vehicle Highway Systems Program in the United States' and 'RTI/IVHS on European Highways' in the ITE 1993 Compendium of Technical Papers and Various Patents.

16. The role of government in introducing automated freight transport systems

Matthias Weber and Claus Seibt

16.1 INTRODUCTION

With the growing sophistication of information and telecommunication systems and their application in transport technology and logistics, new opportunities have emerged to develop and introduce automated transport systems for both passenger and freight transport. In particular in the second half of the 1990s, there has been a wave of enthusiasm which – after serious consideration of costs, risks and potential benefits – gave way to a more sceptical assessment of their short- to medium-term potential (IABG 2000). This kind of enthusiasm is well known from past experiences with new transport systems which seem technologically promising and fascinating, but then take a long time to be realised or even get never realised at all.

Therefore, automated transport systems are seen today with a lot more realism than in the last decade. Niche applications have been introduced for passenger transport in special areas (e.g. Lille, Paris Orlyval, Toulouse, etc.), and significant potential is seen in freight transport, where several new concepts are being developed (see Part I of this volume). Recently a number of concepts, plans and feasibility studies have been presented for automated freight transport (AFT) systems. For instance, several schemes have been suggested in the Netherlands, mainly based on automatically guided vehicles. The most well-known example is probably the scheme envisaged to connect Schiphol Airport with the Dutch flower market and other time-critical goods deliveries.[1] But in the US, the UK, Germany and Japan concepts are also being developed, using both automated guided vehicles and rail-based systems for higher speeds and distances. In this chapter, we will concentrate mainly on freight transport systems, but take links to automated passenger transport into account as far as there are synergies or conflicts to be expected between both types of systems.

The growing interest in automated freight transport systems is motivated mainly by two concerns:

- Cost reductions in the operation of freight transport and logistics. Personnel costs represent in many cases the largest share of freight

295

distribution costs. Automation represents a major opportunity to reduce this cost component;
- Reduction of congestion. In particular in urban areas, the demand for freight transport and distribution services is still growing. Production logistics require reliable delivery times, which can often not be guaranteed in congested cities. The expansion of existing infrastructures is difficult to implement, due to limitations of space and resistance on the part of citizens.

Automated freight transport systems can be described as socio-technical system innovations, i.e. as innovations that are characterised by major changes in both technological as well as behavioural, organisational and symbolic terms.[2] It is well known from historic case studies that the introduction of system innovations is a complex process during which many different barriers have to be overcome. The construction and implementation of new infrastructures are long-lasting processes and the investments can only be recovered in the long term. Therefore it is often hard to make a business case out for new transport systems, unless under very specific circumstances. Typically, new freight transportation systems have to compete with operating systems which they aim to complement. Major technical and economic difficulties have to be overcome, not to speak of legal and organisational requirements implied by new systems and standards.

Appropriate long-term policy strategies are thus needed to accompany the introduction of automated freight transport systems, and this chapter will look at some of the issues that should be taken into account when aiming to support the introduction and uptake of automated freight transport systems. After introducing and typifying automated freight transport systems in the next section, we will look at what theory and previous empirical evidence can tell us about barriers to innovation diffusion in large socio-technical systems and the role that can be played by government policies to promote innovation diffusion in a socio-technical context. We will then look more specifically at the innovation barriers with which automated freight transport systems in particular are confronted. Building on these findings, we will examine the role government can play with respect to the advancement and uptake of AFT. We will conclude with some remarks on possible policy strategies to promote the wider introduction of AFT while at the same time taking precautionary measures against the risks and uncertainties inevitably involved in the emergence of a new large-scale technology.

16.2 TYPES OF AUTOMATED FREIGHT TRANSPORT SYSTEMS

In a broader sense, automated freight transport covers a wide range of technical systems. However, most visions of automated freight transport refer to fully automated and driverless systems within dedicated infrastructures. In this chapter we will focus on surface and underground transportation concepts and exclude naval concepts as well as pipelines, which – in principle – could also be regarded as automated freight transport systems.[3]

Fully automated transport systems can be further differentiated into those operating in a dedicated or a non-dedicated infrastructure and those in a disturbed or undisturbed area. Systems with dedicated lanes (stilt built, suspension, roll-way or underground systems) offer better safety standards than those without. If, moreover, infrastructures are not accessible other than to specific users, we speak of undisturbed infrastructures (e.g. factory sites, shunting yards), where safety issues are much easier to deal with. In both cases the infrastructure itself can be a major element in the safety concept.

The technical modules for fully automated transport systems are developing very quickly at the moment. So-called 'by wire' technologies are the main technological driver (steering by wire, braking and accelerating by wire etc.). In road transport electronic steering devices without any mechanical components between steering wheel and axle will in a few years replace mechanical systems completely. The systems give truck drivers good assistance to achieve a better driving performance and advanced opportunities to improve road safety with various kinds of driver support. These technologies are an important module for future highway concepts with automatic speed and path control, thus opening up new opportunities for the 'automation' of road freight transport. For fully automated transport systems advanced visual and acoustic information devices and high-range computer-based identification modules, also increasingly using wireless technology, are required. However, the question remains open whether these modules have already reached the necessary reliability for this purpose. In general terms, sophisticated visions of fully automated systems in disturbed infrastructures are regarded with a lot of scepticism and have given way to an approach to using the new technologies mainly as driver support systems. As a consequence, the euphoria about fully automated driverless freight transport systems on roads[4] and railway tracks has given way to more modest expectations. Nowadays fully automated driverless freight transport systems are expected to play a significant role mainly on undisturbed infrastructures, for instance at production sites, in logistic centres in harbours and at shunting yards (see Box).

Automated transport systems are being developed for urban areas, especially underground solutions, as well as for interurban, longer distances.

Scaling down expectations: Automated freight transport on dedicated lanes and infrastructure

Example 1 – Automated trucks
In 1999 Daimler Chrysler introduced a new truck technology, equipped with remote control via a satellite system. Since October 2001 this system is reality in the logistic concept of a large company in Germany. For a distance of 190 metres at the company's site, two fully automated trucks carry goods from the production site to a logistic centre. Both trucks are equipped with a special device combining different actors, an additional brake-system and an onboard computer. To maintain the direction precisely the trucks orient themselves not only via satellite but also via antennas or transponders and wires on the road surface. The onboard computer calculates with the data the actual position of the truck. For safety reasons, the trucks are equipped with laser scanners and mechanical bumpers at the front, the side and the rear, which stop the truck before it hits a barrier. The loading and unloading appliance is fully automated with a special roll-way system.

Source: Zapp (2002).

Example 2 – Driverless railway systems
Fully automated driverless railway systems are nowadays mainly used for shunting work at low speed and in dedicated areas like shunting stations or at industrial sites. These technologies have been successfully tested because it is easy to position the systems via satellite control (while the fine positioning is done by the track) and they fulfil the safety conditions in undisturbed areas. Fully automated driverless railway systems for heavy freight transport crossing the huge plains of Alaska, Australia or China are envisaged but there is a lot of reluctance to introduce driverless systems in densely populated areas. Recently a driverless railway concept was suggested for regional distribution of goods with fully automated rail wagons, but the initial demonstration project has not been followed by larger-scale implementation (Hoogma 1998). The EU-funded research project INTELFRET (Intelligent Freight Train) offers different opportunities to automatize single functions of trains like braking, coupling and decoupling, wagon monitoring (tracking and tracing), etc.

Source: ERRI (2000).

Example 3 – Underground freight transport systems
The most advanced technical concepts for automated freight and passenger transport for long and medium range distances are underground transport systems, like the Dutch Schiphol Airport concept (Schiphol Airport to the Aalsmeer flower market), the Swissmetro (passenger and freight transport between the major cities of Switzerland) or the Talpino concept, an underground freight transport system crossing the Alps from Austria to Italy. For these concepts, feasibility studies have been assigned or already published. The most advanced is the Dutch Schiphol concept, which has been the subject of different studies. However, so far none of these concepts has been implemented or entered a concrete planning stage.

However, the majority of systems considered are promising for short to medium distances of up to about 30–50 km. Currently, the most important types of systems under development are planned to operate in undisturbed infrastructures. They can be differentiated as follows:

- Automated underground freight transport, based in the first instance on rail-guided or wheel-guided systems, possibly also using magnetic levitation or pneumatic technology;
- Self-guided rail vehicles, operating on dedicated tracks or (at least in principle) in combination with normal rail traffic;
- Road vehicles on dedicated lanes; for road transport, mixed traffic is usually not considered for safety reasons.[5]

Without going into detail with respect to the pros and cons of these different approaches, it is worth pointing out that underground systems neither consume much surface space nor cause major visual intrusion. They are thus of particular interest to highly developed and densely populated regions where traffic and freight flow density is sufficiently high to justify the large amounts of investment needed. Next to technological and market uncertainties, investment costs are one of the main barriers to the introduction of underground AFT.

Self-guided rail vehicles have a certain potential to be operated even on non-dedicated infrastructures because access to rail infrastructures is much more restricted and controlled than to road infrastructures. Beyond shunting operations, direct medium-distance delivery services seem to be realistic in the medium term (see also Siegmann and Heidmeier, chapter 3 in this volume), not least because the investment in 'hard' infrastructure is limited.

While the operation of automated road freight transport systems on non-dedicated and disturbed infrastructures may be technically feasible, the safety issues involved are regarded as too problematic to promise their introduction in the foreseeable future. Preliminary schemes operating on dedicated infrastructures have been tested successfully, and others are currently being considered for large-scale operation (see also Shladover, chapter 2 in this volume). Important developments are also under way to combine and integrate automated and manned freight transport, where switching from automated to manned mode represents a major research issue (see also van Binsbergen, chapter 15 in this volume).

AFT systems are usually not operated in isolation, but comprise part of the larger freight transport system. The automation of transshipment and intermodal interconnections of AFT with other transport systems is thus a critical element in ensuring that the expected gains in efficiency, resources and time expected from AFT can really be reaped.

16.3 INTRODUCING SYSTEM INNOVATIONS AND THE POSSIBLE ROLES OF GOVERNMENT

Standard literature about innovation diffusion highlights the typical S-shaped diffusion curves as a characteristic of the introduction of new technologies (Rogers 1983). While ex-post and at an aggregate level this general pattern may still serve as an orientation, it neglects many important features of innovation and diffusion processes. Modern innovation literature interprets innovation diffusion as a complex and interactive process during which several barriers and constraining forces need to be overcome to establish a new concept on a large scale. This is captured e.g. by the recent literature on innovation systems and networks (Lundvall 1992, Edquist 1997, Pyka and Küppers 2002) as well as on large socio-technical systems (Hughes and Mayntz 1988, Summerton 1994, Coutard 1999, Weber 1999), which points to the multitude of interdependencies and systemic effects (e.g. path-dependencies) in the dominant technological regime that tend to prevent major new solutions to be introduced. As a consequence of the emphasis put on interaction in recent innovation research, the management of actor networks and the building of the necessary constituency behind a new socio-technical system has been strongly emphasised (Marin and Mayntz 1991, Callon 1992, de la Mothe and Link 2002).

New technical systems like AFT require a socio-economic, organisational and legal system to be in place before they can actually enter into operation in a public environment. As a consequence, long lead times are common in establishing the necessary embedding systems, often unexpected to those coming from the technical realms. Therefore a wide range of factors (and their interaction) needs to be taken into account to understand the introduction process for AFT.

For the subsequent analysis, we use the notion of 'barriers to innovation' to capture the range of factors influencing the innovation diffusion of AFT (HLG 1999, van Zuylen and Weber 2002). This is certainly a rather crude simplification and does not do justice to the open, interactive and complex character of innovation and diffusion processes. However, it is a useful approach to systematise factors of influence. The following barriers should thus be interpreted as the main types of factors intervening in the process of socio-technical shaping needed to realise AFT:

1. Technical barriers, i.e. the current state of development of a technology is not yet sufficiently advanced to realise full-scale operation of the new system. Problems may be related to infrastructure, vehicles, control systems as well as to the necessary base technologies or issues of interoperability and standardisation.
2. Lack of awareness of available information, i.e. in spite of innovative technical solutions being available, information about their performance

and operation is not received by decision-makers, stakeholders and the public. This can be due to inaccessibility of the information (e.g. due to secrecy concerns) but also to the selective mental framework of potential adopters.

3. Financial, commercial and market-related barriers, i.e. a lack of incentives or perceived market demand to ensure cost-effective investment in R&D, infrastructure or operation. Insufficient competitive pressure in a given market may also represent a major barrier to innovation.

4. Regulatory, institutional and legal barriers, i.e. ranging from unsuitable regulations and administrative procedures, to intellectual property rights and liability issues. In the transport sector, incompatible organisational and industrial structures can prevent the uptake of innovations.

5. Societal barriers, i.e. barriers related to a lack of acceptance of new large-scale or other risk-prone technologies, or to other societal phenomena such as the necessary level of qualification required to operate a technology properly.

6. Decision-making barriers, i.e. the fragmentation of power at several levels or domains of decision-making prevent coordinated actions in favour of a new technology, e.g. to solve mobility problems in a city.

7. User resistance, i.e. incompatibility of the dominant practices and preferences of users with the requirements raised by the new technology, or a lack of skills needed to use a new technology.

8. Dynamic barriers, i.e. mechanisms that result from the interaction of several of the aforementioned barriers in the course of the innovation diffusion process.

This last type of barrier may require some additional explanation. It is necessary to look at the joint impact of different factors over the innovation cycle and the dynamic effects their interaction may have. For example, inferior technological pathways may be taken and consolidated as a result of self-reinforcing or delaying mechanisms at play in technology dynamics. Such 'lock-in' effects (Arthur 1988) may occur, for instance, due to first- and second-order learning processes (Schot and Hoogma 1999) or as a consequence of the interdependencies between infrastructure and vehicle development. Once a pathway is taken, it is very difficult to switch to better alternatives at later innovation stages. In a similar vein, the existing transport system is the result of reinforcing mechanisms and lock-ins that have developed over decades. In order to overcome the barriers inherent in such an established system and introduce new system innovations such as AFT it is not sufficient to address the existing barriers individually, but a timing strategy is required for policy measures aimed at stimulating the uptake and development of a new system over the innovation cycle.[6]

Piloting and experimentation are necessary to develop a promising technological option the exact potential of which we do not know in advance nor what implications it may have. In particular close interaction with potential users is crucial to shape a technology so that it is compatible with their still emerging needs.[7] Here, not only single-loop, but also double-loop learning processes are at play between users and suppliers of a new system, i.e. the technology developers not only need to learn about what users want, but also users need to learn what benefits an emerging technology can bring them and feed those insights back to the technology developers. Close cooperation even during the R&D phase can be helpful to speed up this adaptation process between users' needs and suppliers' plans. RTD policy that imposes corresponding requirements for funding can thus contribute to more efficient and swift innovation processes.

Beyond users and suppliers, those in charge of defining framework conditions for a new socio-technical system in the making also play an important role. The process of defining framework conditions is often linked with a societal discourse about the new system. The uptake of new systems depends on the existence of appropriate regulations and legal permits, as well as on economic incentives (taxation) and formal administrative procedures. The anticipation and implementation of necessary adjustments of framework conditions, by public policy as well as by voluntary agreements or standard-setting, is important to avoid delays in later phases of uptake of a technology.

To capture the essence of such combinations of user-driven and supplier-driven learning for this and similar purposes, the concept of strategic niche management has been developed (Weber et al. 1999, Hoogma et al. 2002). More recently, this approach has been further developed into the concept of transition management as a guiding concept to lead to regime shifts in socio-technical systems (Kemp and Rotmans 2005). Government can take different roles with respect to technological innovation (Table 16.1). A more differentiated overview of government roles during different phases of innovation diffusion is given in Table 16.2, assessing the compatibility of different possible roles with the phases. Government can and does make choices regarding the roles it is willing to take, ranging from a passive role to that of a technology or niche manager (van Zuylen and Weber 2002). In principle, policy can play a role with respect to all barriers mentioned; they would just be addressed by different policy areas. To overcome technical barriers, RTD policy can play a pivotal role, but uptake and diffusion may depend on safety regulations as well as competition policy in transport. This situation highlights the need for policy coordination to enable innovation to happen.

Our objective is to analyse which roles of government would be appropriate to enable and support the development, introduction and wider uptake of AFT. Although government can make important choices and decisions to contribute to the shaping of future technological pathways it needs to take into account several contingencies. Future developments depend also on other actor's preferences and choices. This points to the importance

Table 16.1   Description   of   the   government's   roles   in   technological
            innovations

Role	Content
Neutrality	The government does not interfere in any way in technological development and does not undertake any action that may relate to it.
Monitor	The government is informed about new technological developments that might be important for certain policy domains. In that way, government can behave in a proactive way and is able to react properly to industrial claims for support. Existing policy can be adapted if new opportunities become visible. The execution of the FANTASIE project is an example of a monitoring activity of the European Union.
R&D agent	The government fosters knowledge development. It takes initiatives to start new research on a national scale and stimulates participation in international research programmes. The knowledge is made accessible to all parties that show interest and knowledge transfer is organised.
Regulator	Creating a legal and regulatory framework for innovations, setting standards for safety, environment and performance.
Innovation agent	The government creates the conditions for the successful implementation of innovations. Pilots and demonstration projects are set up, and a niche market is organised where an innovation can grow out of the embryonic phase, become mature and competitive. The government can make covenants with trade and industry, i.e. agreements for realising certain improvements. Regulations can be made to enforce innovation. In some cases the government also has to further favourable technological conditions for technological innovation e.g. by promoting standards, the development of a common architecture and interoperability.
Implementer	The government uses the innovation for the execution of its own tasks, e.g. government departments use certain technologies to manage infrastructure, to enforce regulations etc. The government may be the 'early buyer' of innovative products.
Developer	Government agencies execute research and development for technological innovations. A research institute owned by the government may invent and develop new technologies.

Source: van Zuylen and Weber (2002).

of a moderating and coordinating function of policy in order to bring the different relevant actors together and stimulate cooperation and learning among them rather than imposing top-down measures – which nevertheless may play an important complementary role.

Finally, the timing of policy measures is a decisive factor. Support measures for RTD may be influential and give direction only during a specific phase of innovation, but be ineffective later on. Similarly, too early a standardisation initiative may prevent superior solutions from establishing themselves; at too late a stage a variety of de facto standards may have emerged, preventing system-wide interoperability. In other words, there are certain windows of policy opportunity that should be captured by policy to make it as effective and efficient as possible.

Table16.2   Compatibility of government roles and innovation phases

	Neutral	Moni-toring	R&D agent	Regu-lator	Innov. agent	Imple-menter	Deve-loper
Invention	+	+	++	–	– –	– –	+
Test	□	+	+	□	+	+	+
First application	□	+	–	+	++	++	+
Market introduction	□	□	–	++	++	++	–
Maturity	+	+	– –	+	–	–	– –
Decline	□	+	– –	+	– –	– –	– –
Replacement	+	+	+	+	□	+	+

Notes:
– –   role conflicts with innovation phase
–   role does not match innovation phase
□   combination role and innovation phase are possible
+   role fits phase
++   role may be most appropriate in this phase

Source: van Zuylen and Weber (2002).

16.4   BARRIERS TO INNOVATION DIFFUSION OF AUTOMATED FREIGHT TRANSPORT SYSTEMS

From a technical point of view, research on AFT systems has made a lot of progress over the last few years. However, beyond technical feasibility, it is necessary to assess them also in economic, organisational, institutional and behavioural terms in order to get an idea of their diffusion potential. Moreover, socio-technical system innovations are open processes that do not depend just on the advancement of technology but – equally important – on contextualisation and agency. In other words, the characteristics of AFT need to be interpreted in terms of the implications they raise for the wider social system context in which AFT is supposed to be applied. These contextual conditions can be more or less conducive to its uptake and thus point to the need for a mutual adjustment of technology and social context. In the following section, some of these facets of the innovation and diffusion of AFT will be discussed along the lines of the eight barriers introduced in the preceding section.

Technical Barriers

Most types of automated freight transport system still pose a number of major technical challenges that need to be resolved before a large-scale implementation can be realised. They range from automated control of individual vehicle components (engines, brakes) via communication and positioning technologies (e.g. distance measurement, visual orientation, etc.) to the optimisation of system operation (e.g. terms of loading/unloading, intermodality).[8] Probably one of the most pertinent issues in AFT is the development of control systems that ensure a safe, efficient and timely service. Control systems have been tested successfully for systems running on dedicated infrastructures, but the mixed operation of AFT and conventional traffic still needs to overcome major technical difficulties. For instance, the switch from automated to manual mode of operation is an important topic for optimising road-based AFT (van Binsbergen, chapter 15 in this volume, Tabibi and Hansen 2000).

While there may be AFT systems that operate independently of other modes of transport, they will usually be integrated in an intermodal freight transport chain, with transshipment terminals and shunting services providing the interfaces. Intermodal terminals thus represent a key element of AFT infrastructure, needed to ensure an efficient interconnection to other modes of transport. In principle, they should be located at or near already existing intermodal hubs. Many of the technical difficulties will be similar to those known from existing terminals for road/rail interoperation. However, AFT adds further difficulties in terms of standardisation of containers and the automation of the loading/unloading process itself. As transhipment costs, not least due to personnel costs, represent a large share of total transport costs in intermodal transport chains, their automation continues to be a major issue for future research.

Standardisation is not only a significant issue with respect to terminals and interoperability, but also once different vehicles are supposed to operate automatically on a common infrastructure (e.g. dedicated lanes).

Vehicle-to-vehicle as well as vehicle-to-infrastructure communication requires common and very reliable standards to be in place.

In terms of vehicle technology, be it for underground or surface-bound solutions, the technical barriers seem to be less difficult to overcome. Experiences with automated rail vehicles in service in passenger transport can be built upon. For road-based solutions, it is again the aforementioned interaction with other vehicles that poses the biggest problems, even if electronic towbars have been successfully tested in the meantime.

Lack of Awareness of Available Information

Although a lot of progress has been made in technical terms, with new AFT concepts being conceived and major components being tested and assessed, the new insights have not necessary diffused beyond the expert communities. While for a long time AFT systems have been regarded as simply too difficult to operate and too costly to build, recent tests with more sophisticated control technologies have shown the new possibilities they offer. Interest in AFT has been further triggered by growing pressure (e.g. due to congestion) in densely populated areas. Among both potential investors and policy makers, AFT has now started to be regarded as an increasingly attractive technology option, including its very costly underground variants.

Most available information about AFT still tends to be of a technical nature and difficult to translate into public or policy debates. However, the progress made over the last few years and the promises that seem to open up in AFT technology have started to diffuse more widely. Evidence of this is given not least by the numerous feasibility studies that have been commissioned in the Netherlands and elsewhere (Pielage 2000).

Another key audience that needs to be convinced of the benefits of AFT are potential investors and transport system operators. Many companies are not aware that AFT could be an interesting option for transporting semi-finished products on their factory sites. Similarly, road construction authorities and railroad operators could in principle have a major interest in AFT, but it may be difficult to envisage the integration of AFT into conventional transport systems.

As it is not easy to imagine the operation of AFT in detail and in practice, pilot and demonstration projects have a very important role to play in order to stimulate interest among different stakeholder groups beyond the realm of technology developers.

Financial, Commercial and Market-related Barriers

Several of the known concepts of automated freight transport systems require major investment in new infrastructures, even if they are operated in parallel with existing transport infrastructures. To build these new infrastructures and to integrate them with the existing infrastructures is very cost-intensive.

Underground freight transport in particular presupposes the construction of very costly tube systems, which can only be justified in densely populated areas where congestion already represents a major problem for service reliability and where major freight flows can be expected. Elevated structures may have equal or even superior characteristics as tube systems, but for reasons of visual intrusion and limitations of space they can rarely be achieved in urban areas. This raises the issue of viable business concepts for AFT. There will only be significant demand for comparatively costly AFT services, if special requirements are fulfilled that give AFT a major advantage over conventional systems. For instance, the AFT system at Schiphol Airport is tailored to the specific requirements of the flower business, where timely and fast delivery is imperative. In this case, the willingness to pay a premium for using a less congested, more reliable and speedier transport infrastructures is justified by the fact that the existing infrastructure cannot ensure the reliable operation of the business. The time-criticality of the delivered goods and the comparatively high profit margins justify investment in and operation of an automated underground freight transport system. However, in spite of these favourable conditions, the Schiphol scheme has not yet been implemented.

In specific cases, there may be scope for fully private AFT underground schemes, but in most cases public interests (e.g. due to congestion, pollution) will be a major driver in the implementation of such schemes. Moreover, investment in AFT systems, especially in underground systems, is very high and risky and requires a long-term commitment. However, the scope for public–private partnership arrangements will depend on the specific type of scheme to be implemented.

Seen from a different angle, existing market structures can also represent a major impediment to investment in AFT. It is known from other technology domains, but also from transport, that a carrier organisation is needed to set in motion the implementation of a new socio-technical system like AFT. Experiences from the energy and transport sectors show that incumbent companies are often not the best carrier organisation for new systems that are competing with the incumbents' services. New carrier organisations may have to be set up by coalitions of potential users or initiated by public bodies. Before the liberalisation of the transport sector, even the establishment of such a private carrier organisation would have presented a problem. Today, conditions for setting up such carrier organisations have improved, but as long as the future conditions and prospects for AFT remain unclear, it will hardly come into being on the basis of private initiative only. A similar 'chicken and egg' problem can be identified with respect to the development of infrastructures and technologies: as long as the perspectives for future AFT infrastructures are not clear, the efforts to develop dedicated vehicles to be operated on AFTs will remain limited. Similarly, new infrastructures will be built only if appropriate vehicles are available to operate on them (see Shladover, chapter 2 in this volume).

Regulatory, Institutional and Legal Barriers

AFT systems have significant implications with respect to regulation, legislation and institutional settings. Most obvious are safety regulations and administrative and planning procedures, which – if not in place to accommodate a new system – can constrain implementation. The mixed operation of automated and non-automated transport systems on existing infrastructures is for the moment a rather unlikely option for safety reasons and given corresponding regulations. At a minimum, separate lanes or tracks are usually required so that automated vehicles can operate safely without interfering with non-automated vehicles. For instance, the safety risks of mixed operation was one of the main reasons for abandoning the plans for autonomous railroad trucks in South East Lower Saxony (Hoogma 1998). Also local and regional planning procedures can be very cumbersome for systems that have not yet been implemented in practice, i.e. for which there is no precedent. There are no standards and design procedures defined which in cases of normal infrastructure planning provide a standardised pattern from initial conception to final implementation of a system.

Of major importance for ATF systems is the issue of liability, a problem that also concerns car manufacturers aiming to introduce sophisticated driver assistance systems. As the driver can no longer be held solely responsible for accidents, it can become very difficult to settle liability claims for damages that occur during operation. In the event of damage with an automated transport system not only the operator but also the manufacturer can be held liable. A severe accident with major repercussions in the media could even put in question the diffusion process of AFT systems at all.

In institutional terms, many of the aforementioned legal, administrative and regulatory issues can only be settled by a process of multi-level policy coordination. For local implementation permits, the local planning authorities may be in charge, but they usually follow general rules, standards and regulations defined at national, in some cases even EU level. The time needed to reach consensus about how to assess automated freight transport systems should not be underestimated and thus represents an additional barrier to diffusion.

Societal Barriers

The barriers discussed so far concern mainly those actors directly involved in the development, operation and financing of AFT systems. Other barriers originate from the wider societal context, and they can be equally important for the future of AFT. Most pertinent among these is the acceptance of AFT by the wider public. As far as underground systems are concerned, this may be less of a problem, but regarding all kinds of surface-bound systems acceptance issues can play a major role.

Probably the most important societal concern is safety. As regards the operation of AFT in disturbed environments or in mixed mode with conventional vehicles, public concerns about safety represent a key issue, to the point that they can put into question the realisation of this kind of system at all. But even with respect to dedicated systems where the infrastructure itself plays an important role in the overall safety concept, AFT raises concerns due to the inability to intervene immediately and directly if a problem occurs. Risk assessments may show that AFT promises to be safer than manual transport operations, not least due to very strict safety regulations, but the subjective perception of risk is nevertheless the decisive factor. Other acceptance issues may arise for elevated AFT infrastructures that create concerns about visual intrusion, in particular in urban areas, or for dedicated truck lanes that may become a major source of noise.

Another kind of societal barrier must be seen in the significant amounts of public expenditure required to realise AFT infrastructures. This raises the issue of priority setting for public expenditure. In view of current budgetary problems, investment in large-scale technologies is difficult to justify. This has also been one of the main reasons why some large-scale AFT systems have been abandoned (e.g. the Swissmetro scheme, but equally some of the Dutch schemes).

Decision-making Barriers

Realising an AFT scheme requires that mutually compatible decisions are taken by a broad range of actors in order to ensure that all the necessary pre-conditions are fulfilled. In practice, decisions about AFT are taken in a multi-level governance system where developers, investors, operators, the public and several levels of public authorities come into play. Both local planning procedures and national regulations (e.g. regarding safety standards) have to be respected. On the one hand, the growing complexity of decision-making procedures is a major achievement in ensuring that potential risks and dangers to people and the environment are avoided. On the other hand, it tends to make system innovations very difficult to realise. In strongly consensus-orientated political systems single stakeholder groups can be in a position to block new initiatives. A high degree of fragmentation of policy domains and levels further contributes to delaying the decision process, and even more so if responsibilities for planning decisions, permits and regulations are unclear.

Decisions about new technologies tend to be subject to major uncertainties about their real technical performance, the size of investment and the benefits expected, but also with respect to the social costs they imply. As long as little reliable information about a new system's performance and impact is available, the construction of large-scale schemes like AFT is difficult to justify, both for private and public bodies. Monitoring, testing and evaluation fulfils an important function with respect to the consolidation of the knowledge base about AFT. Moreover, this information should be publicly available in order to ensure the transparency and legitimacy of public policy decisions in relation with AFT.

Behavioural Barriers

It is known from automated passenger transport that operators were surprised that passengers still preferred to have a 'driver' sitting at the front of the train, although train operation was fully automated. This anecdote shows that user-sided barriers are often neglected in the discussion about impediments to the uptake of innovations. In fact, new socio-technical systems such as AFT can give rise to unexpected user behaviour; involving users in early stages of the development process may thus be helpful. We know from case studies in transport (Hoogma et al. 2002, Weber et al. 1999), that close interaction between technology developers, operators and users is a useful mechanism to learn how to specify and refine a new technology so that it is compatible with the final users' emerging requirements. For example, industrial users of AFT systems will most likely have to adjust their logistics operations in order to be able to make most effective use of the new system. Similarly, the design of the AFT system should take the logistics concept to be applied into account. In order to enable such learning processes, appropriate and conducive settings need to be provided where the new technology can be tested under real-world conditions, but without subjecting it immediately to market forces. This means that pilot and demonstration projects should not only be used to test the technical feasibility of a system, but also to learn about users' changing requirements. Examples of such application niches, where AFT is protected from competition in freight transport, would have to be created to enable learning processes. Schiphol Airport could be a promising example, because congestion problems seem to put in question the reliable and efficient operation of the flower market. As a consequence, there are strong allies on the supplier side. If realised, it could be used to learn more about AFT systems' operation, better specifications of user requirements and the direct economic and indirect societal costs and benefits of new AFT systems.

Dynamic Barriers

Dynamic barriers are a difficult issue to capture in advance of the actual introduction of a new system. In the early phase of defining AFT systems, certain basic decisions about their design need to be taken, which will fix to a significant extent the technological pathway that will be followed later on, even if at a later stage this path turns out to be less promising than initially thought. For instance, a decision to use magnetic levitation rather than another acceleration system for an underground AFT system determines large amounts of subsequent investment and R&D work. Thus path-dependencies are created and stabilise a chosen development path. A different mechanism to stabilise a technological pathway is based on cognitive effects. Realised technical systems provide an orientation, a model and a heuristic for further research and development work. If, for instance, a decision to operate AFT on a dedicated lane is favoured, this will be taken into account in all subsequent development processes. However, in the course of the time, using AFT on shared infrastructures may well turn into a serious alternative because rail and road vehicles are increasingly supported by interoperable support systems (e.g. driver support systems), reflecting a general tendency towards transport system automation. Switching to mixed mode operation on disturbed infrastructures may nevertheless not be an attractive option to some key actors, because of the massive sunk investments in dedicated infrastructure and the advancement of vehicle technology for operation on dedicated lanes.

There are many examples of these kinds of 'lock-in' effects in the history of technology. They show how the power of key choices can shape technological trajectories for long periods of time. Current technology choices with respect to AFT may be equally critical for its future development path.

16.5 THE ROLES OF POLICY IN THE EMERGENCE OF AUTOMATED FREIGHT TRANSPORT

In order to get a better idea of the appropriate roles for government policy with respect to AFT, it is first necessary to identify the key challenges and implementation barriers which AFT is facing. The preceding section has given a number of hints in this respect. High infrastructure costs, long standard setting procedures for intermodal integration, compliance with safety regulations, the establishment of carrier organisations and the setting up of pilot and demonstration applications to learn more about the costs and benefits of AFT were pointed out as key issues, next to the difficulties of coping with the inherent uncertainty and openness involved in system innovations.

Many of these issues are typical of AFT's current development phase, i.e. somewhere between the early testing and the market introduction phases. This is a situation where government policy can have a critical influence on the future development path and uptake of AFT. After an initial phase of creating a variety of possible technological options, further investment in larger-scale projects will only be made if the longer-term framework conditions for AFT are sufficiently stable to suggest that they can be operated in an economically viable way in the future. There is a small window of opportunity where targeted policy actions can shape the direction of change and thus contribute decisively to collective technology choices. Government can contribute to reducing uncertainty for investors in several ways, ranging from formal policy statements in support of AFT to concrete measures to improve regulations and other framework conditions (e.g. regarding safety). The concrete design and orientation of these measures can also be critical for favouring specific variants of AFT systems. For instance, current safety and liability regulations make it extremely difficult to operate AFT in disturbed environments, i.e. jointly with non-automated vehicles on the same infrastructure. A weakening of these regulations would improve the perspectives for mixed mode AFT and might lead to a stronger concentration of R&D and investment on this technology trajectory, but there are obviously also important counter-arguments. Moreover, a clear definition of the application space for AFT could help establish a lead market for this technology (Beise 2001). However, there is also a danger in favouring specific technology trajectories. The inherent uncertainty of technological change implies that the option favoured may well turn out to be a dead end, made obsolete by new competing options. There is no fixed set of clearly defined AFT options at the outset, but individual options evolve in the course of time, and high initial expectations may have to be revised in the light of practical experience. If, for instance, the reliability problems of mixed mode operation cannot be solved satisfactorily and severe accidents happen, acceptance of this specific variant of AFT would decline rapidly, and with it acceptance of AFT in general. In other words, a 'robust' policy approach that focuses on a few significant options while keeping other alternatives open by modest investment in further R&D is preferable.

In principle, government has the choice of whether it wants to pursue an active or a passive policy approach with respect to the introduction of AFT, but these choices ought to be well justified. An important pre-condition for defining the policy approach is thus an assessment whether by and large AFT is actually a desirable future technology or not. There is a need to assess the potential benefits, risks and uncertainties involved in the creation of different types of AFT before a decision on an active or passive approach is taken. Although these general policy approaches tend to change slowly, they are not definitive and evolve in the course of time. Therefore regular performance and impact analysis needs to be built into the policy process in order to avoid the system being rejected in the long run for having neglected important side-effects. A key element of both government approaches is thus to perform continuous monitoring functions in order to provide better information on AFT to prove (and question!) its promises.

Within each of these fundamental approaches, government can adopt different roles and promote automated freight transport by using different types of instruments during the phases of the innovation diffusion process. The more specific roles and instruments may be revised regularly in the light of new findings on the progress of AFT development, based on a continuous monitoring and evaluation process against key criteria such as socio-economic benefits, environmental impact, investments costs, etc. Obviously, these criteria tend to change as well in line with the priority of political objectives. For instance, environmental concerns may grow significantly in importance over the coming years and boost investment in more sustainable transport systems.[9]

If a passive approach is chosen, the means to promote the uptake of AFT are restricted to setting conducive framing conditions and putting market-based incentives into place. In other words, government could take action that would facilitate the benign operation of market forces, in a way that is conducive to the advancement of AFT. Apart from the neutral position, regulatory and monitoring roles would be compatible with this passive approach.

If, on the contrary, an active approach as a promoter of AFT is sought, government can adopt a wide range of roles and corresponding instruments at its disposal that are applicable during all phases of the innovation diffusion process (see Table 16.2). This brings us to the question of what kinds of roles and instruments would be appropriate in view of the current state of development of AFT and the perceived barriers to innovation diffusion. Some of the known AFT concepts have been led by industrial actors who had a keen interest in the realisation of such a system in order to ensure the efficiency of their operations. However, in spite of industrial interest in AFT, the large amounts of investment needed and the significant degree of uncertainty (technological, regulatory, financial, safety, etc.) seem to require at least a clear backing by government before a decision to go ahead with a large-scale AFT scheme is taken. Even in the past, public sector organisations – often motivated by government policy – had to compensate for a lack of private initiative and investment. However, this only makes sense if sufficient interest in AFT can be generated among potential developers, operators and users.

In the current innovation phase, the role of an innovation agent seems to be most appropriate as part of an active policy approach. This does not mean that government through one of its agencies necessarily has to take the lead itself, but it would have to take care of identifying and supporting a lead actor/organisation that is able and willing to coordinate a longer-term process of initiating the necessary technical, economic, regulatory and institutional improvements needed.[10] The task of such an organisation could be quite close to that of a 'niche manager' for the different types of AFT applications (Hoogma et al. 2002, Weber et al. 1999). A niche manager is an agent who builds networks and aims actively at providing conducive framework conditions that open up a testing and learning space for AFT. This role can be compared to that of a facilitator or moderator of innovation processes that involve a wide range of actors. Network building is thus a key task of the niche manager.

Government policy should not be understood as fully coherent, but rather as being composed of often contradictory interests of different government bodies. An active government role as an innovation agent would thus also aim to better coordinate initiatives in different policy domains. RTD-programmes and pilot projects would have a role to play alongside the introduction or adjustment of regulations and specific sectoral policies. In other words, there is a need for policy coordination in order to fulfil a support function for AFT. Critical in this respect is also coordination between policy levels and coordination of policy impulses over the innovation cycle.

Some of the potential roles of government seem to be less appropriate in the case of AFT, although according to Table 16.2 they are in principle possible and recommended for transport innovations. The development of AFT clearly needs to be done in close cooperation between research, industry and end users, where government-led research and development work has little to add. Similarly, implementation can only be successful if it meets in the first instance with user needs and market demand. Government, in its role as innovation agent, can contribute to pilot implementations by means of specific grants and facilitate adoption by preparing early on conducive regulatory and legal framework conditions, but there is very limited scope for government involvement in private special purpose infrastructures for AFT (e.g. on individual production sites). To draw a comparison with telecommunications, automated freight transport systems offer value-added services for special customers, but they do not fall under the universal service requirement.

In the course of the innovation process, the role of government is supposed to change, but it is very difficult to find the right moment at which to change roles and instruments. The role of a regulator will become more important once the pilot and demonstration projects with initial AFT applications have provided more evidence with respect to appropriate safety standards and regulations. Similarly, standardisation initiatives may be taken by government after a preliminary period of testing different applications. Also the adjustment and revision of existing legislation may be an important task in enabling the operation of AFT, which may be illegal under present legislation, but it will only be addressed once the feasibility and acceptability of AFT has been proven. Also in this respect, monitoring and evaluation have a key role to play. Overall, it seems rather unlikely that AFT will come into being if government takes a passive stance. The need for coordination with competing systems and modes, the establishment of common standards, safety regulations and carrier organisations point in the direction of an active policy role being necessary to accompany the innovation diffusion process of AFT. Some of the many pitfalls of an active policy approach favouring AFT have been highlighted in this section.

16.6 CONCLUSIONS

AFT technology has made significant progress over the last few years and today represents a viable technological option for specific small-scale application niches, for instance on factory premises or marshalling yards. Larger-scale applications or general purpose schemes are still difficult to realise, in spite of the promising characteristics of AFT. After a first phase of conceiving a large variety of schemes, we have now entered a consolidation phase where a limited number of AFT concepts are under closer scrutiny, mainly automated underground freight transport, self-guided rail vehicles, and road vehicles on dedicated lanes and areas. AFT operating on public infrastructures in a mixed mode, i.e. jointly with manually guided vehicles, meet with a great deal of reluctance.

Several types of barriers, ranging from technical to institutional issues, affect the advancement and uptake of AFT, not only in the sense of inhibiting the evolution of AFT in general, but also by determining the likelihood of the different AFT concepts being realised. For instance, liability issues are one of the main reasons why the operation of AFT on non-dedicated infrastructures is unlikely to happen. As long as it is unclear whether operators or manufacturers would be held liable for accidents and fatalities, they will not take a serious lead in promoting and advancing AFT. As a consequence, semi-automated driver assistance systems are more likely to be introduced for use on public infrastructure than fully automated freight and passenger transport systems.

This shows that AFT is currently in a phase of development where government intervention could make a real difference, both in terms of promoting the advancement of AFT in general and with respect to the choice of specific technological trajectories. However, making this difference presupposes first of all the willingness to pursue an active policy approach. It is rather unlikely that AFT could be realised on a larger scale without a supportive and active stance from government. Stable and conducive framework conditions, for instance in terms of safety regulations and liability rules, are essential for improving the market perspectives for AFT and attracting private investors. Financial support through RTD programmes is needed to give incentives in the early phases of the innovation diffusion process. Moreover, there are several major coordination matters involved that will not be solved in a market environment and require government to play a moderating and facilitating role, for instance to bring manufacturers, potential operators and users together to define viable AFT concepts. And also within government, several policy areas contribute to the shaping of AFT and ought to be consistent with one another.

What is needed is thus a set of coherent activities to be implemented by a range of actors and stakeholders. The notion of an innovation or niche manager has been introduced to capture the coordinating role needed to put such a network into practice. This implies not only the initiation of specific policy measures (i.e. legislation, regulation, R&D programmes) but also the building of the necessary coalitions able and willing to carry the implementation of AFT forward.

Due to the open character of innovation processes and the high degree of uncertainty (technological, market-related, regulatory, acceptance, etc.) involved in the setting up of AFT schemes, critical technology choices should not be made and realised in a linear planning mode. Instead a robust and adaptive policy strategy is needed that facilitates learning about and adjusting to new opportunities and insights with respect to the risks and advantages of AFT, and the effectiveness of policy roles and measures. This also implies keeping alternative options open and avoiding concentrating entirely on only one of the different AFT options under discussion.

In order to inform government about experiences and policy impacts, pilot and full-scale applications should be continuously monitored and evaluated. This is not only important for reconsidering the technology choices made, but also to identify the right moments in time when government needs to change its role and shift the focus of its measures with respect to AFT.

NOTES

1. See also IPTS (1999), Pielage (2000) and in particular Pielage and Rijsenbrij (in this volume). Next to the Schiphol case they refer to feasibility studies for Utrecht, Twente, Arnhem/Nijmegen, Tilburg and Leiden.
2. See for instance the definition of system innovations by Schot et al. (2002), who characterise them as 'co-evolution of a number of related elements, including technology, infrastructures, symbolic meanings, regulations, scientific knowledge, industry structure, etc'. Usually, the term system innovation implies that in addition to radical changes in technological terms, the innovation also entails significant changes in terms of user behaviour, organisational and institutional setting.
3. For a wider review of underground freight transportation systems (including pipeline systems) see Pielage and Rijsenbrij in this volume.
4. See for instance the PROMETHEUS demonstration project and the long-term visions associated with it (Prätorius 1993).
5. In Europe, road trains, i.e. trucks that automatically follow each other so that only the first truck needs a driver, are usually not considered an option in mixed traffic, i.e. in a disturbed environment. However, in Australia or other world regions with a low population density it is regarded as a feasible option.
6. See Erdmann (2005) for a discussion of the issue of time strategies. He points out that there are only small 'windows of opportunity' when policy measures promise to be effective in shaping the direction of technological change. Examples are given from the chemical industry in Europe and Japan during the 1980s, but other work is in progress dealing with cases from the automotive sector.
7. See the research work on interactive learning in innovation systems (Lundvall 1992) as well as the broad range of literature on the social shaping of technology (Rip et al. 1995, Sorensen and Williams 2002).
8. C.f. the technical challenges described in this volume by Shladover who focuses in his assessment of technical barriers on road-based AFT.
9. We do not address here the question whether AFT should indeed be regarded as a 'sustainable' transport system or not. This would require a separate analysis.
10. Setting up a carrier organisation that is operating as a lead actor and network node in a specific sector or technology area, is a policy approach frequently applied in the Netherlands. See for instance the case of combined heat and power generation where the Projektbureau Warmte-Kracht PWK was created as a carrier organisation in the 1980s.

REFERENCES

Arthur, B. (1988), Competing Technologies: An Overview, in: G. Dosi, C. Freeman, G. Silverberg and L. Soete (eds), *Technical Change and Economic Theory*, London: Pinter, pp. 590–607.

Beise, M. (2001), *Lead Markets. Country-Specific Success Factors of the Global Diffusion of Innovations*, Heidelberg: Physica.

Callon, M. (1992), The Dynamics of Techno-Economic Networks, in: R. Coombs, P. Saviotti and V. Walsh (eds), *Technological Change and Company Strategy: Economic and Sociological Perspectives*, London: Academic Press.

Coutard, O. (ed.) (1999), *The Governance of Large Technical Systems*, London: Routledge.

de la Mothe, J. and A.N. Link (eds) (2002), *Networks, Alliances and Partnerships in the Innovation Process*, Boston: Kluwer.

Edquist, C. (1997), *Systems of Innovations. Technologies, Institutions and Organisations*, London: Pinter.

Erdmann, G. (2005), Innovation, Time and Sustainability, in: K.M. Weber and J. Hemmelskamp (eds), *Towards Environmental Innovation Systems*, Berlin: Springer, pp. 193–204.

ERRI (2000), *Intelligent Freight Train, Final Report*, Brussels: European Rail Research Institute, January.

HLG (1999), *Working Paper on Innovation in the Field of Transport*, Brussels: European Commission, High-Level Group Directorate General VII, October.

Hoogma, R. (1998), *Towards Autonomous Railroad Trucks. Rail Freight Transport Innovation in South East Lower Saxony, Case Study Report for the EU-supported Project SNM-T*, Enschede: University of Twente.

Hoogma, R., R. Kemp, J. Schot and B. Truffer (2002), *Experimenting for Sustainable Transport. The Approach of Strategic Niche Management*, London/New York: Spon Press.

Hughes, T.P. and R. Mayntz (eds.) (1988), *The Development of Large Technical Systems*, Frankfurt: Campus.

IABG (2000), *Policy and Market Synthesis, RECONNECT Deliverable D5*, Munich: IABG, March.

IPTS (1999), *New Means of Transport Survey and Preselection, RECONNECT deliverable D1*, Sevilla: IPTS, May.

Kemp, R. and J. Rotmans (2005), in M. Weber and J. Hemmelskamp, *Towards Environmental Innovation Systems*, Heidelberg: Springer/Physica, pp. 33–54.

Lundvall, B.-A. (ed.) (1992), *National Systems of Innovation: Towards a Theory of Innovation and Interactive Learning*, London: Pinter.

Marin, B. and R. Mayntz (eds) (1991), *Policy Networks. Empirical Evidence and Theoretical Considerations*, Frankfurt am Main/Boulder, CO: Campus/Westview.

Pielage, B.-J. (2000), *Underground Freight Transportation. A New Development for Automated Freight Transportations Systems in the Netherlands*, Research Paper, TRAIL, Delft University of Technology.

Prätorius, G. (1993), *Das PROMETHEUS-Projekt. Technikentstehung als sozialer Prozeß*, Wiesbaden: Gabler.

Pyka, A. and G. Küppers (eds) (2002), *Innovation Networks. Theory and Practice*, Cheltenham: Edward Elgar.

Rip, A., J. Schot and T. Misa (eds) (1995), *Managing Technology in Society. The Approach of Constructive Technology Assessment*, London: Pinter.

Rogers, M.E. (1983), *Diffusion of Innovations* (second revised edition), New York: Free Press.

Schot, J. and R. Hoogma (1999), *How Innovative are Users? A Critique of Learning-by-doing and -using*, Paper prepared for the Fifth ASEAT Conference 'Demand, Markets, Users and Innovation: Sociological and Economic Approaches', Manchester, 14–16 September.

Schot, J., G. Verbong, F. Geels, K. Green, R. Kemp, B. Elzen and M. Weber (2002), Transitions to Sustainability through System Innovations, Keynote paper for an International Expert Meeting, Eindhoven/Twente.

Sorensen, K. and R. Williams (eds) (2002), *Shaping Technology, Guiding Policy: Concepts, Spaces and Tools*, Cheltenham: Elgar.

Summerton, J. (ed.) (1994), *Changing Large Technical Systems*, Boulder, CO: Westview.

Tabibi, M. and I.A. Hansen (2000), *Dedicated Lanes for Automated Freight Traffic. A Solution for Rapid Increase of Freight Transport in the 21st Century*, Research Paper, TRAIL, Delft University of Technology.

van Zuylen, H. and M. Weber (2002), Strategies for European Innovation Policy in the Transport Field, *Technological Forecasting and Social Change*, Vol. 69, pp. 929–51.

Weber, K.M. (1999), *Innovation Diffusion and Political Control of Energy Technologies*, Heidelberg: Springer-Physica.

Weber, K.M., R. Hoogma, B. Lane and J. Schot (1999), *Experimenting with Sustainable Transport Innovations*, A workbook for Strategic Niche Management, Sevilla/Enschede: JRC-IPTS/University of Twente.

Zapp, K. (2002), *Vom Fahrerhaus zum Telearbeitsplatz*, Verkehrs-wissenschaftliche Nachrichten, 7 August, Hamburg: Deutscher Verkehrsverlag.

Index